& Louche

FAST
& Louche

Confessions of a **flagrant sinner**

JEREMY SCOTT

P
PROFILE BOOKS

Four or five of the names in this memoir have been changed to spare embarrassment to the living and because of the author's characteristic discretion.

First published in Great Britain in 2002 by
PROFILE BOOKS LTD
58A Hatton Garden
London EC1N 8LX
www.profilebooks.co.uk

This paperback edition is published in 2003

1 3 5 7 9 10 8 6 4 2

Printed and bound in Great Britain by
Bookmarque Ltd, Croydon, Surrey

Typeset in Stempel Garamond by MacGuru
info@macguru.org.uk

A CIP catalogue record for this book is available from the British Library.

ISBN 1 86197 666 6

Photographs: **Nanny** © David Scott; **Jeremy with two models** © Terence Donovan; **Jeremy and Peter Mayle** © Jennie Mayle; ***Gortyna borelii*** © Natural History Museum; **Tania, Jenny Beerbohm and Jamie** photographer unknown

To Jamie, with love.
And for Ernest and Christie, Peter and Jennie,
The Fishers and Ramage;
the best friends imaginable.

Contents

Prologue

On Easter Sunday Father killed and ate a dog. He and the man with him cooked it on a Primus in their tent after yet another unsuccessful day spent searching for their companion, buried alive 8,000 feet up on Greenland's ice cap.

In 1930, four years before my birth, Father, J. M. Scott, was one of a party of fourteen young men who sailed to the Arctic to pioneer a route for the first commercial airway from Europe to North America. The party was led by Gino Watkins, aged twenty-three, who like Scott had just come down from Cambridge but had already led two expeditions to the Arctic. With a love for jazz, dancing and sports cars, foppishly dressed, Gino did not resemble most people's idea of an explorer. One fellow undergraduate said he looked like a 'pansy'.

The proposed air route lay over the coastal mountains which were of unknown height, then for 500 miles across

Greenland's unexplored ice cap, the most hostile environment on earth. Gino's plan was to survey and map the coastal range but, crucially, to set up a meteorological station high on the ice cap, which – manned in shifts for one year – would record temperature, wind and weather conditions six times a day. Nobody before had ever passed a winter on the ice cap, much of which is in 24-hour darkness. No one on the expedition or elsewhere knew what to expect.

That August Scott guided a party up the glacier leading onto the ice cap. Winching up the sledges and hauling up their dogs by rope, it took them six days to travel the first fifteen miles. In the next ten days they sledged a further 112 miles into the frozen desert to set up the weather station, a nine-foot tent equipped with a full range of meteorological apparatus – but no radio or communication with the outside world.

The two men left to man the station were replaced by two others in late September while the weather was still good. In November the party which set out to relieve them was pinned down for so long by blizzards they had consumed most of the food and fuel intended for the station by the time they finally reached it. Either it must be abandoned or one man alone must staff it through the winter until he could be relieved. Courtauld, another Cambridge undergraduate and heir to a family fortune, volunteered to do so.

Arctic winter closed in. On 8 December the sun failed to rise, not to be glimpsed again for weeks. Gales raged continuously. The Base anemometer recorded 129 mph before it blew away. At the weather station high on the ice cap conditions were worse.

At the end of February Gino said to Scott, 'I'm afraid someone will have to go and fetch Courtauld while the weather is still bad. I'd like it to be you.'

Scott took one man; each drove a dog sledge. One of these

broke in half on the glacier, then a blizzard pinned them down for days. It took three attempts to get going. After seventeen days travelling in appalling conditions he calculated they were on the latitude of the station and within a half-mile of it. Marking off a grid with flags, they began to search for it. Most of the time the weather was atrocious and visibility reduced to a few yards. When the low sun did appear the snowscape became a zebra pattern of bright crests and dark shadowed troughs. It was like looking for a man overboard in a rough sea. They spent the next three weeks searching the area ... and could not find Courtauld.

By 15 April, having already eaten two of their dogs, there remained three-quarter rations for only four more days. The decision to abandon the search was Scott's as leader of the party. Having taken it, they raced back to Base, travelling in any weather and running the crevasses blind in darkness. On the final stretch the exhausted dogs were no longer able to pull the pathetically light loads. Dumping the sledges, men and beasts stumbled the last miles to Base where Scott gave Gino the news.

Taking two men Gino set out at dawn on the 130-mile journey to the weather station. Scaling the glacier, he and his party raced towards where Courtauld lay buried. On 4 May they knew they must be near; almost at the same moment the three saw a dark speck half a mile away. As they hurried nearer it became a very tattered Union Jack, three-quarters hidden by the snow, but everything else was entirely buried beneath a huge drift. There was no sign of life, but as Gino climbed the drift he saw an inch or two of ventilating tube projecting above the surface. He knelt over it, shouted ... and a voice came back. Entombed beneath the ice cap, Courtauld had been isolated in his tent for 149 days.

Gino, Courtauld and Scott were changed for ever by the Arctic. They'd lived in a vast white empty world of cruel beauty and truth. To face the adversities they encountered there required comradeship, resolution and courage; their lives were simple, pure, their purpose clear. Afterwards, what could match the intensity of that experience?

Along with the others Scott never adjusted to everyday life. But he was also changed in another way. His failure to find Courtauld altered his personality, turning him into a misanthrope who needed drink to become whole. Forever afterward he believed himself a failure and the conviction would poison and ruin his life.

While together in Greenland he and Gino had at one point been caught in a jam they thought they might not escape from. Gino was not without responsibilities. His mother was dead, his father expiring from TB in a Swiss sanatorium. His sister Pam and brother Tony, both younger than he, were living almost without funds in a rented house in London, looked after by Nanny Dennis who had been with them for over twenty years. By nature insouciant, Gino had inadvertently become head of the family. Now in Greenland he said to Scott, 'If anything happens to me, look after Pam'.

The two managed to extricate themselves from that particular hazard, but on the second phase of the Air Route Expedition in 1932 something did happen to Gino. He went out alone in his kayak, hunting seal among the ice floes to feed his party ... and disappeared. His kayak was found floating half full of water, and his trousers soaking wet on an ice floe, but his body and rifle were never recovered. The accident – if accident it was – remains a mystery.

Scott was a representative of his period and class; he believed in duty, honour and the manly code. He did the right thing and married his drowned leader's sister, Pam – a woman whose temperament and tastes could not have been more different from his own.

In the year following the couple's wedding they had a son, whom they christened Jeremy Gino Scott – myself.

1
Dumbleton

The day started with Nanny drawing the curtains in my bedroom to let in the sun. 'Come on sleepy-head, let me get your togs on,' she said fondly, dressing me in girl's clothes as was the fashion in the late 'thirties.

I lived in two rooms, the day nursery and the night nursery, at the top of a house in a quiet tree-lined street in South Kensington. Breakfast was with Nanny and Mrs Reeves the cook in the basement kitchen; my parents ate theirs in the dining room on the floor above. Father, who had the square jaw and rugged handsome looks of an action hero, champed on salted porridge behind his newspaper while Mother chattered brightly and unsuccessfully. Finishing his oats in silence, he slipped a climbing rucksack over his suit and set off for the *Daily Telegraph* in Fleet Street, today as every day 'by Shank's pony', as Nanny put it.

My own walk came later in the day. Pursuing a life which, even then, inclined to be more idle than his, I took it in a pram. Through streets almost free of traffic Nanny and I walked down the Fulham Road past run-down shops selling hardware and artists' materials, a dairy with a stable, and the Boucherie Chevaline, a horse butcher, though we never went down Park Walk as she said 'rough people' lived there.

After lunch I took a nap and played with my toys in the day nursery while Mother visited art galleries and exhibitions and met for tea at Harrods or Fortnum's with her numerous and all much richer cousins. I was taken to join her when she returned. 'Hello, my little treasure,' she cried in her piercing upper-crust voice as Nanny brought me in, 'And have you been utter utter blissikins today?'

'More trouble than a barrel-load of monkeys, I do declare,' said Nanny, and I'd be delivered over.

Mother was a thin dark-haired woman with a delicate bird-like face, a nervous distracted manner, and a small inheritance. She was uncomfortable with touch or people too close to her. She read to me from *Babar the Elephant* or we did a jigsaw puzzle until Father came home. We shook hands as he wished me goodnight.

Nanny took me upstairs, put me in nightdress and tucked me up. 'Now off to the land of Nod,' she said.

One of eight children of a Leicestershire farm labourer, Nanny had gone into domestic service at the age of fifteen, working for Mother's cousins in their country house. She'd had to provide her own uniforms and trunk; her family had gone short to buy them. Her wage was £12 a year, paid quarterly in arrears. She had risen from the job of skivvy, getting up at 4.30 am in order to clean the grates and lay the many fires, to that of nursemaid. She went to work for my grandmother in Eaton Place in 1909, on my mother's birth, remaining with Mother until her death in 1973, by which time she was earning a wage of £5 per week which often went unpaid.

Throughout those sixty-four years of unbroken service Mother had no idea in which drawer her own underclothes were kept. As a child it was Nanny who raised me, not my parents, and her I loved, not them.

Our weekends were passed at the country houses of relatives, usually at Dumbleton in Worcestershire. We drove there in the rickety car Father had bought for £20. Nanny and I travelled in the back with the luggage; Mother rode beside Father, wearing around her neck a dead fox with angry red eyes and a cruel jaw snapped shut on its own tail. 'I wish you wouldn't overtake,' she said at times, 'It uses up a frightful lot of petrol.'

Dumbleton was a twenty-bedroom Victorian Gothic pile set in a park containing its own church, cricket pitch, pavilion and lake with water lilies and a punt. It belonged to Mother's uncle, who was First Lord of the Admiralty, and Aunt Sybil.

Uncle Bobby, Viscount Monsell, had risen to eminence and wealth from unpromising beginnings. The sixth child of an impoverished Irish family, his grandfather, a clergyman, had written the rousing hymn 'Fight the good fight with all thy might'. Entering the navy as a midshipman at the age of fifteen, Bobby set out to fulfil its exhortation to 'lay hold on life' in his own way. Almost wholly uneducated, he possessed enormous charm. Barbara Cartland, who knew him when she was a debutante, called him the most handsome man she had ever met. Inspired not only by the hymn but through the example of his father, who had wed an heiress, he married an heiress of his own when only twenty-two. For his bride Bobby chose Sybil, the large, ungainly, pathologically shy only daughter of the Birmingham industrialist who had invented the zip fastener.

A gregarious and witty man, he enjoyed entertaining. At weekends Aunt Sybil sat at the foot of a table set for twenty-four, picking distractedly at her food and tortured by embarrassment while trying to think of something, *anything*, to say to those beside her, as from the other end of the table gales of delighted laughter reached her from the charmed circle of animated guests grouped around her husband.

Appointed First Lord in 1932, Uncle Bobby's job and social life kept him mostly in London while Aunt Sybil remained at Dumbleton giving birth over the years to four large children of which Graham, the only boy, became Comptroller of Military Intelligence during the war and, according to Mother, a Soviet spy. Uncle Bobby did not play a major role in their upbringing for family life failed to enthral him and, in time, he left Aunt Sybil to marry a younger and smaller woman.

By then he'd retired from his country's service. The summit of his political career was to negotiate and sign for Britain the Anglo-German Naval Agreement of 1935, criticised by Sir Winston Churchill as 'a most surprising act ... it effectively removed all restraint to German naval expansion and set her yards to work at maximum activity'. In the Second World War which followed, it resulted in the deaths of hundreds of British and American seamen and the loss of countless tons of Allied shipping. The German negotiating team was led by von Ribbentrop, who was a frequent guest at Dumbleton during the protracted negotiations in the course of which he and Uncle Bobby became close friends. Indeed the house's drawing-room curtains, a set of heavy velvet drapes covering the french windows and decorated with a bold motif of Nazi swastikas, were a personal gift from von Ribbentrop at the conclusion of the agreement and proved of such enduring quality they still hung in place thirty-five years later when I visited Dumbleton after it had been bought by the Post Office for use as a residential country club for its employees.

But as an infant I was unaware of Uncle Bobby's illustrious career. I spent the weekend segregated upstairs in the nursery, while Nanny's life centred on the servants' hall. I was a year old apparently before I had the pleasure of meeting Uncle Bobby face to face. The story is Mother's, for I don't remember the occasion, but it seems that one morning I was in my pram on the gravel sward outside the house attended by herself and Nanny when Lord Monsell stepped out the front door in tweed suit and hat, carrying a cane and pair of gloves, about to start on his own morning constitutional around the park. Sitting in my high pram I was on my part equally well dressed in an attractively embroidered lace smock and looking my best. As indeed was Mother, who positively glowed with pride in the little treasure she'd borne into the world.

Emerging from the house, the First Lord threw a brief glance towards our little group before setting off briskly in the other direction. But Mother wanted to share her bounty. 'Oh good morning, Uncle Bobby,' she carolled as he was about to step off, '*Do* come and see my little baby.'

He balked, then very reluctantly he approached, though no closer than was absolutely necessary. Stopping well short of the pram, he leaned forward a little to examine what was inside and his handsome features contorted into an expression of the utmost revulsion as he looked at me. '*Ugh!*' he exclaimed in a shudder of intense disgust, then turned and walked away.

2
Arisaig

'If you know how to hunt with a rifle, ski well and climb an overhanging rock face you'll be all right whatever happens to you in life,' Father told me. He said it with conviction and, aged seven, I did not question the proposition's truth. Skiing was out for the moment as there was no snow, but he started me at once on the other two skills he considered essential to prepare a boy for the modern world. For we lived then in the ideal situation for him to teach me both – Arisaig – a tiny village in the west highlands of Scotland. At the start of the Second World War he'd been sent by the army to this remote spot as a commando instructor.

The whole stretch of some 900 square miles of coast and wilderness had been taken over by the Special Operations Executive. To seal it off from the outside world was not difficult, only a single-track railway line and one very bad road led into the region; an official permit was necessary to enter it and the men who examined these permits, although in military uniform, were not soldiers but security agents and police detectives.

Arisaig House, Inverailort Castle and the few other large isolated houses in the area were requisitioned as schools of mountain and guerrilla warfare, and used for training male and female agents. The SOE had come into being after the fall of France, in order to foster and support resistance groups in occupied territories. Its function was to supply agents skilled in the tactics of unorthodox warfare, including destruction by explosives, silent killing and unarmed combat. When their training was completed they were smuggled into occupied territories by parachute or submarine, equipped with the explosives and weaponry required to inflict maximum damage and disruption.

The resident instructors in these arts were an oddly assorted group of men which included a Norwegian champion ski jumper, a Russian professional wrestler and the 'Heavenly Twins', a cheerfully sinister pair who had come from the Shanghai police. One of them, Captain Bill Sykes, specialised in throttling people with his enormous hands, while the other, Captain Fairbairn ('Murder made easy, that's me!'), had developed an individual style of killing from a combination of black-belt karate and the night-time techniques of the Shanghai waterfront. And then there was Father.

He was chief instructor at Inverailort. A damp, gloomy, Victorian monstrosity, the castle stood at the head of a sea loch, facing due north and situated beneath a mountain which cut off all sun except for a few hours in high summer. But Father was in his element – for he enjoyed discomfort and physical challenge. To be wet and cold and hungry made him feel real. He was resourceful, courageous, tough and a crack shot. He led his men on gruelling treks through the mountains, sleeping out without tents both winter and summer.

They carried no food but lived off limpets and mussels gathered from the shore, which he taught them to eat raw – as he did me.

Arisaig was very cut off from normal life. It stood in a landscape of astonishing beauty and grandeur, a savage wilderness broken up by lochs reaching far between the mountains, by treacherous bogs, ravines and streams swollen with rainwater cascading from the cliffs. It was a place inhabited only by sheep and deer and birds and the dour descendants of those Highland families who had not been evicted from their crofts and shipped to North America to make room for livestock.

The village and its outlying crofts had a total population of 450. Its inhabitants, the native Highlanders who were our neighbours, were a wiry, short-legged people with toffee-coloured hair, closed faces and a guarded manner. Only after we'd been there two or three years did they return a greeting or acknowledge us in the street. Few owned a bicycle, none possessed a car. There was no electricity, people lived by the light of paraffin lamps and candles, warmed their damp cottages by peat fires or (rarely, because it cost money to run) a smelly paraffin heater. Except for a handful of jobs on the Arisaig estate, which owned all the cottages and land, there was no work and never had been. The villagers dressed in ragged clothes and lived out their austere existence in a state of poverty, at times near to destitution. Conditions in the area had changed little over the last hundred years.

Arisaig was set on a bay of the sea enclosed by steep heather-covered hills and backed by range upon range of mountains. Its single street ran along the rocky shoreline past a small inn built the previous century, past cottages, a tiny one-man post office and a blacksmith's forge where the estate carthorses and crofters' ponies were fitted with metal shoes, to turn up a steep hill and skirt a walled garden containing a run-down church and its manse, then continue out of the village on to the wooded slopes beneath the mountains.

That manse was my home. A square, solidly built four-bedroomed house, Mother had bought it for £1,000, though the price did not include the Wee Free Church standing in its garden. By 1940 the sect was so long out of favour most of its followers were dead. Only one service a year was celebrated in our little church; the minister came from Fort William on a motorbike to take it. That first year five elderly celebrants hobbled through our garden to attend it; the second year three; the next, only one. After that the abandoned church was used only to store our kayaks, Father's Arctic sledge and harness, his harpoons, boomerang, eighteen-foot leather dog whip and our bicycles. On VE Day I tugged the bell clear off its tower, pealing it too exuberantly in celebration of Allied victory, and after that the building decayed in silence through the years beneath an ever-deepening layer of dust marked only by a trail of footprints to our stash of toys.

A track ran past the manse's garden, leading up to the tiny railway station on the lower slopes of the mountain range behind the village. Set back from this track, two small houses and the Protestant church stood overhung by large trees. Built of dark granite which turned black in the rain, one house was the church's manse, the other the Protestant school.

The school had eight pupils; I was one. Its only teacher was Miss Gillies. Small and old and shapeless under layers of clothes to protect against the chill, she kept order with a leather strap. The classroom was low roofed and dark, the heavy trees outside the window cut off the light. It contained a dozen hinge-topped wooden desks, battered, heavily scarred and carved with names, which faced the blackboard and a cast-iron stove. During winter and spring terms each pupil would bring a clod of peat or lump of coal to feed the stove, as well as the wrapped 'piece' which was their midday meal.

Two of the pupils were sons of the estate ghillie who lived in an isolated croft three miles away on the far arm of the bay. Thin bony boys with wary eyes and the ferocious manner of maltreated dogs, they walked the distance barefoot on an unsurfaced track, carrying their hobnailed boots which they put on when they reached the school. At the end of class they removed them for the walk home – which for half the year was made in darkness. Another boy, who had a mad mother, owned no clothes but wore a woollen blanket which hung in folds around his scrawny little body, his head poking out through a hole cut in its centre.

The pupils were between six and fourteen years old. All spoke with Highland accents, hardly moving their lips. My first weeks there I could understand nothing that was said to me; to them my English accent was incomprehensible. It did not make for a cosy relationship. They had every reason to hate the English. Arisaig was the very centre of the 1745 rebellion. Bonny Prince Charlie had landed here, in the rocky bay below Arisaig House, to raise the clans and march south on his doomed adventure with the bagpipes skirling. And it was here he returned as a fugitive with a price of £30,000 on his head, pursued over these hills, hidden in these same caves and woods, fed on scraps from these same crofts ... and from here finally he fled by a boat to France, a drunk and broken hero.

And it was here the worst reprisals of the vengeful English army had been perpetrated on the local population. Crofts had been torched, the inhabitants' tools and poor possessions tossed on to the fire. Their cattle had been stolen or killed, their land confiscated. Living in caves and holes in the ground, they had starved or frozen to death.

I wasn't popular with my fellow pupils in the school, but I wasn't bullied. I was an alien lifeform, a representative of the occupying power which had oppressed them for two centuries. I was looked at with suspicion, resentment and a wary hostility – but I was left entirely alone.

I was more than ready when class ended at 4.30, and ran the hundred yards to home. Throughout the winter I read, for the manse was filled with books. The rest of the year I lived outdoors. Most days I spent by myself scavenging for food, which was severely rationed. There was no fresh meat or fish, no fruit, and no fresh vegetables except cabbage and potatoes. What was available in the only shop, which sold coal, rope, tools, paraffin and boots, was extremely limited.

The loch contained fish, but no one fished it because no one in the village was rich enough to own a boat. Its rocky coves were thick with mussels clumped beneath the seaweed; there were oysters, and at low tide you could find clams and dig for razor fish in the sand, though with the stubborn perversity that characterises the Highlander, the locals refused to eat shellfish. But we did, and I was the family provider. And to a nine-year-old boy whose head was filled with others' fictional adventures the sea also carried far greater treasures. Outside the bay where the village was situated, the coastline fronted the open ocean; any wreckage from a ship torpedoed in the North Atlantic was washed up eventually on this rocky shore. Over the course of the war I found a crate of lard and two of margarine, each containing a fifty-pound slab of edible fat beneath a skim of marine growth. I came on large battered tins of tea, a case of American K-rations half buried in the sand, a German mine … and more. One day, scavenging the shore beyond the mouth of the bay, I came across what looked from a distance like a heap of sodden rags half-hidden among the sea-wrack. Scrambling down the rocks to where it lay, I saw it was a dead body. His hair was twined with weed, the flesh of his face slimy white beneath a wet swatch of kelp, and his eyes had been eaten out by crabs. I stared at him with horror and fascination, unable to approach closer or to run away. On getting home I told no one, I don't know why. The drowned sailor haunted my mind, I saw him in my dreams. Almost every day I walked the four miles to look at the decomposing body and check if it was really there. Then one morning it was gone. I have no idea if it was found and taken away or what happened, for no one ever spoke of it in the village.

During the school holidays I stayed out all day, walking miles over the hills to scavenge remote beaches the locals never harvested. Alone, I was happy. Less so at weekends when Father's dog-weary troops at Lochailort slept off the gruelling exercises he'd put them through and he was home and free to train *me*.

In his early thirties, fit, strong and of great energy, he was leading the vigorous outdoors life he so enjoyed. The climate in western Scotland, which has the highest rainfall in Europe, was particularly stimulating to him. His greatest pleasure in life, he once told me, was walking long distances in the rain. Wet weekend on wet weekend, blinded by the driving storm, I found myself clinging to one vertical rockface after another with frozen fingers, inching myself in terror towards his impatient figure outlined on the summit high above me. 'Anchor yourself before you reach, never look down,' he yelled. Roped to him, I finally reached the top. 'Now without the rope, you have to learn to depend on yourself alone,' he said.

The other skills he taught me I took to with greater pleasure. The arsenal of weaponry in the manse was extensive. The Mannlicher had been one of Gino's hunting rifles, and the two .22 rifles, twelve-bore and Greener gun dated from those Greenland expeditions. A beautiful long-barrelled .22 revolver had belonged to his father. The rest had been liberated from Inverailort: a Colt .45 automatic pistol, a .303 army rifle adapted to fire grenades, a flare pistol, a Sten gun, boxes of Mills bombs and, later, plastic grenades. He'd assembled this collection with a deliberate intent and kept it in his study together with other more specialised equipment in daily use at the castle. A plywood cupboard contained a crossbow, weighted throwing spikes, a flick-knife, a telescopic spring cosh and a garrotte.

These were the ideal toys for a boy in his view – he taught me to use all of them. 'You have to do it from behind. Not very sporting but it's him or you remember. Right arm over his head ... cross the wires ... yank back hard!' he instructed.

Father enjoyed weapons, but the collection had been put together in case of the unthinkable – Britain's occupation by Germany. Though no one spoke of Allied defeat, this looked quite possible at the time. Had it occurred it's unlikely the Hun would have stayed long, finding it as profitless and inconvenient to subjugate Highland Scotland as had the English and the Romans before them, but while they remained Father planned to continue the struggle from caves and mountain hideouts from which he'd lead a guerrilla band on raids to harass the enemy's garrisons and ambush their transport. He'd chosen these spots already and took me on long hikes to show me the advantages of their position and nearness to fresh water, which in many cases was dripping down the walls. I viewed our future habitations with childish dismay. Wouldn't it be better just to surrender with everyone else and stay in the manse with our books, I wondered. But I knew better than to ask.

Perhaps Father saw me as heir to his guerrilla band, the son of the chief, but I think it was more that he believed everyone in the tribe must be trained to maximum usefulness. And it was certainly useful that I should shoot rabbits and game for the pot. We were always short of food; I was permitted to shoot anything so long as I and the family could eat it. With his tuition I became a fair shot, and we moved on from these basic skills to further abilities he believed a growing boy required. I learned camouflage and fieldcraft, to read footprints and to track, to use rough terrain in stalking game or a human enemy, how to set up an ambush or mount a raid. He coached me in techniques of silent killing: the throat jab, Japanese strangle, bronco kick and knife work. A keen pupil, I took to my lessons eagerly, learning how to use a culvert to mine a road, where to place charges to blow a bridge, and the way to derail a train.

Under his supervision I became handy with a sten gun and moved on to grenades. 'Bowl it, don't throw it like a Mills bomb. This is an impact grenade, you have to bowl it straight arm,' he ordered. The first time I flung one the explosion and effect on the target, and emotionally on myself, was awesome. Far and away my most satisfying experience to date.

He was a demanding tutor, but I was a keen pupil always ready to practise what I'd learned while he was at work rehearsing his troops at Lochailort. Then, in 1943, following the Allied landings in southern Europe, Father was posted to Italy to teach British and US troops to cross the Alps and fight on skis ... and the ordnance at the manse was mine.

With Father gone away to war and his entire arsenal at my disposal I was blissfully and wholly content. By that time I had a baby brother, David, who occupied much of Mother's and Nanny's time. My role in this well-armed but now leaderless family was a traditional one. I had become the hunter, I brought home the meat.

Mother did not worry what I was up to, so long as I was out of the house all day. Nanny fussed as she gathered up the sodden clothes I'd discarded on the floor on my return, scolding me for slovenliness as she tidied away the Mills bombs in the toy cupboard. Then she'd poach one of the salmon I'd brought home from the day's fishing; next morning she and Mother would smoke the rest of the catch in a primitive contraption Father had built in an outhouse.

I didn't always fish with grenades, normally I used a hand line towed behind my kayak in the sea loch. In summer darkness did not fall until 11.00 pm. Some days the wide bay, enclosed by mountains, would be flat and smooth as a mirror reflecting the intense blue of the sky, the sea floor distinct and clear twenty feet below the canoe, alive with streaming weed and the bright red glint of sea anemones. A rifle across my knees, I paddled through a world of dazzling light; seals basking on the rocks drowsily raised their heads to look at me as I went by, yawned, then flopped back into somnolent after-lunch siesta. The only sound was the splash of my paddles, the cry of gulls and piping of the oyster catchers.

An archipelago of small islands was slung across the mouth of the bay, at low tide they were linked by beaches of shell-white sand. Scrawny grass, bracken and heather clung between their rocks, and here I collected gulls' eggs, searched for flotsam among the sea-wrack on the beach and swam among the seals in the clear cold water in the channels between the cays.

Other days I spent tramping the broken coastline, looking for eiderduck. Deep-cut burns plunged down the mountain-side to the sea, their banks in spring scattered with a carpet of bluebells. In late summer wild roses bloomed, flag irises spread along the foreshore, the bracken on the hills turned rust red and crimson berries blazed in the rowan trees growing between the rocks.

Usually I carried my .22 rifle or a shotgun with me on these hunting treks, but once I took the Sten gun instead. It required subterfuge, for I was not supposed to use an automatic weapon unsupervised. I carried it from the manse wrapped in an oilskin together with a couple of loaded magazines and hid them beneath a tree in wait for a suitable moment. The next day a storm blew up and hunting was impossible. For a week I hung about indoors while the wind howled, shaking the house, and long Atlantic rollers smashed on the rocks across the mouth of the bay.

The first day of good weather I started out early. Nanny made me a 'piece' to take with me. She knew I was up to something, she had an uncanny nose for it though she didn't always know what. 'Now you be careful or you'll be getting yourself in a real pickle,' she told me.

Recovering the Sten from its hiding place I went towards the mouth of the bay, keeping to the heather and bracken covered slopes behind the shore. The short, all-metal gun felt heavy and lethal in my hand. I carried it openly; if I came across anyone I possessed enough fieldcraft to disappear into the heather without being sighted. There was a small bay opposite the islands where I'd found duck before and I approached it carefully. Peering over the crest I saw a covey by the far end of the cove. Pulling back, I slithered on my belly to peer down to where they floated. There were seven, out of range but swimming in my direction. I inched the snub barrel of the Sten through the bracken to take aim. Midges buzzed around my face, my bare legs prickled in the bracken but I dared not move. When the covey was at thirty yards I let loose, emptying the magazine in a shuddering sustained burst which scattered a rain of bullets all over the sea.

To my astonishment I got three. I swam out to recover the family dinner before it sank. Flushed with pride I carried the ducks home and handed them to Nanny in the kitchen. 'Gracious me, they're cut to ribbons. I'll have to make a stew of these,' she said.

I shot nothing we didn't eat, and we had need of food. That beautiful savage landscape of mountains, woods and sea was my own habitat, as it was of the game I hunted. What I did seemed natural; I was part of an elemental world, the hunter on the hill, and before my childhood ended I went after the biggest game of all.

Between spring and late autumn basking shark appear off north-west Scotland. The second largest fish in the sea, they grow thirty feet in length and weigh up to seven tons. One-seventh of that weight is their liver which, refined, yields 30 per cent in edible oil. After the war there was a shortage of such oil, used in making margarine, cooking fat and soap; it trebled in price.

Recognising the potential, two men equipped boats to hunt basking shark commercially. One of these was Gavin Maxwell, an SOE instructor at Arisaig whom I remember only as a vaguely sinister solitary figure loping around the village – but perhaps this was coloured by Father's dislike of him: 'Frightful little pansy, wears dark glasses.' The other was Mother's brother, Tony Watkins.

Tony's first successful attempt to catch a basking shark had been with a hand-held harpoon from a rowing boat, the two on the oars backing off fast the instant he'd planted it in the fish. Diving, the shark towed the boat for thirty-six hours. They brought it to shore at last on the Irish coast. Slitting it open, they measured the liver and took a sample for processing. The results had encouraged Tony to continue with the venture.

Mother's modest inheritance had been safely invested, and

never touched. *Never spend capital* was an article of faith to her, emphatic as *thou shalt not kill*. Tony used his to buy three West Coast fishing smacks, each capable of sleeping three in considerable discomfort, and a trawler which he equipped as a factory vessel. The hunting boats were fitted with a specially strengthened bow platform, solid enough to absorb the recoil of the Norwegian whaling guns mounted on them. Aged twelve, I passed a summer working on one of those boats.

Each day was spent at sea searching for shark, and in the evening the small fleet made its way to one or other of the little harbours on the islands or mainland coast. No more than villages with a jetty, they consisted of only a pub, a shop, and a few cottages. Situated at the edge of the world, and in many cases connected to it only by sea, these were extraordinarily primitive places. All the inhabitants came to stand on the quay in silence watching us as we put into harbour. Once there, we used the 'bathroom', a bucket on a rope, then ate supper fried up on a Primus stove.

After the meal some of the crew went ashore to try their luck with the local girls – often with success, for to them they were rare and exotic visitors – while Tony, three crewmen and I sat on deck in the endless northern twilight and played poker. He taught me the game, 'Never draw to an inside straight ... If you're going to bluff you must come in strong.' He was skilled in poker, he'd published a book about the game and played professionally.

During the days at sea I passed the time belayed securely to the top of the boat's wheelhouse, scanning the waves with binoculars watching for prey. In the rain with a sea running it was almost impossible to make out the black dorsal fin rising clear of the water that betrays the fish. Like the rest of the crew I was on a bounty system, paid a pound for any shark I spotted and that we succeeded in catching. It was an enormous sum of money to me, my pocket money at the time was a shilling (5p) a week.

After days aching for the opportunity, Tony asked if I wanted to take my turn as harpoon gunner. Thrilled out of my mind, I was worried by the responsibility. To fire at a shark and miss meant hours, even half a day lost before we were in position for another strike. The whole crew would be let down; it would be unbearable to flunk it.

Next morning it was light at 4.30 am. Our little fleet sailed an hour later, the hunting boats spreading out a mile apart in search pattern with the factory trawler following well astern. A breeze was blowing and the sea quite rough, but as we rounded the southern tip of Skye the sun pierced through the clouds to light up the mountains on the Isle of Rum ahead of us on the horizon.

Just before noon one of the boats radioed that they'd sighted shark and we closed up into a pack behind the fish. I felt a thud of excitement as I spotted their fins in the troughs between the waves.

Moving at a speed only slightly faster than our quarry we crept up behind the school. One shark separated from the rest, and it was this we went after. Tense with thrill I took my position at the bow, freeing the lock of the harpoon gun so I could move it.

The shark was directly ahead of us now. It was hard to judge distance on the broken water, at times the tall black fin looked like a sail, then it would disappear beneath the waves. I was terrified it would dive before we were in position. Minutely increasing speed, we moved up on it. The steady pulse of the low-compression engine seemed to lull the fish, but I knew any sudden movement could alarm it. As we nosed up slowly behind the fin the monstrous bulk of the shark became visible beneath the surface, its black hide streaked with algae. It was vast, awesome in its size. I trained the gun on it but the boat was pitching in the waves and I couldn't keep aim. My heart was locked up in my throat as I guided the man at the wheel behind me with careful handsignals until we were right behind the slowing waving tail. Ten feet short of it I fired, aiming for a spot just behind the dorsal fin. With a loud *bang* the twenty-pound harpoon arced out, the tie line snaking after it. In a rush of exhilaration and terror I saw the harpoon bury itself in the shark, the shaft fall free. For a second I was overwhelmed by panic, then tumult broke loose in front of me. The water churned in spray, the tail rose eight feet clear of the surface, swiping the boat a blow that shook the deck and buckled the metal band reinforcing the bow. The shark went down fast, the coiled harpoon rope whipping across the foredeck as I jumped clear.

Towing the boat, the shark swam strongly for the open sea. Astern of us the other hunting boats were still stalking the pack, and far beyond them I could make out the distant mountains of Scotland. We let the shark tow the boat for an hour to tire it. Then, slipping the rope when the pressure built, the skipper winched the fish up cautiously, taking twenty minutes to do so. At last I could see its huge shape below the bow, the tail moving strongly in slow broad stokes ... to become a flail as it broke clear of the surface, smashing repeatedly at the boat in a storm of spray, confusion, thuds and shouts of warning. Tony and I struggled to sling a chain around the tail so the shark could be secured.

We made fast the catch. The great fish was the length of our boat, it lay tied alongside while we sailed back to the factory vessel to deliver it. As I stood on deck looking down at the shark different emotions streamed through me. Triumph, pride – but also something close to dread. A horror that I had done this, that this gigantic sea-creature had been swimming along quite happily in the ocean ... and I'd killed him.

A year later, while hunting in the mountains with a rifle, I wounded a rabbit which I could not reach to finish off but had to watch and listen to it die. Unable to put it out of its pain, I was torn apart by pity and guilt while I heard it suffer. The experience had such an effect on me I never killed any animal, fish, or bird again.

For me Arisaig was the kingdom of heaven, a savage unpopulated wilderness of beauty and adventure where wild roses bloomed behind the reed beds on the loch's shore, where calm blue sea lapped white island beaches and the empty hills rose steep and silent but for the harsh cry of the raven and hooded crows. At the time we moved there, few of those remaining in the depopulated village had ever left it. Most had not travelled even as far as Fort William. Now, because of the war, no able-bodied men between eighteen and fifty were left. Those few I saw loitering in the village, who when it wasn't raining sat on stones by the shore outside the shop, were physically handicapped or soft in the head.

The lives of all were governed by the Church. All pleasure and enjoyment was frowned on – the only recreations available were watching the single street from behind lace curtains, gossip, and drink. And, every two or three months, a ceilidh.

This took place in the village hall, a ramshackle wooden building with a leaking roof, separated from our manse's garden by a hedge. It had an old petrol-driven generator which often broke down but usually produced enough power for a dim electric light. Seated on hard wooden chairs, or on benches fixed to the walls, the whole village attended, even the infirm and mad. All had dressed in their Sunday best. The men had wet-combed their hair flat; in threadbare suits and shirts without a collar they perched stiffly along the benches, silent and attentive. Almost all were smoking, either pipes or thin handrolled cigarettes they held cupped in the hand. Seated apart from the men in the body of the hall were the women. They wore woollens, long skirts and heavy shoes, their capes and oilskin hats stowed neatly beneath their seats. None of the women smoked. None wore make-up and their stern craggy faces showed an impregnable fortitude. Even the young looked middle-aged.

The hall filled up with cigarette smoke as the ceilidh continued, it coiled in the beams of the rudimentary spotlights trained on the small stage. The talent was native to the village, the acts familiar: Donald the Post dressed up in kilt and sporran played the bagpipes; Marjorie Post, his daughter, performed the Highland fling and sword dance in full costume, kilt, ruffled lace blouse, tartan stockings and buttoned shoes; Bella Shop did recitations she composed herself; Wee Ian, a retired seaman whose eyes floated in sagging pouches filled with blood, reeled off epics in a hoarse wrecked voice, coughing abominably between verses. But mostly the evening was song.

Illuminated by the flickering yellow light, in itself a novel luxury, these evenings in the hall were magical. The performers sang of doomed causes, slaughtered clans, defeat and loss, and their laments were of a piercing sadness:

Ye'll take the high road
And I'll take the low road
And I'll be in Scotland afore yee …

In the past they'd left their crofts only to accompany their clan chief as a warband in which many would perish, hacked to pieces on alien soil. They had to find their way back to their ancestral home; 'the low road' was death.

The villagers were not a happy lot – poor souls, they had little to be happy about. Their voices were held low, they rarely met your eye, showed no reaction. Their harsh lives had taught them to endure, but not to smile or ever to show emotion. Yet listening to those laments of parting, failure, loss and death, whose words they knew by heart and murmured as they heard, they were transported. Their faces became rapt; many wept. Despair unsealed their true being and they came alive.

Although it was our home, as a family we were never accepted by the villagers; only Nanny was asked into their houses. I was always the foreigner, the English boy. I left the place aged sixteen, not to return until I was sixty. Then, on my second day back I walked down to what was still the only shop to buy bread and milk. Having got what I needed I started home; while climbing the hill from the village to the manse I drew level with an old fellow resting on his stick while regaining his breath for the ascent. I glanced at him as I went by and within the broken-veined wreckage of his face I glimpsed the ghillie's son I'd been at school with fifty years before. 'Good day,' I said, and he peered at me.

'Och it's you,' he said after a few moments in an absolutely flat voice. 'You blew up the wasps' nest with a bomb; you've been away.' He paused and asked accusingly, 'When are you leaving?'

It was the sort of welcome I was used to, but I persisted; we lingered and we spoke, and over the dram or two in the manse which followed our chance encounter on that rain-swept slope I told him something of what had happened to me in those four and a half decades since I'd left the kingdom and headed south into the world that lay outside its bounds. In time he departed, but in the ensuing days the gist of the personal history I'd related to him spread around the village for, despite TV which now almost everybody possessed, gossip and prurient curiosity in others' lives still remained the principal activity of the place.

Over the next week as I went about the village (now more populous, prosperous and better dressed, with street lighting but essentially unchanged) I became conscious of something extraordinary taking place around me. Running into people I hadn't seen since childhood, I met not hostility as before but instead cordiality and welcome. Their stony natures softened, they warmed to me in a way they never had before. In my defeat and destitution, which all now knew about, I'd proved myself to them. They could accept me; I was received as a native son come home; the prodigal had returned, suitably ruined.

3
Stirling

Hurst Grange Boarding School for Boys, in Stirling, was not a 'good' school. It would not be true to say it came bottom of the league of Britain's prep schools, for the sad truth was it didn't even feature. No pupil from it had ever been known to win a scholarship to a public school and, though its cricket and rugby teams did compete against two equally unknown prep schools, they resolutely failed to distinguish themselves. But Hurst Grange had one compelling advantage, it was cheap. For with Father still away at war, the remainder of my education had been safely left with Mother, and Mother was pathologically stingy over money. She was stingy in the way some people are born with green eyes or the Y chromosome in their blood. She couldn't do anything to alter it, it was part of her. And the fees at Hurst Grange were just so temptingly lower than anywhere else.

This trait was certainly not inherited. Her grandfather had been rich; his only son, her father, Colonel Watkins, recklessly extravagant. As a child she and her brothers, Gino and Tony, had been brought up in a house in Eaton Place and cared for by Nanny. Colonel Watkins was in the Coldstream Guards and spent little time at home. Jennie, his wife, ran the household on accounts with local shops, principally Harrods. When the bills were sent in at the end of each month they were forwarded to her husband's elderly mother to settle.

Colonel Watkins was a lean man with a thin straight nose and moustache, who looked the world boldly in the eye without particularly liking what he saw. His regimental duties were undemanding but he enjoyed an active life, travelling, skiing and hunting chamois in the Alps. Hopeless in business, he soon lost the capital he'd inherited. Leaving the army at the age of forty, he became a king's messenger. On an errand to Moscow he bought two half-grown bears as a present for his children. On a later mission he was despatched to Cairo by sea. It was inconvenient to participate in the liner's social life with a briefcase chained to his wrist so he removed it, and on arrival in Port Said it could not be found. When reporting to the British ambassador, he had to explain that he'd lost it. The ambassador roared with laughter, assuring him that anything of importance was sent by cable, but on his return to England he sadly found himself without a job.

By this time in life he knew he had TB and moved to a sanatorium specialising in the illness in Davos, Switzerland. This became his home and his wife, children and Nanny joined him for skiing holidays. When they were not with him, which was most of the time, he led the cosseted life of an invalid, sat in the sun with a rug across his legs, and increasingly coughed blood. An entertaining if capricious man, he took up with a glamorous Austrian in her thirties, Countess Hoyös. After a time it became clear he would not be returning to England.

In Eaton Place Jennie, his wife, found herself in an impossible situation. She had three children, Nanny and the servants to support, and school bills to pay. For money she depended on intermittent cheques from her husband's ancient mother in Florence. One morning after breakfast Jennie Watkins put on a hat and coat, kissed her children goodbye and caught a train to Eastbourne. There she took a taxi to Beachy Head, a headland plunging to the sea below. Then she simply disappeared. Presumably she walked to the cliff's edge and jumped, but her body was never recovered and she left no note.

The effect upon her three children and on Nanny must have been devastating, but her death was never admitted. As with Gino's in the Arctic a few years later, it was not mentioned and her name never brought up in conversation. Mother and her two brothers continued to live at Eaton Place, looked after by Nanny. Although the house was large, Nanny slept in a cot in Mother's bedroom until Mother was eighteen years old, was presented at Court, and 'came out' as a deb to do the London Season.

Hurst Grange consisted of a pair of stern nineteenth-century houses overlooking Stirling Park, joined together by a cheaply built wooden annexe. The once-white paint on the rickety plank façade of this annexe had over the years turned grey, flaked and curled back in scales, but the severe frontages of the twin houses supporting it were built of dark, almost black granite like the rest of the town. In the wet their appearance was particularly forbidding.

To get to the school from Arisaig at the start of my first term involved a six-hour journey, two trains, and a linking country bus. 'Now you stick up for yourself,' Nanny told me as I set off, aged ten.

It was necessary to do so. Again I was the only English boy, surrounded by two dozen Scots. Understandably I was regarded with extreme suspicion from the start. My memories are of being almost always cold and always hungry. Fees were so low it must have taken diligent planning and strict control for the school to break even, let alone show any slim margin of profit. Mr Pope, the headmaster, played his part by selecting teaching staff whose personality or academic shortfall made it impossible for them to find other work, while the domestic and catering side was administered by Mrs Green, the housekeeper, who ran it as a private fiefdom. A large woman with swelling forearms, she was married to Mr Green, the small fox-faced French and games master. Their 18-year-old daughter, a repressed bad-tempered miss who cuffed the heads of boys she had it in for, was school matron.

But the syllabus and spirit of the school was set by the headmaster, Mr Pope, a one-armed zealot and crusading Christian fired by such ecstatic fervour he'd beat the edge of the pulpit as he preached and the empty sleeve of his tweed jacket would jerk free from his coat pocket in a frenzy. When he taught class or walked the school's dingy corridors and shabby dormitories he held himself upright and stiff. He twitched though, and even to a child – perhaps particularly to a child – he looked to be in a state of extreme tension. At times his control snapped and, scarlet and perspiring, eyes swelling from his face, he gave way to bouts of almost insane rage. It was an alarming sight, and fortunately these occasions were rare. Usually he remained imprisoned within a tight constricting rectitude destined one day to shatter under the strain and bring him to disgrace.

Letters we wrote to our families were censored. Those we received were opened and read before they were passed on. Tolerating no interference from parents, Mr Pope ruled the school fiercely in a tradition of muscular Christianity, *Mens sano in corpore sano*. Though he possessed neither himself, he believed in a healthy mind and a healthy body for others. And a healthy body meant cold showers, outdoor exercise and sport.

It rains less in Stirling than it rains in Arisaig; yet it rains a lot, as it does throughout Scotland. Daily, after we'd wolfed the pitiful snack called lunch, we were marched across Stirling Park to the playing fields which lay beneath the baleful edifice of Stirling Castle, its black granite silhouette backed by a leaden sky either threatening or delivering rain. There I played rugby in the wet, running across a muddy field after an odd-shaped ball, barging into people and trying not to catch up with it. At the end of the game, bruised and cold, soaked, filthy and bored, I marched back with the rest across the park, its slopes and trees already fading in the damp twilight of a winter dusk.

Reaching the school we stripped off our mud-soaked clothes in the changing rooms, then raced naked and freezing to the white-tiled area and sunken bath that was the communal shower. There was no question of the water being *hot*, there wasn't even a tap for hot.

Mr Pope 'took' the showers, he always took showers. Until my last days there, I don't recall this duty ever trusted to another master. As we scampered naked from the changing room he was waiting for us, standing above the sunken bath his one hand resting on the single lever that controlled it. In a shivering bunch we massed beside the bath. On command, the first eight jumped down to occupy it. Mr Pope's fingers would tighten convulsively on the lever and he'd shove it to full spurt. Twice a day Mr Pope discharged this duty. Twice a day he watched groups of pre-pubescent and pubescent boys dance and shriek and quiver in frozen anguish beneath him.

Hurst Grange didn't simmer with unlawful lust, the weather in Stirling was too cold for anything to *simmer*, but repressed sexuality oozed in a dank tide through the school's narrow corridors and chill high-ceilinged rooms. In the fiery blaze of his ardent religious conviction Mr Pope knew the flesh was evil. From the pulpit every morning, and twice on Sunday, he inveighed against carnality. Miss Green the matron shared the same horror of the flesh, though it was a trial she faced only once a week, rather than twice daily as he did. On Friday we were allowed our weekly bath in hot water; it was her job to 'take' bath night.

The communal bathroom was an unheated lino-floored room fitted out with hand basins and two freestanding tubs. Each had a line drawn around the inside four inches above the bottom, to mark the level to which it could be filled. One ration of warm water served four boys in turn.

'Taking' bath night involved Miss Green in not just impatient supervision but active participation in the event. A tall, bossy girl with long legs and a good figure but mean mouth and face pinched in constant irritation, she stood over each pair of boys as they sat in the puddle of soiled water in the bottom of the tubs, snapping out instructions and brandishing a large rough-bristled scrubbing brush of the kind used to scour floors. If they didn't move fast enough she'd use it on them hard to scrub their dirty necks.

In the same bath rota as myself was a boy named Forsyth who was in his last term and captain of the rugby team. Popular, he had a swagger and air of self-assurance we envied; we admired him particularly for the wispy but undeniable beard of pubic hair that grew above his genitals. One night as Forsyth sat in the tub while Miss Green stood over him in her customary threatening fashion, he got an erection. And Forsyth's erection was no mere twitch or sluggish thickening of the member; in the space of seconds it rose erect in rampant adolescent glory, aimed directly for Miss Green.

For an incredulous moment she stared at it hypnotised, frozen into shock. Then her sallow face went bright red, her mouth flew open. 'You filthy, filthy, disgusting little boy!' she shrieked. Pouncing on him she attacked it with the brush, scrubbing at his cock with the coarse bristles in a frenzy of disgust, reviling him while he yelled in pain, floundering in the bath and struggling to escape.

There is a time and a place for everything, I learned, and observed all that was happening around me with fascinated attention. I believed that I was the first person to have invented masturbation and that one day I would become rich and famous when I chose to reveal my secret to the world.

I bought a watch. I'd spotted an ad for it in a newspaper claiming it would function fifty feet underwater, which I thought would be useful in the explosives work I was planning for the holidays. I saved for eight months to get it; it was the first thing I'd ever bought and I was immensely proud of it. That watch meant a great deal to me and when it broke I cried.

I hadn't dropped it, I hadn't overwound it, it had just stopped. Mr Faulkner said he'd get it fixed for me in town and I gave it him.

Mr Faulkner taught maths. I was seeing him twice a week for coaching. These tutorials took place in his room among the warren of narrow, dark-varnished passages and winding stairs on the far side of the school. In his late twenties, he had sandy receding hair and a walrus moustache. Narrow chested, he wore an old tweed jacket with leather patches on the elbows, one of them coming detached. The Players Weights he smoked, thinner and smaller than normal cigarettes, had marked his finger and thumb with a sepia stain. He taught standing in the classroom, seedy and dejected with shoulders stooped and on his bad days gave off an air of such furtive desperation you felt sorry for him.

It was hard to concentrate during his tutorials; the room was heated only by a single-bar electric fire and the windows kept tight closed. The damp fog was pungent with old tobacco, a smell of stale beer from the empty bottles stashed beneath his bed and an odour of something else that was Mr Faulkner's own. At times I felt a little sick.

Spotting my discomfort he was always ready to take a break and talk about something else. 'If you ever put a foot wrong and come up against the law, I'll tell you one thing,' he said to me one evening. His offer connected with nothing we'd been discussing before, but I listened carefully to what he had to say. 'I mean it *can* happen,' he continued, 'You make some slight mistake anyone else would get away with but they go after you and you find yourself in front of the beak.' He paused and gnawed on the ragged fringe of his moustache, groping in his pocket for a packet of ten. 'Well, just say it happens and just because of rotten beastly luck you're found guilty and sentenced to a fine of £200 with the option of thirty days in prison ...' He jabbed at me fiercely with the Weights packet, '*Always* choose to pay the fine. If you have to beg, borrow or steal, pay it. *Never* choose prison – *the stigma stays with you always.*'

My watch, which he'd given to a shop in Stirling, took ages to repair. 'Foreign – a question of the spare part,' Mr Faulkner explained. Two weeks later it still had not been fixed. We were nearing the end of term and I asked him to recover it, I'd get it done in Fort William during the holidays. Just before breaking up I asked again. Mr Faulkner seemed flustered. 'Turned out to require a specialist, had to send it to Glasgow. Be ready waiting for you when you get back next term,' he promised.

It wasn't, and when I did return to school a month later Mr Faulkner was no longer on the Hurst Grange staff. The town was permanently off limits, but I got permission to ask after my property at its three jeweller/watchmakers. None had record of it. I don't believe Mr Faulkner had intended to steal it, but his solitary pleasure – drink – had proved hard to support on the pathetic wage the school paid him. I think he'd pawned the watch, then found himself too pushed for money to redeem it before he and his stigma had to move on.

Winston Churchill claimed that he found private school an invaluable experience: nothing one goes through afterwards can ever be as unpleasant again.

Quite early in my time at Hurst Grange I worked out my own technique to survive the place: hypochondria. My supposedly delicate health got me off games, allowing me to indulge my one true pleasure – reading. The skill I'd developed at turning sheet white and dropping in a dead faint to the floor won me spells in the sick room, and these gave me as much pleasure as I found later in weekends of luxury in five-star hotels. There was privacy and peace – even a primitive form of room service. Lying in its narrow bed with the coverlet pulled up to my chin I read compulsively, and the books I read transported me to another place. At first it was Henty and John Buchan – many of whose stories were set in the Highlands I missed so painfully – then Saki, Osbert Sitwell and Ronald Firbank. School was a dank prison to be endured, but I knew somewhere out there existed a world of capital cities and sparkling lights, a world of dazzling possibility.

Some afternoons, alone in the school while everyone else was at games, I'd go down to the cramped passage off the changing rooms where our tuck boxes were stored. These were kept padlocked. We had the keys, though the boxes were subject to arbitrary searches for contraband by Mr Pope. However, I'd constructed an ingenious false bottom to my own which remained undetected. In it I kept the fudge Nanny had made for me, a medicine bottle filled with gin decanted from my parents' drink cupboard and my .22 revolver together with a box of fifty rounds of high-velocity ammunition.

I'd sit in the dark-varnished, dimly lit changing room, nibble a square of fudge, nip on gin flavoured by toothpaste, and think about God, Arisaig, and that world of wit, glamour and romance which one day would be mine. Regularly I broke down the revolver to its separate components, cleaned and reassembled it. I'd punched a hole in the lining to the inside pocket of my school blazer to fit the barrel, and if I felt low I'd wear the gun to class.

Twenty years later in New York City when a man described to me how carrying a concealed pistol had changed his life, I understood exactly what he meant. He faced the world from a place of power; he gave off different vibes which others sensed and reacted to with respect. I never showed the revolver to anyone at school, never drew it and never fired it. Yet the feeling it was there, heavy in my breast pocket, cheered me enormously. In over three years at that school I learned little, but I did discover that carrying a gun is an excellent way for a boy to gain self-confidence.

Every morning for ten minutes, and at much greater length on Sundays, Mr Pope preached to us from the raised pulpit in the assembly hall. Twenty-five small boys stood below listening to him rant, their hair still wet from the morning shower.

He preached of damnation and hell fire, of the flaming pit and eternal torment that awaited us ... *unless*! It was the same severe Calvinist faith as I'd heard in the Presbyterian kirk in Arisaig, but afterwards could run home to the manse where Nanny was cooking Sunday lunch. There I'd been able to discount its uncompromising message, here I could not. Mr Pope's impassioned delivery made his words impossible to ignore; he became so excitable he frothed, spittle flew from his mouth. *Choose Christ or burn in hell.*

I resisted for a year – and then I cracked. I remember vividly the sermon that did it for me. Coming towards its climax Mr Pope declaimed, 'Suppose I were to step down from this pulpit and go amongst you with a rope ... winding that rope in and out between you where you stand, so some of you are on one side and some upon the other ... And all of you who are on *this* side of the rope will go to Heaven, and all on *that* side will burn for ever in everlasting punishment ... All you have to do is choose. *All you have to do to be saved is step over the rope.*'

Well ... some choice, I thought. And stepped.

Soon after came my last term at Hurst Grange – and also, rather more surprisingly, Mr Pope's. One evening, final assembly was taken by Mr Green – something that had never occurred before. Next day Mr Pope was still missing from the school; the evasive but exhilarated behaviour of the staff and lack of normal supervision told us something was amiss. A thrill ran along the frigid corridors of the school. First through wild rumour, then confirmed, we learned the reason for the headmaster's absence. He had been arrested for an act of gross indecency in Stirling Park.

In the letter sent later to all parents, encouraging them to keep their children there under a new headmaster, the school's principles were spelled out: academic excellence, respect for discipline and, above all, dedication to the moral and physical health and well being of the boys put into its care. The letter reiterated this code of honour, it had always been and always would remain in place. Mr Pope's little lapse was regrettable, of course, *but* – the letter pointed out – to the very last and even in the heat of passion the headmaster had himself remained faithful to these self-same high ideals. His 'indiscretion' had been with only an idle working-class lad from the neighbouring estate, *not*, it was stressed, absolutely *not* a pupil at the school.

Mother seemed flustered when I turned up at the manse. 'Darling, you're supposed to break up *tomorrow*!' she said.

'I told Mrs Scott she was wrong but she just won't listen,' Nanny said crossly as I hugged her.

I felt a huge relief that Hurst Grange was over and that I was home. It was already dark outside, rain was rattling against the windows but it was wonderful to be back.

'Well, darling, how did you *do* last term? Did anything super happen?' Mother asked.

'The headmaster buggered a boy in Stirling Park,' I told her.

'I'm sure he deserved it, darling,' she answered vaguely, her mind on what she had to announce. 'Your father wants you to learn to ski before you go to public school.'

It was thrilling news. 'Where?' I asked.

'Davos, we're joining him there after Christmas. He's got his hands on some money from a novel he's written but he's not owning up to how much, the swine!'

4
Davos

Mother and I travelled out to Davos by second class *wagon-lit*, taking a large Thermos of tea and food for the journey. Both of us wore skiing clothes. Mine had belonged to her brother Tony and been stored away by Nanny when he outgrew them.

Father was waiting at the station when we arrived and we drove to the hotel in a horse-drawn sleigh. He was in very cheerful spirits, which was not how I remembered him, but then neither Mother nor I had seen him for many months.

He loved winter sports. While training Special Forces in the war he'd never missed a season's skiing; he'd ended it in Italy commanding a school of mountain warfare. Following the Allies' victory he'd returned to England annoyed that hostilities had ended without his leading his specially trained killers across the Alps and *schussing* into Austria. Already in bad humour, he'd taken one glance at post-war Britain and detested it. Though rationing remained in force, signs of returning affluence were already evident in London. Big cars, restaurants which got round the restrictions to serve elaborate meals, a thriving black market, fur-collared coats, and a few expensive-looking people. He didn't care for the look of them at all. 'Spivs and profiteers,' he pronounced. Or 'bolshies'. Bolshies were the worst. He returned to Italy to run the British Council in Milan and write books, encouraged by the success of his first, a biography of Gino, which had been a best seller when it came out in 1935.

The place where we were staying in Davos turned out to be a large luxurious hotel, and this was a wonderful surprise. On the rare occasions I'd spent a night in a hotel in the past Mother had been paying, and the places we'd put up at hadn't resembled this in the least. Here, Father was standing treat. His finances fluctuated; usually broke, when he got money he'd settle the school bills and the liquor account, and for a few months rejoice in affluence with no thought for later. Besides, this was a special occasion, our first family holiday ever and an opportunity to teach me the final skill he felt I required for adult life: to ski.

He took me out on the nursery slopes next day. These were crowded with colourfully dressed people whizzing effortlessly down the piste but, unlike them, I was not allowed to use the tow lift. Edging my skis across the ascent, I had to climb. 'Strengthens the thighs,' Father said. 'Skiing is *all about* thigh muscles, the rest is just *style*.'

He was an excellent skier himself, but wholly self-taught and contemptuous of what he saw as current faddish technique. Skis wide apart, he'd come down the mountain steady as a table. He was used to skiing with a Bren gun strapped across his back.

Davos was a fashionable resort. Just turned thirteen, I was uncomfortably aware that we were dressed differently from everyone else. They wore well-cut tunics slashed with vivid colour, the trousers tapering to fit inside their boots. 'Frightful pansies,' said Father scornfully, throwing them a dismissive glance as they flashed by.

Mother's and my ski clothes dated from the thirties. Unearthed by Nanny from a cobwebbed trunk in the manse's loft, they smelled strongly of mothballs and had shapeless baggy trousers which fell loosely to overlap the ankles. Father, who never fell while skiing, had on a fishing sweater and old tweed jacket. And a large rucksack.

At his insistence, and very much against my will, I wore a rucksack myself. On his orders I'd filled it with my spare clothes and a blanket from the hotel bed. He inspected me critically when I came out onto the slopes on our first morning, weighing the rucksack in his hand. 'Won't do,' he pronounced. 'You can't go into the mountains without the right equipment. Weather may close in on you ... may have to hole up. You need a Primus, soup, groundsheet, sleeping bag.'

The nursery slopes stretched only 200 yards from their crest to the lively restaurant at the bottom, it seemed unlikely we'd be forced to bivouac half way down to pass the night. I tried to dissuade him. 'Well, we'll have to get those from a shop then,' I said.

'Don't be ridiculous! It's the *weight* that matters. Put some stones in your rucksack tomorrow,' he told me.

I wanted to learn how to ski with knees and skis glued together, coming down the slope in a series of perfectly timed interlocking parallel turns, while dressed in the latest fashion – not to invade Austria. But I knew I had to obey him or there'd be an ugly scene the next day.

That evening found me standing outside the hotel's entrance, staring forlornly at the high banks of frozen snow stacked up beside the driveway and wondering how I was going to dig through all that to find stones. The doorman, who was in an impressive floor-length all-weather coat and cocked hat, asked me what I wanted. I told him. 'For stones you must ask the hall porter,' he advised me.

Going back into the hotel lobby I hesitated, then approached the uniformed concierge standing behind his desk and explained my problem. The Swiss are impeccable hoteliers, it is their national métier. The hall porter showed not a flicker of surprise at my request. 'Will bricks do?' he asked me. By the time, a few hours later, when we'd finished dinner and I went upstairs to bed they'd been delivered to my room, wrapped in brown paper and tied with string.

Our hotel was situated in the centre of the resort, standing among others like it close to the funicular where the principal ski runs terminated. It was an opulent, old-style place with ornamental plasterwork and high moulded ceilings. Apart from one couple – war profiteers, Father decided – we were the only English people staying there. Other guests were French or Swiss, plus a few he looked at hard, suspecting they were German. We didn't get a chance to know any of them. One or two said good morning to us after we'd been there a few days but Father was deliberately rude to discourage them. 'You have to snub them *right away*,' he explained to me.

He didn't like the hotel, considering it too showy and grossly overheated. He made his feelings clear by ostentatiously removing his jacket when we had a drink in the bar. And he didn't care for the look of the other guests at all, but to me they appeared enormously glamorous. I'd grown up surrounded by adults in utility clothes – usually the same ones, for they had to be bought with clothing coupons. But the people in the hotel had elegance and grace, the women wore high-heeled shoes and make-up, and an intoxicating trace of expensive perfume wafted on the air behind them as they passed by with their equally dressy partners, in the direction of the restaurant.

The restaurant! It was a large, high-ceilinged, elegant room with tall windows which overlooked the mountains and which at night were covered by heavy drapes with swagged pelmets. It seated fifty or sixty people; the tables were set wide apart, the chairs were upholstered and comfortable. There was a dance floor, and a four-piece band played in the evenings after dinner.

But the *food*! The food was a revelation to me, it was *delicious*. The thought certainly didn't strike me at the time but it surely is quite *odd* that, instantly the war ended, in the newly liberated countries of France, Belgium and Italy restaurants were serving meals of pre-war excellence, while in Britain, co-victor in the struggle, people went on eating sausages, potatoes, boiled cabbage and a once-a-week egg for years afterward.

In the hotel restaurant I quickly mastered the significance of the bewildering array of cutlery and forest of wineglasses set out on the white linen tablecloth in front of me. By the time I sat down with my parents for the New Year's Eve gala dinner, I'd come to feel quite at home.

My new-found poise took a major knock when I saw that everyone else there was in evening dress. We, of course, were not. Mother, who gave no thought to her clothes, wore a utility frock bought several years before in Fort William. Father had on his usual tweed jacket with poacher's pockets large enough to accommodate a dead hare and a couple of trout. I was in my school suit.

But we'd had a bottle of champagne already, and he ordered several bottles of wine during the meal, of which I got enough to relax a little in my embarrassment at how different we looked from the other guests. Father was born two drinks behind the rest of the world and it took a lot to raise his spirits; habitually of few words and those disapproving, with drink he thawed a little. On New Year's Eve by the end of dinner he'd thawed quite a lot.

With the meal ended, and coffee and liqueurs served throughout the dining room, the band had segued from a medley of American show tunes into romantic dance music – slow, smoochy and pre-war French. Father had been talking cheerfully to Mother and myself, even laughing. He was jolly – 'full of beans', as Nanny would have said – but the mood of this after-dinner music didn't suit him, and my heart sank. He didn't *like* smoochy music, or French music, or anything French except their wine. He didn't want to listen to this sophisticated rubbish, he wanted something noisy, ethnic, *real*. Music of the mountains. His dissatisfaction become so expressive that, by the time he'd half risen impatiently from his seat to call over the waiter, several people at nearby tables were looking at us.

'Tell the band I'll buy them all a beer if they'll play the "Tyrolean Yodelling Song", he ordered the waiter.

I knew it was a mistake, *knew* it. In dismay I watched the waiter move off across the restaurant. In the distance I saw him whispering to the bandleader. A little later he came back to say none of the band drank beer; they'd ordered three large brandies and a crème de menthe frappé. Unfortunately they didn't know the number Father had requested.

At the hotel in Father's company time passed awkwardly, but I did learn to ski. Skiing lit a passion in me – I fell in love with the sport and stayed faithful to it throughout my life. That blue sky and glittering, all-white world ... the brilliance of the light ... the dry crisp air of the mountains ... that exhilarating sense of flight swooping down the fall line with mind and body one and concentration total ... Later in life it remained the one sure therapy to burn away the dross and restore me to myself.

Teaching me to ski was a priceless gift – I can forgive Father everything for that.

5
Stowe

Stowe was an eighteenth-century palace set in an exquisitely laid-out park containing lakes, woods and ruined temples buried beneath undergrowth uncleared for years owing to the lack of able-bodied gardeners during the war. The classical landscape had returned to wilderness.

The school's first headmaster, J. F. Roxburgh, was still running the place when I went there two years after the war ended. A flamboyant classics scholar, he owned thirty-two suits and dressed impeccably in a different one every day, a fresh silk handkerchief blooming colourfully from the breast pocket. The rule that the teaching staff must all be unmarried had relaxed a little by the time I got there, but the faculty was still dominantly homosexual. 'One man's meat is another man's passion,' Dr Humphries, the divinity tutor, lugubriously informed us. 'David and Jonathan …'

A number of the boys there lived in Kenya, Nassau or Bermuda, and many of my fellow pupils had parents who were what Mother termed *nouveaux riches* and Father called 'revolting spivs'. Well-dressed, sometimes rather raffish couples turned up at school on Sundays to whisk their sons off to lunch in shiny new Lagondas and Jaguar saloons – Jewboys' Bentleys, Father called them. To my relief, my own parents visited seldom. When they did they came by train as we had no car. After Sunday morning chapel I walked three miles down the dead straight drive to meet them at the White Hart in Buckingham, and it was disheartening to do so with other boys flashing by in expensive motor cars, headed for the same destination. And it was embarrassing to lunch in the White Hart's restaurant with parents dressed so differently from anyone else, a mother who spoke in such a piercing upper-crust accent, and a father who insisted on stowing his rucksack under the table and invariably had a violent row with the waiter.

My contemporaries at Stowe were more sophisticated, travelled and experienced in the world than I. Their parents gave them an allowance and bought them good clothes, the latest skis, sometimes a horse. They appeared more fortunate than myself, and the *very* lucky ones, I noticed, had not just one set of parents but two competing for their affection with the offer of holidays in St Moritz or Bermuda.

I had no experience in mixing with my peer group, but during my time at the school I made two friends I would continue to see on and off for the rest of my life. Nigel Broackes was a tall blond boy with a grave manner and measured voice, the same age as myself. Our bond sprang from a shared fascination with explosives. His prep school had been requisitioned by the army during the war and the grounds were littered with detonators, ammunition and unexploded grenades. More enterprising than myself, he manufactured his own gunpowder and was looking for a source to supply him with hydrochloric and nitric acid so he could produce gun-cotton. I was wildly impressed to learn he'd set fire to his prep school's gym.

'What charges did you use?' I asked, fascinated.

'For that an incendiary bomb,' he replied, and roared with laughter. He'd found it in the bushes and taken it to the gym to dismantle it when it ignited.

'What happened?' I asked, enthralled.

'Thirteen strokes on the bare bum with a steel-tipped dog whip.'

'Better to be expelled,' I said.

'No,' he corrected me firmly. 'Then they wouldn't have accepted me at Stowe.'

Another friend was Alex Howard, who intrigued me from the first because he dressed differently from anyone else. Slight, square-shouldered and stiffly upright, he sported a cravat in place of the usual tie and wore stylish lace-up ankle boots in tooled leather. 'Finest Northumberland calf. Hand-made,' he told me proudly. He had an oddly explosive way of talking, staccato and emphatic.

'Where can one get them?' I asked.

'Lobb. Can't now. Made for my grandfather,' he explained. They were the most beautiful shoes I'd ever come across but they were a little tight for him, you could see they pinched in the way he walked.

While getting to know him I learned his mother was a novelist. She'd published several books, but the literary life she and Alex's family lived in London didn't sound remotely like Father's or our own. 'She throws parties. Sort of open house. Lots of interesting types, John Davenport, Dylan Thomas, Gerald Hamilton, who was the model for Mr Norris in Isherwood's *Mr Norris Changes Trains* ... You must come along sometime,' he suggested.

'I'd love to,' I told him.

Alex was promising. Mother had said to me, 'You mustn't accept any invitations, we'll only have to ask them back,' but I'd deal with that when I came to it, I thought.

I had a home in London now, we used Arisaig only for summer holidays. Father was living in Milan but Mother had bought a house off The Boltons in South Kensington. An eight-bedroom, one-bathroom Victorian mansion with garden, it was an imposing house but in poor condition, for the building had been damaged when a bomb had fallen further down the street, and the masonry had been glued back in place with cheap mortar.

It was here that Nigel came to tea one day, meeting Mother and my nine-year-old brother David over toast and margarine with Marmite. We'd been talking for a little while before Mother asked, 'Don't you find it lonely being an only child, Nigel? Don't you wish you had brothers and sisters to play with?'

'Not really, Mrs Scott,' Nigel answered in the slow considered way he spoke even then. 'You see, I will inherit a trust fund of £30,000 when I'm twenty-one, and if I had brothers and sisters I'd have to share it with them.'

Later during those same school holidays I was asked by Alex to *his* home. We'd been to the cinema and afterwards walked there along the Fulham Road. Part of a terrace of what once had been workmen's cottages, the house stood back from the street in a small untended garden.

Margot, his mother, had long dark hair, a pale thirties face and a distracted manner; the living room where she sat knitting was untidy and cluttered. Alex had breezed in cheerfully to introduce me but I felt we weren't really welcome. Perhaps it was a bad moment. Papers were scattered over the floor and the walls were scrawled with notes written with soft pencil in a large spiky hand. Alex gamely did his best to get a conversation started but there were awkward pauses. In one of them the ball of wool Margot was using rolled off her lap on to the floor. Reaching out a hand to the table beside her, she picked up a hypodermic syringe, leaned down to spear the ball and fished it back on to her lap to continue knitting.

Soon afterwards Alex said we would move on. 'Not one of her good days,' he observed when we were in the street. But I was thrilled, I felt I'd penetrated Bohemia, and my impression of the exotic was enhanced by meeting Alex's father a few days later. Formally dressed in blue suit, stiff collar and Guards' Brigade tie, he radiated a smiling bland imperturbability. In fact I got the impression he actually enjoyed the chaos of his household. 'What does your father do?' I asked Alex.

'Works for the War Office. Can't say more,' he explained succinctly.

Was he a spy? I wondered, and couldn't wait to be invited again to this tumbledown house where people led such emancipated lives and I might meet Dylan Thomas. It seemed to me a place of infinite possibility.

Decadence was harder to come by during term. Classes took up the morning, evenings were filled by prep, and in the afternoons sport was compulsory.

Father was disgusted by my loathing of all games. I'd made the mistake of telling him I thought competitive sport brought out the very worst in people, and he'd been so incensed I thought he was going to have a stroke. But the school contained an active anti-hearty movement and I was not alone in my views. Nigel disliked team sports as much as I did, but when we'd been there two years he was made captain of the house rugger team. I was shocked to read the announcement on the bulletin board and challenged him about it.

'I detest rugger,' he admitted. 'But when I leave here I'm going to have to lead people – and that means to inspire and organise them. I despise games as much as you do, but one needs to learn how.'

Instead of playing rugger or cricket, I ran. Living among so many people felt alien to me and I longed for privacy; running, I was alone. Each afternoon I jogged for miles through a classical landscape, across a Palladian bridge, down the Graecian valley overlooked by a temple standing in a grove of trees ... all of it man-made, overgrown and ruined. When I returned to shower and change, the rest of the school would still be at games. Taking a book with me, I walked through the woods to where a small stream tumbled into one of the lakes. A mossy grotto had been built here overlooking the water and here I sat and read:

Now as I was young and easy under the apple boughs
About the lilting house and happy as the grass was green ...

I was addicted to poetry and Dylan Thomas's words spoke directly into my open heart; I reached a strange exalted state as I murmured them, a sort of ecstasy. I could achieve the same mood at evensong: *O Lord support us all day long of this troublous life until the shades lengthen and the evening comes, the busy world is hushed, the fever of life over and our work done ...*

We attended chapel twice on Sunday, and evensong three times a week. Services were taken by two ordained ministers who were masters at the school. I was drawn to neither, put off by the mournful lechery of one and the jaunty worldliness of the other. Unlike Hurst Grange the thrust of the sermons was not spiritual but reflected the purpose of the school: to train a boy for dominance in whatever field, for power. Success meant wealth, position and authority. But by then I knew I didn't *like* power or authority. I disliked being told what to do, and I loathed the obvious relish those with power derived from exercising it. I had no wish to push others around myself.

And, though I dreamed of entering a more glamorous and amusing milieu, I had no desire for riches either. I wanted some stylish clothes and enough cash in my pocket to pay for drinks, but I didn't want *wealth. It is easier for a camel to go through the eye of a needle than for a rich man to enter the kingdom of God* ... The faith in which Mr Pope had ensnared me was explicit on the point. And money was what my parents had been arguing about constantly for as long as I could remember; I'd determined never to talk about it myself or to let it affect me. But the sermons at Stowe struck a different note. Yes, the eye of the needle is a narrow gate but it was perfectly possible for a well-laden camel to get through it, the mournful minister assured us. It depended on the skill of the camel driver.

I yearned to be grown up, to be a part of that scintillating world I'd read about and briefly glimpsed in Davos. Most specifically, aged fifteen, I longed to lose my virginity. The opportunity to do so was presented by a visit to Paris during the summer holidays. The place seemed absolutely appropriate, for what I knew about sex came from reading Henry Miller and his books about untrammelled life on the Left Bank.

I was in Paris for only one night, a stopover on my way to the headwaters of the river Loire. Father had by now moved on to run the British Council in Belgrade, but even from that far away he continued to exert a baleful influence upon my life, devising adventure holidays it took all my ingenuity to avoid. This latest, which coincided with one of his brief visits to England, had proved inescapable.

From some army-surplus depot he'd bought me an inflatable rubber boat. It was a dismaying present. Designed to carry the entire fourteen-man crew of a B52 Flying Fortress obliged to ditch in mid-Atlantic, even deflated the thing barely fitted into two gigantic rubberised sacks. Father's plan was that I should haul the unwieldy mass of it to the source of the Loire, fill it with air, and sail down to the sea 400 miles away. He gave me £30, telling me not to return to England for a month.

I needed someone with me, if only to carry the other rubberised sack. Nigel emphatically did not want to come, Alex was equally appalled by the idea. Brian Calvert was a late choice, I didn't know him that well.

The rubberised bags and our rucksacks meant each of us was carrying a load of about sixty pounds. Arriving at the Gare du Nord in the early evening, we had a fearful job getting the inflatable boat across Paris on the *Métro* during the rush hour. We checked into a cheap hotel on the Left Bank, us and the boat. The narrow street contained a seedy bar and a poky restaurant, the area had the authentic Henry Miller ambience, I thought. Over the set menu I told Calvert of my intention to lose my virginity after dinner.

Discouraged by the boat/train journey and the problems we'd had getting the huge rubberised bags across Paris, he was less thrilled by my plan than I'd expected. 'So what am I supposed to do while all this is going on?' he asked.

'You can lose your virginity too,' I suggested helpfully, but he remained cool to the idea. 'It's beastly inconsiderate of you,' he complained.

Dinner over, Calvert returned sulkily to our hotel room and the blow-up boat, and I set off alone for the Champs Élysées. Crowded with people *en promenade*, the wide avenue with its bars and sidewalk cafés looked a vision of glamour to me. Emerging from the subway, I'd hardly started up it before being propositioned by an Arab. Badly dressed, unshaven, with rotted teeth, it was obvious he was what Nanny called a 'ruffian'. I thanked him politely for his alarming suggestion and continued on my way.

Already in a state of considerable disquiet at the idea of what lay ahead, looking back I realise I was not as composed or discriminating as I should have been. And of the many women in the street which, if any, were prostitutes? How did you recognise one for sure? When a middle-aged woman in mesh stockings, high heels and a great deal of make-up swayed out of the crowd to murmur, '*Bon soir, tu veux faire l'amour avec moi*?' I was wound so tight I said yes at once.

I began to regret it as I walked with her to a nearby hotel. She had already told me the price, and when we'd climbed the stairs to her squalid room I paid her the 50 francs she'd asked for. 'It's normal also to give a tip,' she said.

A tip! Henry Miller hadn't mentioned that. I explained about the long voyage downriver that lay ahead of me, I really couldn't afford a tip.

'Huh, Monsieur Minimum,' she said scornfully. 'OK, I must wash you.'

I sat on the bidet while she did so. I was appalled by the woman I'd chosen, she was stout and old and hideous. Overcome by dismay, my heart was still thudding with terrified anticipation.

Having done with washing me, the woman dried my already overheated parts with a skimpy towel. Then in a bored, vaguely resentful way she removed just her skirt, putting it on to a hanger before clambering a little stiffly on to the bed. 'OK, come here,' she said wearily, and spread her legs.

I stared in awe, terror and horrified fascination at a huge black animal covered in coarse spiky hair, crouched upon her belly. 'Come *here*!' she repeated impatiently.

I climbed on to the bed. So alarmed, so tense I could scarcely breathe, I positioned myself on top of her. Every muscle, every tendon in my body was stretched to breaking point. We lay there still, I did not dare to move.

'*Il faut faire jig-jig*,' she said crossly.

Jig-jig! the time it takes to say the word already was too much. One *jig* ... and that was it. Instant deforescence. It was all over in less than five seconds.

Next day Calvert and I took the train to Roanne, some distance from the source of the Loire. Hauling our unwieldy baggage to the riverbank, we spent an hour inflating the several compartments of the boat with a foot pump, launched it and set sail downstream.

My disillusion and disappointment with sex lasted for several days and the incident hung heavy between us, but our voyage down the river proved so magical it finally drove the unhappiness from my mind. The weather was hot and sunny, beneath blue unclouded skies we drifted through an idyllic countryside of trees and fields and cows, occasionally passing through a small town.

Blown up, the boat turned out to be circular – it was impossible to steer. Wearing only swimming shorts, we sat opposite one another, straddling the inflated sides and using a paddle to keep the craft more or less in the middle of the stream. Towards evening, when the light filtering through the trees dappled the smooth surface of the water with shadows, we watched out for a riverside inn. Spotting one ahead that didn't look too grand, we paddled hard cross-current to reach the bank and tie up there. We rented their cheapest room and ate dinner in the restaurant.

It was too good to last, of course. In ten days most of our money was gone and it began to rain heavily. It continued to rain while we shopped for the cheapest food and camped by the riverbank. On the towpath a man ran his bicycle over the tomatoes we had bought for lunch. It went on raining and I became discouraged. The river had grown wider as we descended, it flowed more slowly now and was interrupted periodically by a barrage. I'd constructed a tent from the rubberised bags and groundsheet and lay under this reading Harold Nicolson while the boat revolved slowly as it drifted downstream in the rain. Every few miles it would bump up against a barrage. I'd emerge to help Calvert carry it round the obstruction and relaunch it below the barrier, then return to my book in damp ill humour. 'You're not even trying!' he accused, and it was true. I must have been insufferable.

A third of our floorspace was now flooded. I'd accidentally burned a hole in one of the inflated compartments with a cigarette. Part of the hull had collapsed and dragged behind us in the water, it was hopeless attempting to control the boat's course. Calvert tried though, perched on the side in the driving rain and thrashing the river with his paddle while I sulked reading in my tent. A man after my Father's heart, he was thoroughly cheered up by our adversities, he loved camping and challenging discomfort and hoarding our diminishing resources. Our daily rations were reduced to subsistence level so we could reach the sea.

We got down to our last 20 francs with twenty miles still to go. I didn't give a damn about reaching the sea by now. I told Calvert we were giving up and going back to England. He was furious. Burning with resentment he would not speak a word to me throughout our train journey to Paris. He seethed in angry silence, but as we were dragging those frightful rubberised sacks across the city his indignation got too much for him and he burst out, '*Fifty francs*! If only you'd *controlled yourself* we could have made it to the Atlantic!'

All actions entail consequences – a lesson I was about to learn. Losing my virginity in Paris led to what Nanny called 'ructions', not with Father as usual, but with my housemaster.

It was a week after the start of term. I'd gone to the doctor because I believed the wages of sin had found me out and that I had tertiary syphilis and was going mad. After a deeply embarrassing test he assured me the infection was not as serious as I'd feared. 'Give you some tablets. Clear it up jolly quickly. But we do need to know you know … I mean, some other chap's got the same little problem as yourself and we have to know where it's coming from and to help him too. Who was it, Scott? Come on, it's best you tell me.'

I hesitated, 'Actually, it wasn't a school chap sir,' I said.

'Not a local chap, surely?'

'Actually it wasn't a chap at all, sir,' I told him.

A girl! He was shaken by the news, though his reaction was as nothing compared to my housemaster's. Mr MacDonald was a shambling, untidy man with a moustache, who spluttered when angry. He was already exhibiting signs of strain as he received me in his study. A few minutes later he seemed completely to have lost control of himself. 'Filthy, degraded thing to do,' he raged. 'You're vile Scott, *you have put your person where I wouldn't put the ferrule of my umbrella*!' He paused, choked by the enormity of what I'd done and struggling to master his emotions. 'I'll have to beat you, of course. Bend over that chair.'

I did. He did. And not for the first time. I'd been beaten for smoking, for drinking, for cutting sport and for reading Henry Miller. Now these were six strokes too far. I ran away from Stowe, never to return. I was just sixteen years old; I had one shilling and two bars of nut chocolate in my pocket, and I was headed for Paris to become a barman in a nightclub and write a novel about lowlife, like Henry Miller.

6
London

The setting in which I found myself was underground, grimly Dickensian and chilly ... a series of low, arched vaults built of ancient blackened brick, poorly lit by naked sixty-watt bulbs. The job was gruelling, we started at 7.50 am and knocked off at 5.00. I was paid ten shillings per week. It wasn't Paris and it wasn't a nightclub, but the premises of a wine shipper, Brown, Gore and Welch, situated beneath the street 200 yards from the Tower of London.

On the run from Stowe I had walked to London in three days, keeping to secondary roads as I thought I might be pursued and caught on the obvious routes to town. To get to France I needed money and fresh clothes; the only person I could count on for these was Nanny.

To my vast relief, when I reached our family house in Gilston Road Nanny was alone; Mother was with Father in Yugoslavia, brother David was away at boarding school. 'Goodness gracious, where *have* you been, Jeremy? I'll run you a bath, you look like you've been sleeping under a haystack,' Nanny said as she let me in.

I hugged her; she was the only person I *could* hug without awkwardness. 'Were there any telephone calls?' I asked apprehensively.

'It's been going the whole blessed time,' she said crossly. 'What a commotion! I won't answer the dratted thing.'

She made up the bed in my room and ran a hot bath from the infirm geyser in the house's only bathroom.

'Will you lend me the money to get to France?' I asked her.

'Why ever are you gadding off to foreign parts again? The rest of you are always doing that, and look at all the good it does them.'

'I have to get to Paris, Nanny.'

'We'll see about that in the morning,' she told me firmly. 'Now I'll make you something to eat and you get a good night's sleep. You look just about done in.'

Next morning at 10 am she served me a breakfast of fried eggs, fried bread, bacon and fried tomatoes. Afterwards I sat in a collapsed armchair in the familiar run-down comfort of the big drawing room, read the paper and looked out at the garden and thought what joy it was to be free again.

I lingered there for three days. Seduced by ease, by tranquillity and the reassuring rhythm of regular meals and mid-morning coffee provided by Nanny, I dawdled on my flight to France and I was caught. The school had contacted Father in Belgrade and Mother flew back to London.

There were ructions. 'Your housemaster's written. He says that in twenty-five years he's never known a boy who's got less out of the public school system than you,' she announced.

They gave up on my education. 'You have to work, but you can bloody well learn a trade at the same time,' Father told me in the course of a stormy telephone call from

Yugoslavia. He'd arranged this job for me through a friend in the wine business.

There were five of us working in the vaults under Mr Twort, the head cellarman, who dressed in a crisp brown overall and rimless spectacles. The rest of us wore heavy leather aprons as we manhandled the wooden hogsheads into position for treating or bottling. Neither the work, the methods, nor the machinery had altered for a couple of hundred years. Bottling was done by hand, holding the bottle to be filled beneath the cask's spigot, then passing it to a man who operated a pump handle and crude metal piston to push in the cork.

My workmates all lived near by in the East End, walking to the job each morning in flat caps. They could not have been nicer to me and I liked all of them enormously. At 10.30 am and 3.30 pm work stopped for fifteen minutes and we were each given a pint of Chablis, doled out into tin mugs by Mr Twort. Every evening most of us went home wearing a rubber hot-water-bottle filled with the same non-vintage.

Living at Gilston Road my social life was restricted by my income, but by now I'd met a few people my own age; I went out some evenings and on those nights when I had no invitation read Sartre, Jean Anouilh and Christopher Fry. This quality of life deteriorated severely when Father returned to live at home; it was upsetting for everyone.

He gave up the British Council to take a job on the *Daily Telegraph*, where he'd worked before the war. Moving back into Gilston Road, he instituted a regime which he followed daily without deviation. Rising at 7.30 am to take a cold bath, he left the house after breakfast to walk to Fleet Street, always wearing his mountaineering rucksack; he walked home in the evening, covering nine miles every day. After dinner with the family, always a frugal meal, he retired to his study to drink and write until 1.00 am. He'd published three novels since the war and was working on a fourth. He slept on a sofa in his study under a single blanket and without sheets. The sofa was not quite long enough for him to stretch out, his feet rested on an orange box set up at the end. Though there were several empty bedrooms in the house, this was the arrangement he preferred.

Mother and he quarrelled continuously, not in a series of different rows but invariably the same row which had been going on for as long as I could remember. The root of the difference between them lay in the fact that Mother had money and was niggardly, while he had none and was wasteful. They had been fighting over the subject for at least fifteen years when, during a particularly mean and detailed exchange, he interrupted her mid-sentence to say, 'Hold it! I know you've told me before, but explain to me again, what *is* the difference between capital and interest? Isn't it all just *money*?'

Their characters were opposed in every way. Mother enjoyed seeing friends and her many relatives. Father hated going out. After one party at which he'd behaved particularly badly Mother had sat silent and chagrined in the taxi home, but he'd been full of beans. '*Well*,' he'd said, grinning with uncharacteristic glee, 'They won't ask *us* again!'

Endemically rude himself, he was outraged by rudeness in others. For the *Telegraph* he had to organise a dinner for 400 guests at the Savoy on election night. The great and the good and more-or-less everyone of note were sent invitations. Father brought home the reply he'd received from Evelyn Waugh. Printed on stiff card, obviously in a bulk run of many copies, its nonchalant message read: 'Mr Evelyn Waugh thanks you for your invitation but regrets that he is unable to do whatever it is you have suggested.' I thought it delicious, but Father was speechless at the slight.

Whenever possible I went out in the evening. If I returned home late, there would still be a strip of light beneath his door. Removing my shoes, I'd creep upstairs, avoiding the treads which creaked and the two eaten away by woodworm. One night he caught me. 'Come in here,' he ordered. 'I want to talk to you about your future. What do you intend to do with your life?'

I knew he would not warm to the few notions I had. I muttered something about getting through two years in the army first.

'That will teach you discipline and already you know something about weaponry, but you should prepare the ground *now*. I've had a word with your cousin Graham. You'll have to get your hair cut, but they're looking for the right sort of chaps.'

Graham Eyres-Monsell was Uncle Bobby's only son. A friend of Kim Philby, he held a job in Military Intelligence, where he'd worked throughout the war. That Saturday I went to call upon him at Kinnerton Street off Belgrave Square. The place he lived in had been a morgue. 'This is where the stiffs were stored,' he explained, showing me into the living room. 'I thought of keeping the *loculi* but it complicated the placement of the furniture.'

He was a large, pale-fleshed man in his mid-forties, with a soft face and a loose mouth full of long yellow teeth. He served tea from a silver teapot in delicate china cups. 'So tell me about yourself,' he proposed, sitting down beside me on the sofa.

I did so, launching into a history of my accomplishments designed to impress him. He listened carefully, looking at me intently as I elaborated on my familiarity with rifle, Sten gun and automatic pistol, my experience of grenades, gun-cotton and practical demolition, going on to reveal the training

Father had given me in hand-to-hand combat, silent killing and garrotting ...

'Ah yes,' Graham interrupted, perking up, 'You like garrotting?'

'Well ... yes, but I haven't actually killed anyone yet,' I admitted.

'How would you garrotte *me*?' he asked keenly.

The skill was obviously important. I didn't want to get the answer wrong. 'It works best at an angle, so from behind while you're seated, you're bigger than me.'

'What would you use?'

'My belt,' I suggested.

He nodded enthusiastically, 'Go on, then.'

Did he mean *do* it? Now? Surely not, I thought wildly. So I continued, speaking knowledgeably of spring coshes, throwing knives, bronco kicks, and that moment of especial intimacy which comes when you break your opponents windpipe with a tightly rolled newspaper, but after a while I grew unnerved by the fixity of his unblinking gaze. My speech faltered and ground to a halt as I felt his plump pale hand inching upward on my thigh.

I stiffened – but sadly not in any way that would have cheered Cousin Graham. He took it well; he was not in the least insistent, but neither did he waste any further time. Once he had regained his composure he said, 'I'm sorry, Jeremy, but I don't think that I can be of help. I'm afraid you're just not the sort of man we're looking for.'

I caught the number 14 bus home, where I had to tell Father I'd been rejected. I'd failed the first requirement for a job in Military Intelligence: To be prepared to do whatever is necessary to achieve the end required.

Leaving the cellar I went to Bordeaux, where I was attached

to Bouchard Père et Fils to learn about claret, to Beaune to learn about burgundy, finally to Epernay for champagne. Work in each place consisted of the same manual jobs I'd been performing in the cellar – filtering, bottling, but mainly rolling casks and stacking crates – interrupted by tastings 'upstairs' and occasional lunches in the directors' dining room. The wine trade was a small, self-consciously snobbish profession and those in it stayed pretty much drunk during the day, not falling about but well oiled and insulated from the world.

I was not paid for the year this apprenticeship lasted, but lived on a small allowance given me by Father on the understanding I should not return to England until drafted. I lived frugally, eating bread and cheese in the cheapest rooms I could rent and reading in the evening. And I learned a little about wine.

At the end of my apprenticeship Nigel Broackes joined me in Biarritz, bringing with him two girls we knew in London, Shirley and Charlotte. For him and myself this was our last celebration of freedom for the next two years: we'd received our draft papers and were due to join the army in less than a month.

He'd left Stowe soon after I had while he was still sixteen, and gone to work in an underwriter's office at Lloyd's. 'Much more useful than remaining at school, we both have commercial experience now. When we go for a job after the army it will prove invaluable,' he said.

Biarritz had been a popular resort earlier in the century and, though no longer fashionable, the little town had an easy, civilised feel to it. We took four rooms in a small hotel, lay on the beach and dipped into a cold sea; Nigel and I spent the evenings trying to seduce the girls. But at that time nice girls didn't, and, frustratingly, Shirley and Charlotte were no exception to the rule. One evening Nigel suggested the two of us struck out alone and tried our luck at the casino.

The casino was a splendid Edwardian building overlooking the sea in the centre of town, but because of our age we were not allowed into the *salles privées* but restricted to playing boule in the outer *salon*, an elegant room with a high, moulded ceiling. Standing in the crowd by the table we studied the game for a while before Nigel said, 'It's unfairly weighted because of the double zero, but I suggest we follow the same method as the greyhound syndicate I set up.'

That had involved a slide-rule which he did not have here, but we tried it anyway, using a joint capital of £10. The system involved waiting for a prolonged run on one of the colours, then starting to bet against it. It worked, though it was quite boring.

But we scored at the table that night, trebling our capital in a couple of hours. Quitting while we were ahead, we had a drink on the crowded terrace. It was a fine night, a dance band was playing and we felt lucky and happy and grown-up. Why take a job if one could live like this, I thought.

A couple of days later I said goodbye to the others and caught the train to Nice. Father had cabled to say I should meet him there, we would take a walk together and have a serious talk.

Our walk would be from Nice to St Tropez. As with all his schemes, it was a poor idea. I don't think he had ever been to the south of France, but he'd studied the ground on topographical maps and the close-together contour lines and rugged terrain reaching almost to the sea had appealed to him greatly.

As instructed, I was waiting for him at Nice airport. In old corduroys, his usual jacket with poacher's pockets, wearing his own mountaineering rucksack and carrying another for me, he was not hard to pick out among the rest. Making our way past other passengers in fashionable resortwear, we came out of the terminal. He'd been faux jovial when we met, but the sight of trim suburban villas scattered over the foothills of the Alps and the busy stream of traffic rushing past on the *littoral* put him into immediate bad humour. The wartime maps he was using gave no indication of such development, *this* wasn't what he'd been expecting at all.

We set off at once, striking inland towards Grasse with the intention of walking parallel to the coast at an altitude of 1,000 or 1,500 feet. Father would not use roads and the route he chose involved scaling fences and making our way through private property and people's gardens, sometimes under the startled gaze of the owners sunbathing around their swimming pool. 'No such thing as trespass provided you don't cause damage or chase sheep,' he announced. I knew it was the law in Scotland; whether it was the same under the Code Napoleon, I doubted.

At night, Father cooked our basic rations on a Primus stove. We slept, each wrapped in a single blanket, beneath a tree. After three days we were forced down to the coast and tramped along the shoreline, scrambling over rocky headlands and traipsing across private beaches set up with *matelas* and parasols ... two hot figures in rucksacks marching in line ahead, one cross Englishman followed by his sullen son.

In time we reached St Tropez. The little port was not then a popular resort. Its name meant nothing to Father but for me had thrilling associations with Guy de Maupassant and Colette. We stayed in a small hotel and next day took the bus to Nice. Seated side by side, the journey provided the opportunity for the serious talk I had been dreading. 'Well, if you don't like the wine trade what *are* you going to do?' Father demanded. 'Sheep-farm in Australia?'

The outback wasn't really what I had in mind. I saw myself in a faultlessly cut white suit and co-respondent shoes, frosted glass in hand, a yacht in the background. I didn't mention my ambition, but I intended to become a professional gambler. In response to my increasingly desperate evasions, Father grew irascible. We were barely speaking by the time we reached the airport. His plane to Belgrade was leaving a couple of hours before my own. Just before his flight was called he said, 'You'll be on army pay from next week so I'm stopping your allowance.'

Wearing his hanging-judge face, thoroughly exasperated, he handed me my ticket to London and £50 in cash. 'That's *it*,' he told me, 'From now on, you're on your own. It's your life. Personally, I don't care *what* you do so long as you don't become *a male ballet dancer*.' It was the worst thing he could imagine, the ultimate pit of degradation and shame.

Father's plane took off. Three hours later I was in Monte Carlo. I'd retrieved my suitcase from the airport locker, dumped my rucksack, blanket and groundsheet in a trash bin, and caught the train there.

From the *Guide Michélin* I'd chosen the four-star Metropole; I took a room with a balcony and view of the harbour. The rate was considerable but I was recklessly indifferent to cost. I had £10 of my own; with the money Father had given me, I was rich. And, thanks to Nigel, I had an infallible system at roulette and was about to win big, I could afford to be extravagant.

After the privations of the forced march with Father, I revelled in the hotel's opulent comfort. Unpacking my rumpled school suit of thick grey flannel, now slightly too small for me, I hung it in the steam of the shower to get rid of the worst creases, then took a long bath in the huge tub. I dressed with care, had one drink in the hotel bar to achieve the right mood, then strolled the 200 yards to the casino.

While in St Tropez I'd soaked my passport in water, then smudged and altered the birthdate. I didn't *look* twenty-one, but I gained entry without problem. In the rococo splendour of the belle époque interior I sniffed the mix of perfume and cigarette smoke and was spellbound with happiness. This was the setting of my new career and the ambience I was meant for.

Making my way to the crowded roulette table I waited for three successive *noires* then began to play. I lost and doubled up, lost, and lost again. My luck was atrocious. In disbelief I watched my pile of 10-franc chips dwindle alarmingly. Doubling up, in mounting panic I continued betting. The stack shrank till it wasn't a stack at all, just a few loose chips, then none. I felt ill, in less than fifteen minutes I had lost everything except the £5 in my shoe.

Horrified, I stumbled from the casino, unable to credit what had happened.

Back at the hotel, mocked by the ornate magnificence of the lobby, I rode the elevator and went directly to my room. I slumped at the Louis Quinze escritoire utterly dejected. I knew that I was ruined; I could not even settle the hotel bill.

Stunned by misery, I stared at the folder in front of me. After several moments I realised it was the room-service menu ... a wild notion leapt into my mind. I was aware of room service. It had existed at our hotel in Davos, where there had been a similar menu in my room, but I had never used it. The very idea of such convenience would have enraged Father. Now my heart was thumping with the audacity and sheer naughtiness of my intention as I planned the meal with exquisite care. Picking up the telephone, I ordered an elaborate dinner and a bottle of champagne.

Twenty minutes later a loaded trolley was wheeled in soundlessly. The deferential waiter set up a table at the window with lots of silver cutlery and a satisfying show of crystal wineglasses. I took my place at table in perfect happiness.

Night had fallen, a moon rode high in the warm dark. Below me the harbour was alive with yachts and light and the distant sound of music. Seated at the window, I enjoyed the finest and most expensive meal I had ever tasted. For the very first time my recently acquired knowledge of wine proved of practical use; the bottle of Roederer '45 I'd ordered was superb.

I ate slowly, savouring every mouthful, each meditative draught of wine. And, while I ate, I wrote a letter on the elaborately embossed hotel stationery describing the experience, the place, the view, the feast I was enjoying. I took my time. Sealing it in an envelope, I addressed it to Conscript J. G. Scott, c/o Hadrian's Camp, Carlisle. I knew enough about army life to realise that by the time I received that letter I would be living in cold discomfort surrounded by adversity, but I thought that reading it and learning what a fine time I was experiencing at this particular moment would cheer me up. I'd signed off, wishing myself the very best in my new life.

Abandoning my suitcase, clothes and possessions in the hotel room, I took with me only the last volume of Sartre's *Chemins de la Liberte*, which I hadn't finished. Royally drunk, I walked down to the lobby. I gave the hall porter my letter and watched him post it in the brass-bound mahogany mailbox for despatch next morning. No mention of the cost of the stamp – it would go on my bill.

Leaving the hotel, I sauntered downhill 300 yards to the railway station and caught the train to Nice. In the airport I slept and hung around for nine hours, then took the next flight to England to join the army.

7
Suez Canal

Hadrian's Camp was a vast parade ground, a quarter-mile square, surrounded by a Third World village of tar-roofed wooden huts set in desolate open country whipped by a cold wind from the north Atlantic. It stood, or rather sprawled, outside Carlisle, a garrison town since Roman times.

I lived in one of the wooden huts together with fifteen other conscripts under the control of a corporal a year older than ourselves, whose bed stood nearest to the smoky coal-burning stove. We slept with every window sealed. One of the few class differences in England persisting to this day, although diluted, is that the upper believe fresh air is good for you, the lower that it should be avoided at all cost.

Reveille sounded at 5.30 am, while it was still dark. All the lights were switched on at once and the corporal began to shout. The muffled shapes in the twin rows of beds stirred into reluctant complaining life. A hand reached out from the malodorous lair of the man next to me, groping for a pack of cigarettes. He lit one with his cropped head still beneath the blankets and emerged blearily in a storm of coughing to greet the fug of dawn.

All day we were drilled, marched, made to run, screamed at and abused. Confined to camp, we polished the nailheads in the wooden floor and swept the parade ground clear of snow with the three-inch brushes issued to apply blanco to our belts.

The conscripts in my hut spoke in a wide variety of regional accents. I too had a distinctive accent. For some reason I had never modified the almost caricature voice I had inherited from my parents; it had never occurred to me that I could, any more than I could change the colour of my eyes.

Class awareness and class resentment were very real in England in the early 'fifties. I expected problems, but astonishingly none arose. Shared adversity makes for a powerful bond, of course, but my fellow soldiers could not have been nicer. I hadn't been taught class consciousness, it had never been discussed at home. Mother believed herself upper class in the same unthinking way she believed she had two legs, and Father, for all his faults, was not a snob. With the exception of the king, Winston Churchill and a handful of dead writers, soldiers and explorers, he disliked everybody equally; his prejudice was impartial.

After four months' basic training I was wrongly identified as a leader of men and sent south to Mons Officer Cadet School. I arrived among an intake of forty others in midwinter. Lined up on the square and shivering at attention, we were welcomed by Sergeant-Major Britain, 6' 6" of ramrod spine, a furious red face with moustaches and a roar that carried for miles. Tired, cold, weighed down by equipment, we heard the list of planned atrocities they had in store for us. It concluded on a final note even more depressing than what had gone before. '... And furthermore,' bellowed Sergeant-Major Britain, 'From your pay will be deducted weekly a sum of two shillings and sixpence to pay for *such little extra luxuries* as lavatory paper and electric lightbulbs ...'

The hut I slept in had only eight beds. The one next to mine was Rodney's. He'd come here straight from Eton and his accent was even more preposterous than my own. Eighteen is young to achieve pomposity, but then his family was rather grand. His mother had been a lady-in-waiting, his father held a job at Court. Rodney and I were seated on our beds polishing our equipment one day when he asked, 'When you're commissioned, what regiment are you going into?' There were Good Regiments and Bad Regiments, he explained.

'Which is better to be in?' I asked.

Rodney said a Good Regiment every time, explaining that *he* was going into the Royal Dragoons. He kindly offered to arrange for me to join him and I agreed, all things being equal.

A few weeks later I received a letter from Rodney's father, who was honorary colonel, summoning me to an interview. He wrote that there was a train from London at 10.05 which reached Swindon at 11.36. He would meet me at the station.

He was awaiting me on the Down platform, a spindly, patrician figure in a tweed overcoat which reached his ankles – not at that period the height of fashion. He said, 'There's a train to London at 11.42. I'll walk you over. What school did you go to?'

I told him.

'*Oh*.' There was a wealth of expressiveness in the way he said it. I would discover later that all except two of the regiment's officers had been to Eton.

He grunted, cleared his throat, poked at a scrap of paper with his stick. Speech did not come easy as we crossed the footbridge to the Up platform.

'Sport? Play games?' he asked abruptly.

'When I can,' I lied enthusiastically.

'Polo?'

'Not actually, no.'

'Hum. Find most of the other chaps do.' We marched on a few paces. 'Can't really live on your pay, you know. Bad form to bring it up … but you've got money of your own?'

'Well, Father …' I began.

We came down the steps from the bridge and stood together on the Up platform. 'And what regiment was *he* in?' he asked.

He was a commando, I told him. Almost imperceptibly he winced; it was as though I'd confided that Father worked below stairs. I realised that going on to explain my ability with Sten guns etc. would be a mistake, this was not what the Colonel meant by 'shooting'. But I had to say something. 'But my Uncle Bobby was in the navy,' I added.

He wasn't mollified, but at least I hadn't said the air force. 'What did he do in it?'

'What *does* the First Lord do? I think he sort of ran it.'

'Hum.' A moment or two passed and then he said, 'Yes, gamble, do you?' His expression hadn't changed but his manner had.

I said I played a little poker.

'Wild cards?' he enquired with a flicker of interest.

'Dealer's choice,' I told him.

'Don't care for them myself. Stick to stud and draw, I say, and you'll be all right. Here's your train.'

In due course Rodney and I were commissioned. One spring morning in 1952 we marched on to the parade ground as cadets and off it as officers while Sergeant-Major Britain saluted us. A fine moment. We were given a month's leave prior to joining the regiment in Egypt, back pay, leave pay and uniform allowance, a total of £190. I was rich.

With unusually good timing, Mother and Father were both out of England. Apart from Nanny and Mrs Reeves, the house in Gilston Road was empty. I moved in. It was an enchanted period, a time of grace. I rose late, read the *Telegraph* over a nourishing hot breakfast prepared by Nanny, then sauntered downstairs to discuss the luncheon menu with Mrs Reeves. A little later, over a cup of coffee in the living room, I'd arrange my ongoing social diary on the telephone, then set out the placements on the dining-room table for that day's lunch party. For a month I entertained lavishly – Alex, Nigel, Shirley and Charlotte, and others I knew by now.

For the first time in my life cash was no problem. The allowance of £120 to have my uniforms made seemed a gift, for I had a Turkish tailor who was confident he could run up the lot for £30. He'd done work for me before. He hadn't *made* me any clothes exactly, but twice had adapted my one suit, nipping in the waist, narrowing the trousers to drainpipe width and adding a velvet collar to the jacket. Wearing the result on an earlier leave, I'd gone to a party and found renown.

The party had been in a cobbled mews warmed by braziers and lit by fairy lanterns, thrown by a man everyone knew as the Bogus Baron. That night, renown appeared in the shape of a small overweight American slung with cameras. 'Hey, I sure like that get-up,' he said. 'How about some photos of your wardrobe. Are you a Man About Town?'

I said I certainly was.

'That's what the article's called,' he told me, 'And I want it to be about you, 'cos you strike me as a very elegant and interesting person. I'll come round to your house at twelve tomorrow. Where do you live?'

Swiftly I gave him a false address. Men About Town do not live at Mummy's and have a nanny.

I woke early the next day and with some difficulty secured the house whose address I had given. Another problem was that I owned only one suit, which I had worn the night before. Moving fast I borrowed a varied range of costume during the morning. There was no time to be selective and the collection was wide, very wide indeed.

Even now, fifty years later, I experience an involuntary shudder, a flush of embarrassment, when I think of those clothes, those photographs, and the article which accompanied them with its toe-curling quotes: Frock coat, cigarette holder, curly brimmed bowler, white tie, green carnation, top hat, tailcoat and a swordstick – the caption underneath read 'I only drink champagne'. Worst of all, the kimono: 'In the evening I generally slip into something *louche* ...' Inadvertently I had invented unisex, which in the early 'fifties was hardly good. But just how bad I didn't discover until later.

With illustrations of the two required uniforms I paid a visit to my tailor in his cramped room in Soho. A tiny, wizened man in a golden toupée, he worked seated cross-legged on his bench, eyes narrowed against the smoke of a hand-rolled cigarette stuck permanently to his lower lip.

'Ever such a nice look,' he said in a cockney accent as he studied the drawings. 'Yes, *very* theatrical. Don't know about the swordbelt, though, I've never worked in leather.'

I explained that I would buy the correct belts, buckles, engraved buttons, insignia etc., and accessorise myself.

'I *do* like the yellow stripe slashing the evening trousers and fitting over the riding boots. Chain mail's a good touch. Spurs are clever.' He picked up the other drawing. 'Now this safari suit ...'

'Service dress,' I corrected him.

He pursed his lips, angling the illustration to the light. 'You can see what they're getting at, of course, but they haven't followed it through. Look at the width of those trousers, *so* loose in the bum. Oh dear, oh dear ... wouldn't suit you at all.'

I agreed that the trousers were unfashionably baggy. It was an old drawing.

He nodded confidently. 'Just you leave it to me, I know what you want.'

Time passed. I went for a final fitting. 'I've done you proud, you have to grant. You look like you stepped out of a bandbox,' said my tailor.

I studied my reflection a little doubtfully in the full-length mirror. The effect was striking, though the chain mail and sword took a little getting used to.

My leave drew to its end. I'd run out of money and was quite glad when one day a telegram arrived inviting me to join my regiment.

I reported to Goodge Street Deep Underground. Twelve hours later my Dakota transport touched down on the military airfield in the British Canal Zone. Two years later President Nasser would nationalise the Suez Canal and, after a brief, disastrous military action, the Brits would be kicked out for ever. But for the moment we were still hanging in there, and I had come to help. Our role was a traditional one: subduing the natives.

Along the noxious, flyblown, eighty-mile length of the canal a series of fortified tented camps contained a garrison of 80,000 men and 33 female telephone operators. Beyond the perimeter of razor wire a barren desert wasteland stretched to the horizon. It was insufferably hot.

The Royals – soon to become the Blues and Royals, the

Queen's household cavalry – had pitched their camp apart from all the rest. Indeed, they never spoke to all the rest – they considered themselves of a different order entirely. Inside this floodlit and guarded compound a group of rich young men were kept in close confinement. Killers of foxes, flingers of bread rolls baying at the sound of breaking glass, corporal restriction was nothing new to them; they had been to Eton.

It was a world of elaborate formal ritual. The night of my arrival we dressed for dinner in ceremonial blues uniform, riding boots and spurs, to eat courses of tinned disgustingness while seated at a long polished table so overloaded with monstrous artefacts – the Regimental silver – that it was almost impossible to see across.

I could not help noticing that nobody spoke to me throughout the meal. At its end a stranger approached. His form-fitting tunic decorated with chain mail had three pips on the epaulettes. 'Bradish-Ellames. I'm the adjutant,' he announced in a strangled voice. 'I'll see you in my office at 9 am.'

I visited him next day. The previous evening I'd worn my blues uniform, now he met my service dress. The trousers were the ultimate in fashion, so narrow and tight it was impossible to sit down – not that I was invited to sit. The arrangement of pockets, epaulettes and buttons was roughly similar to his own, though the material was of lighter weight more suitable for the local climate, and any impartial observer must have agreed that my choice of a subtly different shade of khaki was an improvement.

Seated at his desk, the adjutant was breathing heavily and appeared to be in the grip of strong emotion. He tore his gaze from me, rose abruptly and made for the window, where he stood rigid with his back to me. Suddenly he wheeled about, stepped to the desk, tugged open a drawer and from it extracted gingerly a disgusting, dog-eared, much fingered magazine, sweat stained and soiled. He dropped it on the desk in front of me, averting his gaze. 'You might as well know. This arrived in the mess two weeks ago.'

It fell open naturally at the oft-read page, the photographs, damp, grubby, avidly pored over. I stared, hypnotised, at the poised figure in the photographs holding the nine-inch cigarette holder, languid eyes half closed in supercilious irony. 'I have to tell you that while you are here none of us wish to speak to you,' the adjutant informed me.

It proved to be the case.

'It's just not *on*,' Rodney whispered to me in my tent. 'Honestly, those uniforms ... simply not playing the game!' But in the mess he avoided me like everyone else; I had been sent to Coventry.

I did not feel comfortable in my exclusion. What swine they are, I thought, pompous, conceited and stuck-up. But it was no use telling myself these people were despicable, I only knew it hurt. And wasn't I a bit ridiculous myself, with my penniless affectations and preposterous uniforms? Yes I was, but they were still swine.

But if there was pain in my situation, there was also compensation. The hostility of my brother officers made me acceptable to my men.

There's a duff troop in every regiment, composed of drunks, the psychopathic, the ornery and the troublemakers no one wants under their command – least of all in a shooting action. Voted shit of the year, it was fitting I should be given that troop to lead. I had nine men under me. Their previous troop leader had been invalided back to England when a turret hatch slammed shut on his hand, amputating three fingers; the question of who had unlocked the hatch to cause the accident remained unanswered. I came to the job with considerable unease, but a fortunate event changed everything.

Scouse Rae, my Daimler's gunner, who came from a Liverpool family of petty criminals for three generations, broke into the NAAFI one night, drank an entire bottle of gin at the bar together with incalculable pints of beer, then left the spigot running to fall asleep in the growing lake of pale ale which expanded to flow in a river across the floor and beneath the hut's front door to cause his arrest, rather wet and smelling strongly, soon afterwards. Charged with stealing government property, he was to be court-martialled.

He asked me to defend him. I did so against Bradish-Ellames, who was prosecuting before a court consisting of the colonel and three officers. In the Manual of Military Law the definition of theft is 'taking away with intent to deprive permanently'. Arguing that Rae had not 'taken away' because he'd passed out *in situ* before being able to do so, I got him off to Bradish-Ellames's visible displeasure and subsequent ill will.

But the verdict's effect upon the morale of my troop and my relationship with them was enormously encouraging. Pincher, the Daimler's driver, became my devoted batman, stealing lightbulbs, lavatory paper, soap, razor blades, equipment and stamps from other officers' tents to furnish my own.

His thievery and my relative comfort went undetected, for no one visited my tent. In the mess my brother officers continued to cut me, and in time I think they came to find my presence there as inhibiting and awkward as I did myself. I was sent away frequently to man the Eskine Line (an imaginary line drawn across the desert twenty miles away) to watch for the enemy who might come pouring over it to seize the canal at any moment.

The idea of seeing hordes of hysterical, out-of-control Arabs charging over the horizon towards me was unnerving. I asked what I should do if they appeared.

'Fire one shell at them, radio their position and pull back,' I was told. The armoured cars could do 50 mph, both forwards and in reverse. I learned to my surprise that the role of the cavalry in war is to run away at first sight of the enemy.

Of course, there was never any real likelihood they would appear. We loaded up the armoured cars with food and water for a week, then drove on to the desert, navigating by compass, to pitch camp more or less in the right spot in an empty, featureless landscape of wadis, rock and ochre-coloured sand. Over the radio I'd report my position to the regiment, calling them every few hours to say no sign of the enemy yet, actually.

The sun was hot but the air very dry – ideal for tanning. My men sat in the shade listening to the radio and playing cards, while I sunbathed and read Anthony Powell. The nights were cool. There was no twilight, darkness came quickly. We'd light a fire and sit around it beneath the stars while Pincher ran up a gourmet meal enhanced with Fortnum's jars he'd stolen from the officers' tents. I provided drink – I felt it was the least that I could do.

In the mornings I usually read for an hour or so after breakfast. Later we'd have gunnery practice, which everyone enjoyed. We'd attach an empty five-gallon jerrycan behind Coates and Tatnell's Dingo at the end of a long wire. Coates and Tatnell would drive off and hide while we demounted the Bren guns from the cars, loaded up and made ready for them. We never knew exactly where they would appear. Suddenly they'd be racing through the broken ground forty yards away. Aiming for the jerrycan clanging and bouncing in the air behind the Dingo, we'd blast it with our combined fire-power of three Brens, my .38 service revolver, and the Colt .45 and .22 revolvers I'd kept with me since Arisaig. The Brens were the best fun, for every sixth round was tracer; you didn't aim the gun but directed it along a stream of light with runaway power rattling in your hands.

We took turns and everyone enjoyed the game immensely. Once, when we'd become really good at it, I suggested we try it with the two-pounder in the Daimler. Rae clambered into the gunner's seat, I took my position in the turret. Coates and Tatnell drove off as usual while Rae loaded a shell in the breech. There was a choice of armour – piercing and high-explosive; we thought high-explosive would be best.

We tried a left and right traverse with the gun turret to make sure it ran free, and got ready. All at once I saw the Dingo lip the crest of the escarpment and come speeding down the wadi. 'Traverse right, right,' I shouted. The turret spun round ... 'Steady! Aim ....' the jerrycan was leaping all over the place .... '*Fire*!'

There was a deafening *crack*. It felt like two open hands smacking my ears hard. Way ahead of the jerrycan and only twenty yards behind the Dingo I saw the flash of an explosion, a burst of blue-white smoke. *Boom!* The shock lifted the speeding Dingo on its way, a hail of grit and stones rattled against its armour plating, chipping the paint.

I felt a lurch of horror and dismay, it could have been a real disaster, yet everyone cheered. They thought it wonderful and wanted another go, but Coates and Tatnell wouldn't play any more. Rotten spoilsports, they sulked and said they wanted to go home.

The philosophy, theory, practice and day-to-day conduct of the army is based upon discipline. Discipline causes the soldier to snap instantly to attention, crying, 'Yessir!' Discipline is what makes him go over the trench top and charge the enemy in the face of certain death.

I don't believe we ever discussed the subject in my troop.

It was understood that when with the regiment we obeyed the outward forms of discipline, saluting and so on, but while out camping in the desert we should not. It was not only Christ's teaching to treat others as you wish them to treat you, in my view it's an effective and more successful way to achieve results. But I came face to face with a problem which provided a further slant on the matter.

A few months after my arrival in the Canal Zone there was a mutiny. It was hardly surprising it should occur. Confined to camp, without access to women or distraction of any kind, life was very boring. One evening one of the Highland regiments ran amuck and for a few riotous hours their camp became a glorious Saturday-night Gorbals in the desert. They set fire to a couple of cars, doused an officer with beer and barricaded themselves in the NAAFI where they drank everything in sight, threw up and were easily overpowered.

A number of men were arrested. No military prison existed in the Zone and briefly three of the ringleaders were boarded out in our cells. An armed escort delivered them shackled together in chains, tiny, tough, glowering little men who looked as dangerous and unstable as wild beasts and who were clearly hungover.

Rodney, who was duty officer, came in late to dinner that night, his face pinker than usual and smudged with black streaks. 'They set fire to the guard house,' he exclaimed. 'And Corporal of Horse Grayson. Too beastly.'

Next morning the prisoners were separated. Two of them were moved on and farmed out elsewhere. That day it was my turn to be duty officer, an event which occurred every ten days or so. One rose early, for it took longer than usual to dress. The ensemble was in blue, lavishly ornamented, and across the chest a gold and silver pouch was slung in the fashion of a telegram delivery boy. A sword was worn.

Six foot two inches of ramrod martinet, the duty colour sergeant, who was dressed only slightly less gorgeously than myself, accompanied me everywhere around the camp, a gleaming, stamping, shouting machine. With him I changed the guard, checked the armoury, examined the vehicle lines and tasted the men's lunch with a shudder.

During the afternoon it was my duty to inspect the cells. The colour sergeant and I marched towards them in step across the beaten sand, unspeaking and glittering in the sun. There were several prisoners, a man who had stolen petrol, one who'd caused a fight, another who had overstayed his leave. Plus, of course, the mutineer. At each cell the ritual was the same. The colour sergeant flung open the metal door, screamed, 'Prisoner, 'shun!' followed me in and lurked attentively while I inspected. Inside, the geometric arrangement of every cell was identical and immaculate. Each item of the man's equipment, cleaned, blancoed and polished, was laid out on the bed in precisely regulated pattern. At the head of the bed the blankets were folded to an exact rectangle, at the foot the prisoner stood quivering to attention.

I would cast my eye over the cell, enquire 'Any complaints?' to which he would answer sharply 'No, sir!' and we would leave. There was never any deviation from this prescribed scenario.

We came to the last cell. The colour sergeant threw back the door and I was already inside before it struck me as curious that he had omitted to shout, 'Prisoner, 'shun!' as he always had before. Then the view drove all thought from my mind.

The place was devastated, an utter shambles. Equipment was everywhere – ripped, torn, mangled, pissed on. The buckled wreckage of the metal bed lay twisted against the wall and a sea of horsehair covered everything. Shaved head and unshaved chin, a beetle-browed Glaswegian mannikin squatted in the carnage wearing only his soiled underpants. Glaring at me from small red eyes, he conveyed an impression of considerable menace. 'Any complaints?' I heard myself ask ineptly.

'Fuck off,' he snarled.

Nothing in the Manual of Military Discipline and Procedure had prepared me for this. I was uncertain how to act. It struck me that the best thing to do was to follow his suggestion. I turned round and strode out the cell. The colour sergeant's boots crashed the floor in an about turn as he followed me. I waited while he locked the cell, then together we marched down the passage into the fierce sunlight and, side by side in perfect step, commenced the 200-yard march across the desert parade ground, flashing and jangling with silver and brass and chain mail and patent leather and spurs, got up like Christmas trees with our boots pounding the sand into a dust cloud rising behind our splendid passage.

The colour sergeant did not speak. He offered no comment, no explanation, and we'd marched a hundred yards in silence before I felt obliged to ask, 'That last prisoner ... *why* wasn't he standing to attention in a spotless cell beside the bed laid out with his equipment in the regulation manner?'

Face steadfast to the front, the colour sergeant's answer rang out loud, clear and immediate. '*Because he didn't want to, sir!*'

The full force of revelation swept over me as I marched. The man had not offered violence, hadn't protested, had not refused; he'd just made his attitude perfectly clear: *No one can make you do anything you don't want to do!* I marched onward a wiser and more disobedient man.

A month or so after this event the Royals were posted back to England en route for the regiment's new station with British Forces on the Rhine.

Handing over its armoured cars to the Lifeguards, who were replacing us, we travelled to Port Said in armed convoy. The men were embarked at once, but the officers passed a half day in the town before the troop ship set sail that evening. Attended by a crowd of importuning beggars, the flower of young English manhood strutted the foreign streets observing the lives of the inhabitants with undisguised contempt.

Returning to the ship, one voice among the surrounding clamour caught my attention. 'Psst, Spanish fly?' it asked. An Arab beckoned from the shadow of a warehouse with a furtive gesture. As I came closer he exposed a glimpse of what lay in his hand – a round resinous ball. 'You want make jig-jig all night all day long?'

He had a sore on his lip, was villainous to look at, and anyway it was not a practical suggestion, the ship was leaving in a couple of hours. Again he drew the thing from beneath his robe. It had the soft consistency of plasticine and a slightly scented smell that was not unpalatable. A lunatic dream took shape.

'How do I know it works?' I asked.

'Oh, him work,' he said, affronted. 'Him work *fucking* well.'

'How much?'

'Five pounds.'

It was a huge sum. I paid quickly and hurried to join the ship.

We sailed at sunset. Soon after the Royals' officers assembled in the first-class saloon, loud with indignation. Conditions afloat were not those to which they were accustomed. Quite large and senior officers found themselves stacked three to a cabin and sharing a shower. I remained quiet in the grumbling storm. The Royals were not the only troops returning on the ship; in the adjutant's list I had as usual been separated from my fellows and assigned to share a cabin with two air-force officers – beyond the pale in regimental terms.

Shown there by a steward, I'd chosen the best bunk, unpacked, and sat fondling my Spanish fly when the ship began to move. Neither of my room-mates had turned up. Quickly I deranged their bunks; with pillows and my suitcase I humped the blankets into the shape of seasick airmen. By nature untidy, I let myself go. Within a few minutes the look of the place was enough to deter the casual visitor, who would have recoiled from what was clearly an overcrowded, unhealthy slum. I sought out and bribed the steward. Back in my revolting lair I practised the sound of fighter pilots throwing up. Privacy was assured.

In ugly mood the regimental herd moved in to dinner. I left the table early, returning to the saloon where the vast silver orb of the regimental coffee urn had been set up and bubbled upon its burner. Around its swollen sides the steaming horses of the Heavy Brigade galloped in bass relief, charging each other's bottoms. Bending to adjust the flame, I raised the lid minutely and dropped the Spanish fly into the scalding contents.

In pairs, in small bellicose groups, the regimental officers tramped into the saloon from dinner, port glasses clutched in their hands and a high colour mounting to their cheeks as they assembled round the coffee urn. I did not take a cup myself, but watched with gleeful anticipation as they served themselves, then with anticipation turning to disappointment, for I saw no change in them at all. They sprawled, they drank, they grunted in conversation. They belched and farted as usual after dinner. And then … and then … Did I imagine it, or did a restlessness fall upon the first-class saloon? They rose to their feet, they paced, they hitched their trousers, they stamped, they roared.

Certainly disquiet had infected them. They called for drink, countermanded their orders, bawled out the barman. Loud, argumentative conversations were begun, only to be abandoned in mid-sentence. A game was started, getting round the room without touching the floor. Normally popular, even over this new course tonight it did not answer. After breaking a couple of coffee tables it was abandoned, their hearts were elsewhere. Restlessly they kicked the furniture, peered from the portholes at the sliding waste of water, impatience in their glance, bloodshot longing in their eyes. For what? A kill? The unmentionable?

And then abruptly they retired, leaving me to stare at the swollen orb of the coffee urn as a vision danced before my eyes ... the officers and gentlemen of the Royal Dragoons in uncontrollable homosexual rut. Aboard ship, buggers can't be choosers.

Alone in my cabin I slept well, waking at 8 am, the sky bright, the sea untroubled. I dressed and made my way to the dining saloon. Tables laid and waiting, the place was deserted. The steward seemed surprised to see me. 'You up, you well?' he said. 'My, my.'

'Not at all well,' I murmured, simulating weakness.

'Not hungry are you, surely?'

'Certainly not,' I answered in a sickly voice, looking ravenously at the crisp rolls, the mounds of butter, the eggs and bacon sizzling in the griddle pans. 'But a coffee might be good for me, perhaps just one piece of toast.'

I retired to my cabin to read, but hunger brought me out again at noon. The dining saloon was still empty. 'My, you're a one,' the steward said, 'The only one.'

'The others ...?' I enquired.

'No *they* won't be eating,' he said quite definitely. He'd gone with beef tea to a couple of cabins and returned shaken.

'Losing it at both ends, spewing their guts up,' he reported.

'Serious?' I asked nervously. Even in my furthest imaginings I hadn't intended to become a mass murderer.

'Nah,' he said. 'Came over a little queer is all, but that's behind them. It'll pass. A few days at sea and they'll be right as rain again, you'll see.'

Yes, I thought, I probably would. Nothing would *change* these people. Whatever happened to them, one couldn't hope for any lasting moral improvement. However, during the time the vessel was mine and before my fellow officers became their unspeakable selves again, I determined to enjoy the voyage.

Studying the menu, I ordered a large and well-earned lunch.

8
Germany

Once back in England most of the regiment sloped off on leave, but I remained in barracks as part of the skeleton force manning the transit camp. 'You're to be sent ahead to Germany,' Rodney informed me one day. 'They think you don't fit in here, that you're not really one of us,' he explained.

I went to the regiment's new station at Wesendorf in Germany as one of only three officers in the Royals' advance party. Bradish-Ellames, Rodney and myself lived as guests of the 15/19th Hussars, whom we were to replace as part of the occupying force of 600,000 men defending civilisation against the Russian army camped on the other side of the nearby fence and minefield stretching from the Baltic to Austria, which partitioned West from East Germany.

The accommodation and mess had been purpose built in the late 'thirties for the Luftwaffe, who clearly were used to a higher standard of taste, comfort and general *aménagements* than British officers. My room, which had an en suite bathroom, was large, well furnished, and had a view over the pine forest. The mess was spacious and high-ceilinged, panelled in dark wood. Embellished with the resident regiment's paintings of cavalry charges, battle scenes, monumental silver artefacts, leather chesterfields and chairs, it looked 100 per cent British: a St James's gentlemen's club.

I mingled easily with the young officers of the 15/19th. My state-of-Coventry had not come with me to this new location. Instead of driving senior officers purple with fury, my uniforms were considered enviably fashionable by some here. Many young men in the outside world were now wearing trousers similar to mine – if perhaps not *quite* so tight.

The 15/19th Hussars weren't such a smart cavalry regiment as the Royals who, occupying the right of the line and standing closest to the sovereign, considered themselves superior to all. The Hussar officers were mainly not Etonians and less obsessively snobbish than the Royals, most of whom had chosen the army for their career and the regiment because their father and grandfather had served in it before them.

Life in the Wesendorf mess was just as formalised and ritualistic as before however. We dressed up in elaborate uniform, chain mail and spurs to swill claret from silver mugs and pass the port down a polished dinner table set for thirty, groaning beneath the weight of regimental silver statuary. But the young officers were a deal more friendly than I'd been used to. These people *spoke* to me, two of them even asked the name of my tailor.

'Don't want to get *too* chummy with them,' Rodney warned. 'It's not on. Bad form, you know.'

A poker school existed in the mess, which played most evenings after dinner. The stakes were higher than I could afford to lose, for unlike the others I was living on my pay of £5 a week, but soon after arriving in Wesendorf I joined it.

Apart from weaponry, explosives and garrotting, poker was the only thing I was good at. The coaching I'd received from Uncle Tony served me well when I came to play in the Wesendorf mess. I didn't play more skilfully than the others, but I played less recklessly and, unlike them, never drew to an inside straight. It's not a help to gamble against people with more money than yourself and in a high-raise game. You can't always risk following your judgement. But often I won, and sometimes I won well.

Holding four jacks against a full house and a flush, I won so well one night I bought a car. I didn't like possessions, owning things made me uneasy; I'd never owned anything except my Colt .45, my .22 revolver and, briefly, my Swiss watch. Even when, later, I could afford to buy clothes everything I possessed in the world fitted into two suitcases I could carry easily by myself. But when I first glimpsed the two-seater supercharged Auto Union Wanderer sports convertible, I fell in love instantly. Above 3,000 revs the noise of the supercharger was a sustained howl. Built for the Le Mans 24-hour race, the car had the acceleration of a startled kangaroo and would do 120 mph on the autobahn.

One of the members of the 15/19th poker school was Ben Fisher, whose studious appearance and wry self-deprecating manner contrasted strongly with the boisterous exuberance of the rest. I liked him from the start, but it was a while before I sounded him out on what he was planning to do when he left the army. Most of the other National Service officers seemed to know exactly what they were going into – generally estate management, stockbroking or banking – and the question featured insistently in the letters I was receiving from Father.

'Haven't a clue,' Fisher admitted cheerfully.

'Don't you have family and relations who can fix it like everyone else?' I asked.

'Heavens no!' he said, explaining that his father was a rural dean. 'We know absolutely nobody and Daddy only has about six parishioners, he spends all his time in his study writing books.'

'What sort?' I asked.

'His last was a Dictionary of medieval agricultural terms used in Essex, it wasn't a best seller, exactly. No, Daddy's no help there at all. The only jobs I've seen are schoolmaster, the Church or the army, and they look so frightfully dull. I'd much rather be a professional card sharp on a Mississippi river boat.'

'*Really?*' I said. Here was a man I could relate to. We formed a working partnership with an operating capital of £150. He owned a car even more impractical and unreliable than my own, one of Detroit's all-time lemons: the Keizer-Frazer. Fisher's did nine miles to the gallon and broke down constantly, but in it or my Wanderer regularly after dinner we drove 140 miles to Travemunde on the Baltic coast. A small old-fashioned resort of boardwalks and wooden houses, its focus was a casino dating from the Belle Époque. Few in defeated Germany had money to gamble at that time; business was poor and the groups of young British officers in mess uniform, booted and spurred, often drunk, were a necessary clientele. In pragmatic fashion the invader was made welcome and here, night after night, Fisher and I played with dedicated concentration at the roulette table. We thought of ourselves not as punters but hard-eyed pros, honing and perfecting our career skills.

Gambling and raffish behaviour appealed to us. Fisher and myself were strongly attracted to the disreputable – only

Nigel was exempt. Our parents were worthy and respectable; they'd done their duty, fought, suffered and gone short to save civilisation from the Hun. But we were the post-Waugh generation, and in the years of drab austerity and rationing in Britain which followed their hard-won victory, the rake had emerged again as a desirable role model.

None emulated it more determinedly than Ivor Mottron, an officer in a nearby regiment, who had ash blond hair and the pale blue eyes of a Weimaraner. Also a Slav wife with a chiselled face of immodest beauty and a nature wilful and unstable as his own. As a couple they were astonishingly good looking. Quite unlike anyone else I'd come across in the army, they gave off a rackety carefree glamour; both were wantonly reckless in their behaviour.

Frequently in pressing debt, Ivor and Natassia were wildly extravagant. He lived then and for years afterwards on the expectation of an inheritance and on credit. By the army, Natassia's sometimes dramatic behaviour was understood because she was 'foreign'. And Ivor's capricious liaisons and excesses were excused, even applauded as 'showing form'. Rather than antagonising, they endeared him to his young brother officers, who were ignorant of his past. She had grown up in Paris and met Ivor in Capri, where both were being looked after by others; but lightning passed between them at first sight and they'd eloped together, penniless and bankrolled only by their beauty and allure. Ivor's patron, devastated by his defection, had pursued him with a telegram. It read: COME AT ONCE DESPERATELY RICH.

I was entranced by their glamour and recklessness and careless style. I passed almost every weekend staying at their house. They had no car, for Ivor of course had crashed it, and we used the two-seater Wanderer to get to Hamburg for the evening. Late at night we drove back crushed together in the sports car's padded cockpit, and there was a highly erotic charge in the feel of her supple body pressed against my own, the smell of her scent, and the long scream of the supercharger as we hurtled along the dead straight road through the Luneberger forest at over 100 mph. High on youth, drink and the exhilaration of excess, the three of us shared an intimacy that embraced everything, including the real possibility of our sudden deaths, and I realised I was in love with both of them.

In due course the main body of the Royals arrived in Wesendorf. Fisher and the Hussars moved on, and the mess was colonised with our own battle paintings of cavalry charges, portraits of the dressy dead, and monstrous weight of regimental silver. The expensively educated squirearchy tramped into their new home to lower their large bottoms into the leather armchairs and bellow for drink.

They formed not so much a tribe as an upper-crust gang, with similar backgrounds, upbringing, tastes and prejudices. They disliked Jews, black people, lefties, 'cleverness' and culture. They didn't like women much, but they loved horses and dogs. Having been born English, they believed they had won first prize in the lottery of life and behaved accordingly. Twice a week, on mess nights, we dressed up in full blues uniform for dinner. After a heavy meal of pork or boar stew, school pudding and a lot of port, everyone would tramp from the dining room with spurs jingling. They'd stamp and fart to dispel their after-dinner lethargy, then someone – usually Birbeck would call for a game.

Birbeck was ruddy faced, burly, boisterous and rich and he didn't give a damn for anyone's opinion. His favourite game involved getting around the room without touching the floor. Birbeck loved this because he was so good at it. Although a heavily built man with a broad bottom and substantial gut, he got around the course faster than anyone else, invariably breaking more furniture than the rest. Rather unwillingly, I came to like him.

One evening I drove with Rodney to have dinner in Hamburg and visit the red-light district. The Four Seasons Hotel, overlooking the Alster, was then an officers' club. Over Tournedos Rossini and a couple of bottles of claret Rodney said, 'We'll be leaving the regiment in a few months. Got what you want to do sorted out, have you?'

'Hardly,' I told him. 'You?'

'Chap's got to think of the way the world's going,' he said. 'Dollars, greenbacks, real money – that's what counts nowadays.'

'You mean go to America?' It was something I longed to do myself. I knew the country well from the cinema; the USA seemed an infinitely more glamorous and exciting place than Britain.

'God no!' said Rodney, appalled. 'Wouldn't want to do *that*! Get the buggers on your own turf. Stick it to them there.'

'Stick what?' I asked.

'Our place. Ship them down for weekends. Polish up the silver, drop the word that Kent comes down to shoot.'

'Rodney! Isn't that selling out on your heritage?'

'Not at all!' The suggestion made him huffy. 'You've no idea how expensive horses and staff are to keep these days – not always satisfactory, either. They'll like old Banks the butler, though – he shuffles well and we could dress him up a bit. Country house weekends! Take it from me, they'll pay through the nose for them.'

Everyone else seemed to know what they were going to do in life. Beyond buying a white suit, becoming a professional gambler and trusting to God, I had no idea myself. Occasionally it bothered me, as it did now.

We were fairly drunk by the time we'd finished dinner. Leaving the supercharged Wanderer outside the Four Seasons, we took a taxi to the Reeperbahn. We walked down the narrow cobbled street, lined on both sides by windows, a half-naked woman in each one. Garishly made up, most were unattractive, fat and middle-aged. The street was crowded with drunk soldiers and smelt of sick. Both Rodney and I had come here before for brief unsatisfying couplings which left me feeling there *must* be more to sex than this or Henry Miller would not have written about it with such feeling.

Tonight we were looking for an exhibition Rodney had heard about and particularly wanted to see. At last we found it, a small, red-lit, overheated room where eight men crouched or stood around a table on which a woman was seated, feet upon its surface.

She hauled up her skirts. 'Gimme a cigarette,' she ordered.

Rodney stepped forward, offering a tin of duty-free Benson and Hedges. She took one and, putting down the tin, he lit it for her. Inhaling deeply, the woman lay back on her elbows and inserted the cigarette between the lips of her vagina. I with the rest in the airless crowded room stared in astonishment as her abdomen contracted, then relaxed. A cloud of blue smoke puffed out, wreathing through the black forest of her pubic hair to float toward the ceiling. My startled glance flinched from the sight to the Benson and Hedges tin on the table between her legs. The brand's advertising slogan, featuring on poster hoardings throughout the country and current for years, slanted in copperplate script across the open lid: *Where Only the Best Will Do*.

Much later we found our way back to the car parked by the Alster. My own drunkenness had by now transmuted into a stoned-out lucidity that welcomed the idea of the eighty-mile drive ahead, but Rodney didn't want the fun to end. While getting into the car he spotted a covey of duck on the water, thirty yards from shore. Grabbing my .22 revolver from the door pocket where I kept it, he rested his elbows on the convertible's soft-top to take unsteady aim. *Bang ... bang ... bang ... bang ... bang ... bang ...* In the absolute tranquillity of the city's dawn he loosed off six rounds, happily missing wide.

In the summer of 1943, exactly eleven years earlier, Hamburg had been bombed by the British and American air forces for nine days and nights continuously. The heat of the phosphorous bombs created firestorms which drove rivers of flame through the streets, incinerating everything in their path. A million people were made homeless, 85,000 burned to death. Many, running from the inferno with their clothes in flames, flung themselves in the Alster and were drowned.

Now Rodney slumped drunkenly by this same lake, shooting duck with my revolver. We were the occupying power. The Germans we met were hard-working, subservient, eager to please; not for another fifteen years would they not us, prove to have won the war. Among themselves they called us 'the Barbarians.'

Eagerly engaged in discovering life, I never thought of death; the idea of it never entered my head. Yet before my army service ended, death would pass by me twice.

The culmination of a summer's training in simulated battle manoeuvres was the week-long NATO exercise in which the US and British armies combined with French and Belgian forces to resist a make-believe Soviet advance into West Germany. At midnight, three days into the manoeuvres, my troop of armoured cars was driving down a sandy track through a pine forest somewhere on the Luneburger plain. The cars were widely spaced, with seventy or a hundred yards between them to make the troop less vulnerable to ambush.

None of us had slept since the start of the exercise. To deprive men of sleep was a deliberate policy, the quickest way to show up those who'd become unreliable in battle conditions, and we had been kept moving continually. In the open turret of the second car I was in that state beyond exhaustion when events have the illusive detachment of a dream. A strong wind was blowing, dragging a tattered wrack of cloud across the moon and rushing through the branches of the pine trees beside the track ahead, which was illuminated dimly by our masked headlights.

A call came through from the leading car, crackling in my handset. 'Motor cyclist. Just passing me.' I saw his light a few seconds later, jiggling unsteadily on the uneven track. It drew closer and my driver pulled over to let the bike pass, but he was as sleep-deprived and bone-weary as the rest of us. The car's tyres were set in deep ruts, and he didn't turn the wheel of the heavy vehicle with sufficient force to haul it free.

The motor cyclist did not see our masked lights until it was too late. At the inquest it was established that he'd passed the evening drinking in a *bierkeller*. His own wheels were set in one of the ruts and he collided head-on with our off-side wing. For the last ten yards I watched him coming in the slowed inevitability of a nightmare, then his bike hit the car. His body flew up in the air in an untidy black bundle, somersaulting straight at me. His head struck the turret just below where my hand was gripping it. The unprotected skull cracked open, the body whirled past into the dark. The armour plating was spattered with his brains – as was my sleeve. The wind was shrieking through the pine trees and torn clouds scudded across the moon.

The sense of overwhelming horror recurred for days afterwards. I would be functioning perfectly, then suddenly the ground would open at my feet and I'd be staring into the abyss, dazed and sick with dread.

My second glimpse of death came soon after. In the week following the NATO exercise there was a regimental mess night. When dinner was over Birbeck and I set off to gamble at Travemunde. We drove in his Jaguar, a new car he'd brought from England which, typically, he had not bothered to run in but caned from the start, indifferent to the damage he was doing to the motor.

Reaching Travemunde before midnight, we played roulette in the casino. Birbeck at first won, then lost heavily, buying more chips and scattering them recklessly over the table. When we came to leave, the drink had soured in his belly and he was in bad humour. He asked me to drive.

An hour later and south of Hamburg dawn leaked into the sky – that light the French call *entre chien et loup* – as I gunned the car down a straight empty road bounded on both sides by the pine forest. I could see almost a mile ahead and was holding the Jaguar in the middle of the road with the accelerator flat to the floor.

In the shadowless light I didn't see the humped bridge at the bottom of a long downward slope, didn't have time to brake. The shocks gave an enormous *bang* as the big car bottomed in the dip, came up the hump and took off. As we flew from the hump I saw a silver Mercedes thirty yards ahead.

We struck head on. I have no recall of the impact ... I was in Arisaig on the heather-covered hill above a ruined chapel, looking out over the bay. The world was silent, absolutely still, and the air vibrated with colour and with light. Dreamlike and shining, this was a place I knew yet did not know, for it had never been like this. I was suspended in peace, and I knew that I was dead.

Then suddenly all was changed and above me I saw the

interlaced branches of a tree, beyond them a sky clearing into blue. 'Fucking hell!' I heard a voice swear. Birbeck lay on the mossy ground ten yards away, his big body half in and half out of the twisted wreckage of the Jaguar which was wrapped round a tree. We were both wearing dress uniform and one of his spurred boots had been trapped in the shambles. As I helped to free his foot the driver of the Mercedes came stumbling out of the forest, white faced as a ghost.

In the collision the two cars had met at an impact speed of about 150 mph. Both were mangled beyond recognition, crumpled wrecks. As if he'd been in an ejector seat, the German had been shot out through his blessedly open sunshine roof. The doors of the Jaguar had burst open as it rolled, Birbeck and myself thrown clear. He and the German were unharmed, I had a gash on my head requiring three stitches.

I never recovered memory of the crash. But it shook me, for I did not understand how we had survived. For a short while it changed me until, in the way of youth, the lesson become submerged in the eager activity of living.

9
Gilston Road

Completing two years' military service I returned to London to embark upon a glittering civilian career – in what, I had no idea.

At Gilston Road the household cast had changed since I'd last been there. Mrs Reeves, our cook, whose legs were so bad she'd been unable to climb the stairs from the basement for years, had finally retired. And Mother had given birth to another son. I'd learned of the event only after it had occurred from a casual reference in one of her rare letters. This was, I think, a last attempt to save her marriage and, as such, misconceived. Hamish had a nursery at the top of the house and was looked after by Nanny. When I went by his pram in the garden I said hello, but unsurprisingly we were not close. Nor was I to my other brother David, for five years is a vast age difference in childhood and we had little in common. He was away at school, Fettes, when I arrived home from the army.

Father occupied a room on the ground floor of the house.

By now he had published six books – none of them successful except the first, his biography of Gino, and was still following the same routine of sleeping on the sofa in his study, walking to the *Daily Telegraph* wearing a rucksack, returning by foot at 8.30 pm for supper, then retiring to write. And Mother's domain consisted of the master bedroom on the first floor and the drawing room.

She was always busy. She looked after Hamish while Nanny did the food shopping, and again at tea time; she went to art exhibitions and galleries; sometimes she painted water-colours at an easel in her bedroom; she read a lot. She was a member of Harrods' library and the store was also her bank. Once or twice a week she'd go there to change books or cash a small cheque. She went by number 14 bus, always getting off at Brompton Oratory, the preceding stop, and walking the rest of the way because that was a 'stage' and saved one penny on the fare.

She still bravely attempted to give dinner parties for her friends and relatives. 'Don't be ridiculous,' she told Father. 'One bottle of wine is *quite* enough for six people. There's one open from last time at the back of the drinks cupboard.'

On these evenings the table was laid with the good silver she'd inherited, and candles set out on its polished surface. She prepared and cooked the main dish herself. There was never enough and the portions were niggardly. 'I got the best off-cuts I could with the money,' Nanny would explain defensively. 'And the butcher *said* they were good.'

Despite the wretched food and lack of alcohol, sometimes these parties began rather well, for a number of Mother's friends were charming and entertaining people, and she herself could be very witty. But Father had perfected a way of ruining them. On one such evening he returned particularly late from the newspaper. The party had already moved into the dining room and started on the meal, served by Nanny in her best apron which she'd had to pay for herself.

Dumping his mountaineering rucksack in the hall, Father entered the dining room with a set face, dressed in the baggy tweed jacket and flannels he always wore. With a curt nod to the guests at table, he strode to the sideboard where the main course simmered in a chafing dish. Raising the lid, he peered inside. His face wrinkled with distaste, he let out an angry grunt. Marching to the kitchen, he returned with the wooden breadboard, a slab of margarine still in its wrapping and a pot of jam. Banging these down on the table as dinner conversation withered into silence around him, he cut himself a thick slice, spread it with jam and began to eat.

Usually Mother chose evenings when he was away to entertain. He was out of England often during the time I served in Germany. At the *Telegraph* he was their Arctic, mountaineering and wine correspondent and book reviewer, as well as handling the paper's public relations – a strange job for a man who detested people so much as he did. As their travel correspondent he made a number of walks, one of these from the Atlantic to the Mediterranean above the France–Spain frontier. Ignoring roads, he followed a high mountain route, sleeping out each night beneath a tree; next morning he would leave a coin at the foot of the tree to pay for his lodging. On two occasions he was shot at by border guards, he believed he had a natural right to cross international frontiers wherever he chose.

'When the east wind's blowing it's cold as charity here, I do declare,' said Nanny.

I was sleeping in my old room on the top floor and the building was in conspicuously worse condition than when I'd last lived there. Nothing planned had been done, and the bomb damage dating from the war had never been fixed. The roof had needed replacing when Mother had bought the house, now the full blast of winter could not be kept out without constant running repairs.

Mother would accept only the lowest quote, and that with great reluctance. A series of cack-handed cowboy workmen had botched their way through the years until she'd found Mr Baines – 'an absolute *treasure*, darling'. Smaller and cheaper and more incompetent than any before, he was chronically depressed; 'trouble at home' he confided to Nanny. One day he was out on the roof, hanging there precariously as he attempted to force in a new slate, while Mother watched anxiously from the garden below. There was no possibility of either of them being insured. 'Oh, Mr Baines I *do* hope you're not going to fall off,' Mother carolled from the ground.

'Quite honestly, Mrs Scott, I don't mind if I do,' Mr Baines shouted back.

It was a cold house that winter. There was only a single radiator in the hall to heat the entire building, but this didn't work, and though some rooms had antique gas fires, their heating elements were no longer manufactured. Nanny passed her weekly afternoon off scouring hardware stores in Battersea for any of the honeycomb china fittings that remained in stock. The temperature sank further whenever Father returned to roost. While at home he questioned me closely on what efforts I was making to find work and had already come up with several unwelcome suggestions.

I had lunch with Alex one day to ask him how *he* was progressing in the search for a job. We met in Salamis in the Fulham Road, where you could eat for two shillings and sixpence (12½p), and he appeared in the most extraordinary double-breasted jacket with twin rows of large, very shiny brass buttons. Built with unpadded sloping shoulders, it resembled nothing anyone else was wearing at the time.

'That's a striking blazer,' I remarked, rather lost for what to say.

'It's not a blazer, it's a boating jacket,' he rebuked me. 'Made for my grandfather.'

He also had on a beret, which he wore throughout the meal. 'Seventy per cent of the body's energy escapes via the head,' he explained. Nigel, with whom he shared a flat in Cadogan Square, had warned me he was behaving oddly and had started sleeping on the floorboards of his room rather than the bed. We'd decided this was because he'd done a course in parachuting and special training, but we wondered what he was toughening himself up *for*.

Over lunch I confessed my disturbing lack of success in finding work. The single job I'd been offered was as a trainee copywriter at Masius – but only if I first spent six months as a shop assistant in Selfridges 'to learn selling'.

'What a preposterous idea!' he said. 'Actually, I'm thinking of going into advertising myself, but only in an executive capacity, of course. Our qualification is *we know how to lead men*.'

'Er, yes,' I agreed, remarking that quite a lot of people in advertising seemed to be women. But Alex said that was all right, we knew how to lead women too.

'How many interviews have *you* gone to?' I asked him.

'Don't be depressing,' he told me tartly. 'I have excellent connections and that's what counts. Some of them will be there tonight, Mother's throwing a party. You can come, if you want,' he added.

I arrived late at Margot Howard's party – I'd already discovered it's better to turn up when the revel is already warmed – and I came bearing a bottle of gin. The living room of the house was packed with people and thick with cigarette smoke. Alex said something when he greeted me, but the noise was so overwhelming, I had to ask him to repeat it.

'I said Dylan Thomas is here,' he told me.

I was thrilled. 'Where? Can I meet him?' I asked.

'Later,' he promised, introducing me instead to a stocky man whose scruffy suit was sprinkled with cigarette ash. 'John Davenport – literary critic, *Sunday Times*,' Alex explained, and alertly I made ready to discuss Jean-Paul Sartre and existentialism, but before I could Davenport muttered in a slurred voice, 'Better pour some of that gin before you put it on the bar, once there it's done for.'

I was used to drunkenness in my peer group but I'd seldom seen older people drunk, and never *en masse* like this. I found the sight vaguely alarming and circulated uneasily for a while. It was a relief to come up against Alex's father Rex, who appeared reassuringly sober and well-dressed. 'I think my cousin may be in the same line of business as yourself,' I remarked as a conversational opener.

His reaction was stony. Rex's Whitehall office was purportedly something to do with Resource Management; was I supposed not to be aware he was in Intelligence? 'Graham Eyres-Monsell, I wonder if you know him?' I continued.

He gave me a long appraising look. He didn't say anything, and his silence was disconcerting. 'Mother insists he's a Soviet spy,' I gibbered on recklessly. 'Do you think that could be so?'

Rex kept on looking at me in heavy silence. A nerve twitched beside his eye. 'And what do *you* think?' he asked at last.

I believed it quite likely. Graham's father, Uncle Bobby, had done so much to advance the Nazi cause during the war Graham probably saw betraying Britain as a family tradition.

But I realised it would be a mistake to say as much to Rex who was glaring at me furiously. I realised I'd upset him.

Then came deliverance. I saw a plump figure in a fisherman's jersey emerge from the scrum behind Rex and stumble toward us ... and my heart leapt as in that ruined face of a sottish cherub I recognised the poet whose verse had so moved me at school. 'Isn't that ...?' I asked excitedly as he lurched closer, and I saw his puffy cheeks were pale and slick with sweat.

'Ah, Dylan, my dear fellow,' Rex exclaimed, turning from me with relief.

The poet halted, staring at us glassily. He belched, and a bubble of froth ballooned in his full loose mouth. Then, quite slowly and almost gracefully, he swayed forward and threw up.

'I say, steady on, old chap. Better in the garden donch'ya know,' Rex said mildly and, taking him by the arm in friendly solicitude, he steered my idol to the door.

Disillusioned and soiled, I was left staring at my shoes, splattered with Welsh vomit.

10
Connecticut

Three months after rinsing Dylan Thomas off my shoes I found myself on board the SS *United States* – the fastest and most modern of transatlantic liners – as she moved slowly away from the quay into Southampton Water at the start of her voyage to New York. I was on my way to take up a rather intriguing offer of employment.

This had come about through Brownie Were, mother of Shirley, one of the girls Nigel and I had taken to Biarritz two years earlier. Brownie's husband, Cecil, had retired from his post as consul general in Basel and the couple lived with their three children in a house in South Kensington. Cecil Were was twenty-seven years older than his wife, whom he'd married in Alexandria when she was seventeen. She'd married Cecil for a security she had never known – and had paid a price for it. 'My wife is uneducated and I'm not sure she isn't drunk,' he said to me at a dinner party. Cecil was self-important and pedantic; she was vivid, witty and very attractive.

Very soon after their marriage she started to take lovers, the latest Christoph Veiel, son of the president of Roche International, in Basel.

I met Christoph at their house. Ten years older than myself, he'd just published a novel set in Capri in which one of the characters was identifiably my old pal Ivor Mottron, whom he'd known in an earlier incarnation. Like myself, he'd found Ivor enchanting and undependable.

Christoph was entertaining company. Living now in Connecticut, he taught at Choate. He told me a family he knew, the Buckleys, had decided it was impossible for their children to receive a sufficiently right-wing education within the US system and had therefore decided to start their own school. He had been invited to set it up and teach there, 'Why don't you come and do the same?' he suggested.

The several sound reasons I shouldn't had not deterred me. I said I'd love to.

There were two classes on the SS *United States*, first and cabin. I had a grub-stake to fund my new life which amounted to only £100 and was travelling cabin. Though small, my accommodation was quite pleasant and the saloon was large and comfortable, but my fellow passengers in their Sta-Prest suits and nylon frocks were a bit of a disappointment.

I'd booked my passage on the *United States* through a girl I'd met at a party, whose father was a vice-president of the shipping line. Though this got me no reduction on the price, it provided a basket of fresh fruit in my cabin and, on the last-but-one night of the voyage, an invitation to dine first class at the Captain's table.

The surroundings here were very different from cabin class. Fitted out in pale leather and chrome, the décor of the saloon was ultra-modern and glossy; the passengers had the air of well-travelled sophisticates. Though not everyone was a member of the *beau monde* exactly, all of them looked rich.

There were ten people already seated around it when I joined the group at the Captain's table that evening. To my left was Mrs Rothenstein, wife of a wholesale garment manufacturer in NYC; on my right Mary Western, a cool American blonde with a husband, Carl, seated on the far side of her. I asked her if they'd been holidaying in Europe.

'No. Carl's been working in Prague, he's in the State Department. We're on our way home to Washington,' she said.

On my other side Mr Rothenstein poked his bald head forward of his large wife to bark, 'Where ya bin then?'

'I'm sorry?' I queried.

'Haven't see ya before. What ya bin doing all this trip?'

Unwilling to confess my lowly status, 'Reading Proust,' I told him languidly.

An outright lie, it didn't deflect him. 'Proust, smoust, where ya bin noshing, then?'

I informed him I'd taken all my meals in my cabin but he wasn't convinced and later was seen interrogating the Purser. Doing my best to ignore him, I concentrated with quickening interest on Mary Western.

Aged twenty-nine, she was tall, sophisticated, very well dressed and strikingly good looking, with the ice-blonde composure of a Hitchcock heroine. I was stricken with a hopeless longing to make love to her. A band was playing in the large saloon, and after dinner we danced. 'Carl won't mind, he hates dancing,' she said, and her husband beamed approval, settling back into his chair.

The band were playing smoochy numbers: 'J'attendrai'; 'La Vie en Rose'. Her body pressed against mine as we danced, she moved beautifully. Her hair brushed my face, I smelled her perfume. I realised with alarm that I was becoming aroused. Would she recoil from me in revulsion?

It was warm on the dance floor. After a couple of numbers Mary suggested we get some air. Minutes later we stood in the chilly dark beside a lifeboat. The sea was calm and the moon threw a speckled road across the pattern of the waves. I was tongue-tied by desire. 'So what does Carl *do* for the State Department?' I asked ineptly.

'He's an ... *operative*,' she breathed and, stepping forward, melted into my astonished arms.

The Buckley dynasty consisted of its patriarch, his wife and five grown-up children, including William F. Buckley Jnr, founder of the *National Review*. These, together with *their* young children, lived in several houses centred around the patriarchal compound, a mansion with picture gallery containing portraits of them all, in Sharon, Connecticut. An Irish Catholic family, churchgoers and ardently political, the origins of its patriarch and the reasons for his conspicuous wealth were hard to make out. An overbearing, rather frightening man, he possessed none of the education and culture he'd ensured for his children. Sometimes after dinner he told rambling stories of the Mexican war and tipping crates of weaponry from a moving train.

Disembarking from the SS *United States*, and on the train to New England, I was exhilarated by my first sight of Manhattan and this new country unreeling past the carriage windows. It was not until we drew near to Cornwall, Connecticut, where Christoph lived, that I started to have serious doubts about my ability to do the job I had undertaken. How and what could I *teach*? Apart from wine, demolition, silent killing and guns, I knew nothing.

I need not have worried. Christoph, who met me at the

little railroad station in a red Pontiac convertible, told me cheerfully that the Buckleys – whom he had been playing tennis with only that afternoon – had completely lost interest in the idea of starting a school. With the same ready spontaneity as they'd conceived it, the project had been discarded.

To learn this within minutes of my arrival was disconcerting. But it taught me a valuable early lesson about the rich: Their whim is not to be relied on. Don't trust them.

I stayed throughout that spring and summer as a guest in Christoph's house. To earn money I tutored a couple of boys in French and mowed lawns. The people I came across were open, friendly and hospitable. Through Christoph and the Buckleys I was invited to parties at their houses and the country club. Charles Addams, creator of the Addams family, had a house in the area and attended some of these evenings. Familiar to me from the *New Yorker*, his macabre humour intrigued me. I believed he had access to some weird vein of truth, but communicating with him proved impossible. A profound melancholic, he spoke only in monosyllables and what he said was incomprehensible.

Another local resident was James Thurber. A brilliantly amusing man, the subversive wit in his writing and cartoons had enchanted me since Stowe. In the flesh not a trace of it was detectable. I found myself listening in dismay to a resentful drunken diatribe. He complained of everything – but mostly about his mother, who was in an iron lung. Nursing care and auxiliary power were costing him $500 a week. So sharp was his sense of grievance, he grumbled about it endlessly. 'The old bitch *won't die*,' he told me furiously.

Thurber was almost completely blind by this date. Always crotchety, when drunk he became aggressive; he was a prestigious though frequently a problem guest. The evening I met him, late that summer, I was going around with a girl, Posy Tyson, whose mother owned a house near by. Soon after my unsatisfactory conversation with him she and I went to leave the house to go to a drive-in movie. Thurber and his wife were ensconced in the hall, both equally drunk. Stick in one hand, glass in the other, he was wedged across the front door. We tried to negotiate our way round him but it wasn't easy. 'Where ya goin'?' he demanded belligerently.

'To a movie,' I said.

'A movie? What ya tryin' to do, wreck the party?' he snarled.

I glanced back at the animated crowd of tanned and laughing people filling the room. 'They seem to be managing without us,' I said.

'*Seem to be managing*, do they? Huh! If you get any more *British* ...' He did a strangled mimicry of my English accent, '... *You won't be able to talk at all*. Party pooper! Get back in there and drink!' he ordered.

We retreated, forced with other departing guests to escape the house through an open window in the living room. Dylan Thomas, Chas Addams, now Thurber ... what a mistake it was to meet the men behind the myth.

It was lovely country around Cornwall and Sharon, pretty rather than spectacular. The Housatonic river burbled through a landscape of woods, low rounded hills and lakes. Villages and small orderly townships were built of white clapboard houses with shingle roofs and close-cropped communal lawns.

People could not have been nicer. They showed an openness and generosity of spirit never encountered in Britain. I had no car. Hearing this, Reid Buckley said, 'I'll lend you one,' and did so freely as someone providing an umbrella. I was wildly impressed by the gesture, it seemed to epitomise America.

Many of those I met at parties and the country club were highly educated, gifted individuals. I'd met intellectuals before at Margot Howard's literary *salons*; they wore leather patches on their elbows and bought gin by the half bottle. Here they owned kidney-shaped swimming pools, became outrageously drunk at weekends and slept with each other's wives.

Throughout that spring and early summer I continued to pursue the affair which had started so unexpectedly aboard the SS *United States*. I travelled to New York City to see Mary Western whenever the opportunity offered. That is when *she* found the chance, for I was always available. I waited with nervous anticipation for her calls telling me where and how to meet.

On the first occasion she'd told me to take a room at the Hotel Taft and call her from the lobby when I got there. I took the train to the city and checked into the hotel as instructed. In room 1010 I hung up my suit, had a drink, lit a cigarette and picked up the telephone.

'I'm in room 1402. I'm taking a shower, come up in thirty minutes,' she said.

Half an hour later she opened the door to me, wearing a bathrobe. 'How did you get here?' she asked.

'Train, taxi, elevator,' I told her.

'I'd rather you didn't use the elevator,' she said. 'And don't call me from your room.'

Room service had stopped by before I arrived, a bottle of champagne stood in an ice bucket. She poured me a glass. As she went to sit down her bathrobe fell open to the thigh. She had long, beautiful legs, and more. I stood there, dazzled and awkward and twenty years old. Lounging in her chair, she glanced me over coolly. 'You look hot in all those clothes, why don't you take them off,' she said.

Mary Western had been around a bit before marrying her husband. A poised, unusually handsome woman, there had been no lack of suitors. She frankly enjoyed sex and was clear about what she liked. Once, while we were making love, Carl called from Washington. Picking up the telephone, 'Hi, darling!' she said, and embarked on a long conversation while her free hand encouraged me to continue in what I was doing. I realised I was part of another and larger agenda, and the thought was oddly rousing.

I was worried at times by the thought of her husband. Not so much by the commandment about adultery and coveting one's neighbour's wife – so compulsive was my new-found fascination with sex that I'd effortlessly managed to isolate it from my Christian beliefs – as by his job. Exactly *what* he did for the State Department in Prague and elsewhere was hard to make out, but from the little Mary let drop it sounded pretty dubious. If he found out I was sleeping with her he had the connections to have me rubbed out, I thought, during occasional bouts of paranoia.

Another spy! It seemed such an overcrowded profession. These were the boom years for it, of course, the Cold War was at its height and there was glamour and a certain cachet in the occupation; not for some while would the invention of the photocopier bring espionage within range of the man in the street.

I was leading an enormously enjoyable life, fraternising with a bunch of people older than myself whom I found unusually interesting. But I didn't have a proper job and was earning only pocket money. I existed on Christoph's generous hospitality, and felt at times a little uncomfortable in doing so.

I knew I had to start in a career. I still dreamed of becoming a professional gambler; I planned to take a Greyhound bus to Las Vegas and apply myself at the roulette tables, but I knew it was pointless without a substantial grub-stake. There was also another job I'd wanted to try for years, though I hadn't felt able to tell Father about it when he pressed me on my plans for the future. While still at Stowe I'd seen a French film in which the suave hero – if such a word applies – wore a white suit and two-tone shoes and was a gigolo. It was not just the clothes but the lifestyle that appealed to me, the mix of lowlife with high gloss, the hotels, international travel and cosmopolitan diversity of people I believed I'd come across in bars. That was how it was in the film, anyway, and the profession had attracted me ever since. I'd never had the faintest idea of how to get started in the work. Presumably, like most jobs, it meant beginning at the bottom – but whose? In Cornwall I was presented with an unexpected opening.

One day Christoph returned from the village with a load of groceries and remarked, 'I ran into Hazel Guggenheim in the liquor store. She says she'll pay you $100 to sleep with her.'

I'd come across Hazel on several occasions during the summer. A member of New York's *haute juiverie*, she'd been born into one of a group of families known as 'Our Crowd'. Both her grandfathers had been foot peddlers who prospered to become bankers and millionaires. As children, she and her sister Peggy had lived in the St Regis Hotel, raised by nurses and governesses. Their father had perished as a passenger on the *Titanic*. Both daughters had determinedly gone wrong from an early age in the inexorable pattern followed by kids of the self-made hugely rich.

What I did not know until later – and which might have given me pause – was her marital record. She was only twenty-five when her second husband, Milton Waldman, left her. The split was bitter and acrimonious, she told him she'd kill their two children rather than let him have them and was mortified when Waldman only laughed; custody was the last thing he wanted. Taking the little boys, aged four and one, with her in a taxi, Hazel went to the penthouse apartment of a friend at the Hotel Surrey on East 76th Street, and flung the children from the terrace on the thirteenth floor.

The year I met her, Hazel was just short of fifty. Grossly fat, she weighed around fifteen stone and looked like a butcher's wife, with meaty arms and frizzy, bleached hair. Suffering from piles, she carried with her a child's inflatable lifebelt which she would place in a chair before sitting down.

Christoph's suggestion of a night with her came out of the blue, I was unprepared for it. Furthermore, the idea of servicing that mountain of very white flesh was extraordinarily unnerving. Christoph stood before me, arms filled with brown paper bags and waiting for an answer. Clearly I must respond. But was I up to this, I wondered in growing panic.

It's impossible to estimate the extent of one's genetic heritage, but I believe it helped me at that moment. Both Father and Uncle Gino were men of action, resolute and decisive. Faced by the unexpected or the hard choice, neither of them hesitated. They went for it boldly. I knew I could not let them down. 'Tell Hazel yes,' I said.

Our date was arranged for the following evening. That morning started ominously with radio warnings, repeated every half-hour, that hurricane Betsy, expected to strike the coast in Massachusetts, had altered its course to veer in our direction. All day people in the village were busy putting up storm shutters and nailing planks across their windows. The hardware store had sold out of candles by lunchtime. Radio reports continued throughout the afternoon, confirming that the storm was headed directly for us. As I drove to Hazel's house in Christoph's Pontiac in the early evening the sky had a strange bruised colour and fierce gusts of wind were blustering through the trees.

Hazel's was a clapboard New England home, standing in its own well-tended land some way from the nearest village. Neat and pretty, it nestled in the woods. Beside it grew a magnificent oak tree, planted when the house had been built 150 years before.

She opened the front door wearing a tent-like cotton print dress reaching to her ankles. Greeting me, she peered up at the darkening sky. 'This storm …' she muttered in her curious adenoidal voice. Leading me into the house, she poured me a stiff drink. We sat down and started on a rather stilted conversation. I was nervous and so too was she, though not because of my presence – this was a familiar situation for her; she regularly ordered up oxboys from the city, Christoph said – but because she was worried about the storm and what it might do to the house. The radio continued playing as we talked. The frequent weather warnings said the hurricane would pass right by us.

We spoke awkwardly; Hazel's attention wasn't on what she was saying but on the mounting storm outside. In stilted pauses we listened to the hurricane banging around the house and the sound of the wind tearing through the trees. After a while Hazel suggested we'd be more comfortable upstairs. Before adjourning she took me to the kitchen, where she laid a tray with plates, two silver forks, a box of Kleenex and a large iced cake from the refrigerator. Carrying this while I followed with our glasses she plodded heavily up the stairs. In the bedroom beneath the roof the noise of the storm was louder. The windows looked out on the immemorial oak tree only yards from the house; its branches were lashing in the wind. Hazel went to the bathroom. Undressing, I climbed on to the bed. I took a slug of bourbon and tried to imagine how

Gino would have acted faced with this challenge, but it didn't do the trick. I thought of the wicked wiles Mary Western had showed me, and that helped a little.

Hazel returned wearing another tent, this time a white lace *peignoir*. Stepping to the window, she stared at the wild agitation outside. 'That oak,' she snuffled, biting on her lip. She came to sit on the bed. Cutting herself a thick wedge of cake, she ate it voraciously. Finishing the slice, she plucked a tissue from the box and fastidiously wiped her lips. Discarding the Kleenex, she hinged forward on her enormous bum and clamped her mouth around my cock.

The radio on the dresser continued with its reports on the hurricane, whose eye passed only two miles from the house in the course of that night. The wind rose. Above its howl and the ominous creaking of the oak tree came two sudden sharp reports. They sounded like twin barrels of a shotgun discharged below the window and Hazel bounded up, quivering all over in mortal terror. 'Go see what it is!' she ordered.

It was rather off-putting, but I did as told. At the window I reported on the two smashed flowerpots blown from the wall and scattered over the terrace. The oak let out a particularly loud creak and leaned towards us. '*Make it stop!*' Hazel shrieked at me.

Naked at the window, I stood there at a loss. I'd been doing my best to please, but this was beyond me. Hazel moaned; grabbing up the cake knife she cut a huge slice and crammed it in her mouth. She chewed it with eyes fixed unblinking on the tossing branches of the tree. 'It's going to fall on the roof and crush us,' she said with her mouth full.

Our night together was restless. It was impossible to sleep. Very conscious that this was my first paid assignment in a profession I'd hankered after for years along with the suit-that-went-with, I did my best. I knew I had to prove myself.

Like a doctor or a barrister, a gigolo's career depends on word of mouth.

At one point Hazel whispered, 'I want you to come with me.'

'Tell me,' I said gamely.

'To the kitchen, I'm scared to go alone.'

I accompanied her through the shaking noisy house to fetch a family-size tub of walnut ripple ice cream. Clutching it to her, Hazel scurried back upstairs. During the rest of the night, while the oak tree creaked and groaned and shingles lifted from the roof, she ate it all. At times, setting down the ice-cream pail, she would daintily wipe her lips and beckon ...

Why should anyone want to climb Mount Everest? 'Because it's *there*,' Father had once explained to me, and in the same spirit I attacked that roly-poly mountain of lard-white flesh with the pubic hair shaved off. I was drunk and distanced. It was as though I was watching a film of what was happening, rather than part of the action. It was grotesque, horrifying even, but in a disturbing way I could not analyse, it was also interesting.

In the morning I made myself a cup of coffee and left while Hazel was still in bed. The garden was a mess, the road littered with broken branches and debris from the storm. It took a while to get back to Cornwall. I found Christoph making breakfast. '*Well*, you earned your hundred bucks?' he asked.

A wave of despair rose up to wash over me. Despite the hurricane and the ice cream and sheer daunting *scale* of Hazel, I'd performed so bravely, I thought. I'd so wanted to be a gigolo, and I'd done my very best. I understood at that moment what Father felt when he'd returned to base camp after forty days tramping over the Greenland ice cap in vile conditions looking to rescue Courtauld – and failed to find him. A failure. And there was no arguing with the fact that *I* was too. I'd been given one shot at the profession I'd yearned after for years. I'd had one go – and blown it. I hadn't been paid.

11
Manhattan

Summer ended. The smart crowd shut up their houses in Connecticut and moved back to the city. With the start of school term my tutoring job ceased, nobody needed their lawns cut, and no second opportunity to become a gigolo presented itself. Christoph was a generous host, but I knew I'd outstayed my welcome; I took the train into New York and found work.

Lehman's, Manhattan's premier wine store, occupied the ground floor of the Racquet Club in Park Avenue, directly opposite the Seagram's Building which then had just been put up. The extensive sales floor was panelled in dark wood, the walls lined with shelves of bottles laid on their side. At one end stood a large leather-topped library table at which customers could sit in comfort while they thumbed through the extensive catalogue and wrote out their cheques. The décor had been artfully contrived to convey the atmosphere of an eighteenth-century St James's wine shop, though expressed on a much larger scale. I had been hired by the store's owners in the same spirit as they had chosen the fittings; I was the right sort of furniture for the joint.

The owner, old Haas, his son Robert and a dusty book-keeper crouched in a corner ran the highly successful enterprise from an office with an observation window overlooking the sales floor. Four salesmen worked there, apart from myself.

Dressed in a white shirt, dark suit and tie, I was standing uncomfortably ill at ease on my first morning there when one of these approached me. 'Fred Zarb-Mizzi,' he introduced himself, shaking me formally by the hand. A stocky, moustached figure, he had oiled-back hair and held himself consciously erect, shoulders back. Maltese, he spoke in a curious off-English drawl, and within minutes I'd learn how proud he was of having served in the British army during the war.

'You can come share my station, old boy,' he proposed generously.

Each salesman had a station, the best of these were nearest the door to seize upon a customer as he or she entered. Fred's and mine was at the far end of the store, where we had a chest-high lectern for writing orders, a telephone and a window looking on to Park Avenue. As the shop filled up with customers and the other salesmen became busy, Fred and I moved forward to take up battle stations by the door.

I lived in a rented room on East 38th Street in a brownstone walk-up smelling of dust and central heating, and I walked to work each day. I had no friends and no social life. Posy, whom I'd been seeing in the summer, had gone off on the European grand tour customary for Vassar graduates, and though the people I'd known in Connecticut had moved back to Manhattan with the fall, my easy acquaintance with them had ended. Every evening I ate dinner in the same drugstore.

The short-order cook was my friend; he was undergoing times as lean as my own and frequently we were the only people in the place. During the meal, and after it in my room, I read: Nathaniel West, Capote, Carson McCullers, Hemingway, Robert Frost. I joined the public library and got through four books a week.

At weekends I walked. I walked that small inner city I knew from Scott Fitzgerald and O'Hara. The bars at the Plaza and Sherry Netherland I visited for a single drink were the hangouts of the Princeton set of thirty years before. At Thanksgiving I ate alone at the Algonquin beside the round table where the *New Yorker* had been put together daily.

On Sundays I sat for an hour or two in the whispery silence of the Catholic cathedral on Fifth Avenue, then ate late lunch in a nearby automat. Coming out into the fading twilight, I crossed the avenue and lingered to watch the couples skating to music on the bright-lit sunken ice rink in Rockefeller Plaza. *We exist as strangers and foreigners on this earth; here is no abiding city, and no true home ...* Forty years would pass before I read Thomas à Kempis, but I knew it to be so then. I felt very lonely at times.

And my job was horrible; none of the customers wanted to ask the advice of a 21-year-old pundit with an asshole British accent. Some were rude and difficult. I loathed the routine and servile nature of the job. I longed to be out adventuring in the world. But doing what?

With no abilities except those Father had taught me, for which there appeared to be no demand, my best move was to put myself in the way of fate, I reasoned. Manhattan was wrong, here I was defined as a shop assistant; I required a new place in which to reinvent myself. It was a question of deciding where.

The plan – if it can be called that – took shape in the course of one Sunday afternoon in the cathedral and over the blue plate special in the automat which followed. By the end of the meal I'd decided to remain at Lehman's until I'd saved a grubstake of $1,000 plus enough for the wardrobe of two suits, white tuxedo, shirts and shoes etc. I believed essential if I was to move easily in the circles I would encounter. I would then take a ship to my chosen destination, book a room in the best hotel and hang out in the bar talking to strangers who would ask me to run their *estancia*, engage in gun-running, or join them on an expedition to search for Spanish treasure. If I could afford to follow this seemingly well-heeled hotel existence for a couple of months, not just one but several such opportunities were bound to present themselves, I thought.

This scheme struck me as in no way impractical and for the next few months I spent my evenings reading Fodor and other books on South America before deciding finally on Buenos Aires and Argentina as the land of romance and maximum opportunity. Meanwhile I saved rigorously, putting away $35 of the $75 I was paid weekly beneath a loose floorboard in my room. I never went out in the evenings except to the drugstore to eat, but shortly before the year ended I did receive one promising invitation to a party in their Park Avenue apartment thrown by a couple whose lawn I'd cut during the summer in Sharon.

I was acutely missing bright company and the social scene by now, so at the close of work that day I scampered back to my little room, pressed my only suit, shook out the shirt I kept for best and prepared for the evening ahead with lively expectation. I loved parties, particularly those I went to alone; they seemed to hold such infinite possibility. With calculated extravagance I caught a cab to this one instead of walking. I'd thought the ride through pre-Christmas traffic would take some while but we reached the address much sooner than I'd imagined.

The apartment was the penthouse of a 'thirties skyscraper block, and one entered it in a way I hadn't met before: the elevator doors opened directly into its hall. So eager was my anticipation of the fun to come that I was the first to arrive by at least twenty minutes.

Waving aside my host and hostess's apologies for being still in the tub or dressing, I laid hands on glass and ice bucket and began to drink enthusiastically. By the time the first guests sashayed sleek and *soigné* from the elevator I was definitely intoxicated. I had hardly tasted liquor in three months. I'd neither breakfasted nor lunched that day, banking instead on the canapés that would undoubtedly be served.

Almost no time had passed, the party had not even properly begun, I'd chatted brightly to almost nobody before I began to experience a coldness on the brow, a chill sweat prickling across the forehead ... that first faint tremor in the upper stomach which tells one that in the not too distant future one is going to be hideously sick.

I started to look for a place where this could be done quietly and discreetly. The bathroom throbbed with vitality and half a dozen vibrant guests adjusting their make-up. In the kitchen a hired butler transplanted ice cubes. My search became increasingly urgent. The event could not be long delayed, I knew. The main bedroom steamed with fur coats, Burberrys and new arrivals removing their galoshes. My hunt grew frantic, desperate. And then, as I swayed faint and poorly in the hall, privacy found me. The elevator hissed open before my glassy eyes. Happy laughing guests gushed out and past me, vacating a small empty room. I stumbled forward. The doors closed. I was alone at last!

A click on its circuit breaker and the elevator released itself into eighteen flights of record-breaking free fall. My legs buckled and my stomach left me. I clung to the wall, slid, crashed to the floor of that plummeting metal chamber. Weightlessly, endlessly, I threw up.

We hit bottom. The doors purred open, drawing wide and revealing to my dulled gaze an expectant group of beautiful people poised to ascend. Elegantly groomed, perfumed and befurred, the careless laughter of the *jeunesse dorée* of the Sharon country club died on their lips as they beheld me floundering in a sea of puke.

Weakly I crawled out, butting an aisle between their knees; nimbly they skipped back to let me through. Yet, close to death, some tattered remnant of deceit remained, for as I passed on hands and knees I turned to face their shoes and muttered thickly in an English accent turned slurred and indistinct, 'Shouldn't go in there if I were you. Someone seems to have been beastly sick. Goodnight,' and crawled on, out of their lives for ever.

Living frugally as an anchorite in my room, I heard no word of my family for nine months except for a couple of letters from Nanny which took a long time to arrive as she'd used a 2½d. stamp, the UK internal postage at that time. She was looking after my revolver and .45 automatic, as I'd been doubtful about bringing them into the country. To be arrested on arrival for carrying an unlicensed weapon would have made a poor start. She wrote that the guns were well hidden in the bottom of her trunk, dry and quite safe, but her letters were short on hard news.

The prodigal son was not forgotten, however, for a week before my twenty-first birthday I received a card from US Customs to say they were holding a gift parcel addressed to me. I could collect it at the West Side Pier after paying the duty of $1.40. Although pleased, I was surprised, for birthdays were barely celebrated in the family. As children, usually we received some practical item like a lampshade – until then in daily use in the living room – which Mother wrapped up and presented at breakfast, 'To brighten up your bedroom, darling, I know you've always liked it.' In the course of the following month the gift would be quietly repossessed and returned to its original place in the living room.

But, to a mother, her firstborn's twenty-first is a significant event. It felt so to me anyway, as, during my lunch hour, I walked across mid-town Manhattan to collect my present. At the Customs building I paid the duty and postage due, and picked up the parcel. Through the afternoon I kept it on the floor by my station and didn't unwrap it until I got home that night.

Rather than a single expensive gift to mark the occasion, Mother had chosen to send me a cornucopia of things she knew I liked. Undoing the brown wrapping, I found a card-board shoebox filled with bunched-up lavatory paper. From its crumpled folds I took out a pad of Basildon Bond writing paper, a half-pound bar of Cadbury nut chocolate, a packet of twenty Dunhill cigarettes and a tin of Nestle's condensed milk. Also an envelope from Nanny with a ten-shilling book of stamps, which had cost a fifth of her week's wages and sadly were useless in the States.

Mother's present was characteristically frugal but thoughtful – she had at least remembered. Her accompanying card – scissored, glued and re-cycled by herself – wished me a happy and prosperous twenty-first, but said nothing of life at Gilston Road. From Father I received no word. Then, a month later, I had most unexpected news.

It was another Sunday afternoon and I was walking up Fifth Avenue in the direction of Central Park. Passing Doubleday's Bookshop I could not help noticing their window display. The entire exhibit was made up of hundreds of copies of a single title, built into a display wall. The book's cover, endlessly repeated, showed four ragged, near-naked shipwreck survivors on a raft in a rough sea, one of them a woman. The title of the book was *Sea-wyf*. The author was J. M. Scott.

I was stunned by the display. Was the work by Father? Since the success of *Gino Watkins* none of his books had achieved anything; it seemed inconceivable that *he* was the author filling Doubleday's window. I went inside. The writer's stern face glaring from the back cover was unmistakable. I'd been saving so hard and living so stingily I hadn't bought a newspaper in weeks. Now I studied the *New York Times*' top ten titles, displayed in the store. *Sea-wyf* had been four weeks in the best-seller list and stood currently in second place.

The following week it moved up to number one, but it would be six months before I learned the full extent of the book's success. By then it had been bought on by Reader's Digest, who sold half a million copies. The film rights were bought by Hollywood; Twentieth-Century Fox produced it as a big-budget picture. During that year *Sea-wyf* was published in nineteen different countries, including Japan. In the space of only a few months the book made Father an enormous sum of money.

Standing in Doubleday's that afternoon, looking through a copy of *Sea-wyf* I was unaware of this. All I knew was that Father had produced a blockbuster; after years of obscurity and failure almost overnight he'd become a best-selling author. It would be a while before I was to learn how success had changed him.

Christmas came and went in New York City. Snow melted from the streets, the new year advanced towards spring. At Easter I went to pass the holiday with Christoph and revealed my plans.

'Buenos Aires? Argentina? It will end in tears, it's a lunatic idea. No, what you should be doing is going after Posy,' he said.

She and I had dated through most of the summer, but never gone beyond heavy petting. Her mother was divorced, but the family was mainline Philadelphia, where they owned coal mines. After Labor Day Posy had gone off to Europe, where she was now doing an art course in Florence. We corresponded regularly and I liked her. But was there a future there?

After Easter I went back to work at Lehman's. Trade following the holiday was seasonally slow, the four salesmen competed for the few customers. Milton the Nark, a hunched mole whose twenty-five years of slavish service in the store had won him the door station, guarded his patch jealously, informing on all to the management.

'He told them you'd used the telephone to call Italy,' Fred Zarb-Mizzi said to me. His blue suit shone at the elbows where it caught the light and the grease spots on his jaunty bow tie showed through despite dry cleaning. 'Milton's a filthy little sneak. You and me, Jeremy, we're the only gentlemen here,' Fred told me.

One afternoon while the store was busy two women entered it from Park Avenue. The other salesmen were occupied, so I stepped forward to serve them. One was tall and ancient, the other stout and middle-aged, with the officious manner of a nurse or minder as she held her employer's arm to guide her into a chair at the leather-topped table. So sure, regal and detached were the old woman's movements it took me several moments to realise she was blind.

Seated at the table with them, I wrote down their order. This was substantial – a dozen bottles of Scotch, bourbon, a case of gin, mixers, champagne – and it required time to list it on the order pad. While I was doing so old Haas crept from his lair on to the sales floor, and scurried up behind me to whisper excitedly, 'You know who *that* is? That's Helen Keller.'

The name meant nothing to me. The cases of drink were assembled while I totalled the bill, which came to almost $1,000. 'Bill it to the Helen Keller Foundation,' the stout woman ordered, giving me a card.

'Have you an account with us?' I asked, but old Haas lurking behind us darted up to say, 'Yes, yes, yes ... that'll be just fine,' fawning over them in an ingratiating fashion all the way to the door.

Our delivery man was out on a job, so I humped the crates out to the limousine waiting on Park Avenue and stacked them in its trunk myself. 'I need the boy to unload,' the stout woman said to old Haas, who told me to accompany them.

I got into the limo and sat on the jump seat facing the two women. We pulled out, heading uptown. No one spoke and the silence grew oppressive. 'Well, you old girls are throwing quite a bash,' I remarked cheerfully, though not quite in those words. Helen Keller beamed serenely, her minder glared at me coldly without replying.

We stopped outside a brownstone townhouse on the Upper East Side. The chauffeur opened the rear door for the two women to get out then resumed his place behind the wheel, leaving me to unload the drink. Removing a case of a dozen bottles from the trunk, I trotted up the front steps after the women. The front door was open; I was stepping through it when the stout woman stopped me. 'Deliver it by the service door,' she ordered.

I halted, the heavy crate awkward in my arms. 'Down there, boy, and get a move on,' she instructed, pointing to the basement. Helen Keller gave me a blind sweet smile; they passed inside shutting the door in my face.

Unloading the limo, I lugged the cases of liquor downstairs as directed. I walked the seven blocks back to Lehman's thoughtfully. The following afternoon in my lunch hour I went to the office of the United States Line on Fifth Avenue and booked myself first-class passage on the SS *America* sailing for Europe in two days' time. I mentioned to no one in Lehman's that I was leaving. Next morning in the store I spent a half hour selecting a mixed crate of twelve bottles from our superior stock. My knowledge of *crus* and vintages came in handy as I put together a case consisting of two bottles of Château Haut Brion '47, six of Krug '52, a bottle of vintage port, Napoleon brandy and a quart of sour-mash bourbon for good measure. Gift wrapping the case myself, I addressed it to my cabin on the SS *America* and took it to Despatch for delivery. I charged it to the account of the Helen Keller Foundation.

The day after, instead of going to work I caught a taxi to the West Side pier where the SS *America* awaited me. Shown to a spacious stateroom, I explored my quarters with delight while the steward went off to fetch an ice bucket. The gift-wrapped case of Lehman's best stood waiting. I read the charming card enclosed, wishing myself Bon Voyage from the Foundation, and set a bottle of champagne to chill while I unpacked.

An hour later, glass in hand, I stood in a happy glow on the liner's stern deck watching the Manhattan skyline recede behind us. Lounging against the rail, I raised my glass to the Statue of Liberty sinking in our wake. I'd be back, I knew, but now I was embarking on my own Grand Tour, on my way to Europe to capture an American heiress. I was 'off to wife it wealthily in Padua ...' as Howard Keel sang so lustily. Or rather – via London – Florence.

12
Vienna

'David, darling,' Mother cried. 'It's an age since I've seen you, where *have* you been?'

'Jeremy,' I corrected her. She'd always had difficulty remembering our names. 'America – but you knew that, you sent me a birthday present.'

'Yes, of course you have, darling. Frightfully enterprising of you, just like Christopher Columbus. Are you staying to dinner? I don't think there's anything to eat.'

I'd sent a cable to say that I was arriving, though she could not recall if she'd received it. I hadn't exactly expected the fatted-calf reception, but the prodigal son *had* been gone over a year and a half. A little later we sat in the chilly living room at Gilston Road nursing a small glass of South African sherry apiece. The house was as I remembered it, cluttered and threadbare, though I hadn't recalled it *quite* so distressed as this. I was sorry to see Mother looking distressed herself. Her hair was uncombed and she had on a knitted waistcoat, the hem of which had completely frayed away. At times in the past she'd been distracted and agitated. She was the same now but worse, so preoccupied by whatever was troubling her that nothing I said held her attention for longer than moments.

'Father's not here?' I asked.

'No, he's *not*,' she said. There followed a long pause. 'Actually, he left some time ago,' she added. Six months or more, it transpired, though she wasn't certain of the exact date he'd finally quit the family home. He'd strode off after breakfast one morning as usual, wearing his rucksack, and not returned. Apart from books, he'd never owned anything except a razor and a toothbrush, and so slight was his impact upon the household that several days had gone by before she'd registered his absence.

'Any idea where he is?' I enquired.

'Haven't the foggiest,' she answered. Obviously she didn't want to pursue the subject and we sat conserving our sherries in rather awkward silence until the door opened and Nanny came in.

'Is Jeremy to sleep in the cold room or the wet room?' she asked.

Next morning in daylight the dismaying state of the house was revealed. It had been in poor shape when I'd left for America and since then no effort had been made to arrest its decline. Streaks of damp stained the ceiling and discoloured the wallpaper. I was sitting on the collapsed sofa after breakfast staring gloomily around the once-elegant drawing room when Nanny brought me a cup of weak Nescafé on a tray. 'Where's Mother, is she up?' I asked.

'Your mother's in the bathroom washing her money,' Nanny informed me.

It was said in the most matter-of-fact tone, yet clearly all was not well. I'd been accustomed to Mother's odd behaviour my whole life, but it had become more than usually bizarre. A pair of beautifully decorated Regency chairs in her bedroom and a marquetry table had been given a coat of green distemper, slapped on roughly with a brush. Questioning Nanny, I learned that Mother had ceased giving her money for shopping; she'd been using her own savings to buy the household's food. Unable to discuss the problem with my siblings, I telephoned Mother's brother, Uncle Tony, who'd always been good to me and whom I liked a lot.

'Oh dear, is she going batty again?' he asked. I told him how things looked. 'We'd better get her into a loony bin,' he said. It sounds facetious, it *was* facetious, but it was not uncaring. They were close; they'd been together while their father absconded, their mother killed herself, and Gino died.

Throughout the course of the next few days, during which he saw doctors and tried to resolve the problem, Uncle Tony's manner and tone of voice remained the same. And so did mine. It was the way I was used to, the way my family dealt with everything. Nothing was allowed to be serious and nobody in any circumstance ever showed emotion.

Nowadays this is not considered to be a desirable approach to crisis, but it does have one compelling advantage. Detached from the event, one is more efficient in handling it. In achieving what had to be done, Tony was pragmatic and effective – and this did not surprise me. When I was a child I'd heard him relate to Mother the experience he'd had in Germany the year before. A lieutenant in the Coldstream Guards, he'd been leading his troop of tanks in pursuit of the retreating German army. Late one afternoon they had surprised an enemy platoon, who surrendered. A tank troop has no facility for keeping prisoners and, even disarmed, these represented a threat, for Tony's troop would shortly be obliged to laager for the night and the Germans could betray their position to the nearby enemy. The soldiers of the surrendered platoon were thoroughly demoralised and no danger, Tony explained, but their young officer was a Nazi and still defiant. Tony told him that he'd release the platoon if he'd give his word to lead his men back to the British lines and give themselves up. But the German officer refused to do so, instead drawing himself erect to say, 'Heil Hitler!' So Tony shot him.

'Oh, darling, how *awful*,' Mother said. 'That must have been terribly upsetting for you.'

'Not really,' Tony told her. He'd been much more upset when he'd had to shoot Jeff, his bull terrier.

Mother went to stay at a private nursing home overlooking Regent's Park, in the care of a psychiatrist who seemed to understand her illness and appeared kindly. Nevertheless, it was saddening; the shadow of the experience lay over me as I travelled to Florence to meet Posy. Together we caught the night train to Vienna, where we took a double room in the Hotel Bristol.

She was a tall, good-looking girl with an independent mind, long dark hair and a loose-limbed American stride. Her father had been arrested for driving an open convertible into a bank in Hertford, Connecticut, while stark naked and drunk, and had played little part in raising her. The coal mines and the money belonged to her mother, who had brought her up.

In contrast to my own minimal luggage, Posy arrived in Vienna with three suitcases of clothes bought in Saks, Bloomingdale's and, more recently, Florence. She'd enjoyed a privileged upbringing and – unlike myself – was long familiar with grand hotels.

'Hey, this is OK,' she said, looking around our sumptuous room with approval. 'Europe's kind of cute, I guess, but it's real dirty in places.'

To her Vienna meant Beethoven and Mozart; for me it was the wildly romantic black and white city of Harry Lime and Orson Welles. For both of us it was *sacher torte* and smoky bars – every one of which had a zither player. I had the best part of $500 with me, the wages I'd saved in New York. It was a fair amount of money at the time, especially when converted into Austrian schillings. I set about spending it with gusto after the long winter of austerity. We went to the opera, to good restaurants and to cabarets. Posy shopped at Herzmansky and the flea market. Spring had come, the chestnut trees were in leaf in the gardens of the Schönbrunn Palace. I basked in the sensuous pleasure of the city, and the opulence of our hotel with its muffled hush and lofty public rooms. Above all in the company of an amusing pretty woman and the fun of doing things together, both in and out of bed.

We'd been in Vienna several days before Posy remarked casually over dinner one night, 'Ma has had a man take photographs of your house in London.'

'Of Gilston Road? Why?' I asked, astonished.

'She wants to find out about you.'

'What do you mean? There's nothing to find out.'

'Sure,' Posy answered calmly, 'But she's like that. She says only flits wear suede shoes.'

We didn't discuss it further, but I found the idea of a private detective making enquiries of our London neighbours unsettling. There was some information I'd prefer not to be set out in a report to Posy's mother. I could see that she might think a penniless, unemployed English adventurer, whose family house was falling down, whose father's whereabouts were unknown, and whose mother was locked away in a lunatic asylum, was not the ideal suitor for her daughter's hand.

A month later I was back in London with Posy, sharing a

flat in Ovington Square off Knightsbridge. Posy was paying the rent from her allowance – she'd told her mother she was doing an art course at the Slade. Three weeks of European travel, good hotels, room service and romance had exhausted everything I'd saved.

Again I was going to interviews and searching for a job but for once luck was on my side. A couple of weeks after our return, I was offered work in a small company producing advertising spots for commercial TV, which had just started in Britain.

I took Posy out to dinner that night. I couldn't wait to tell her my news, but she was far from thrilled. 'Five pounds a week?' she repeated. 'How can we possibly live on that?'

We could use her money, I suggested.

'Why don't you come and work in the corporation in Philadelphia?' she asked. 'Then we could get married.'

I'd thought about it a lot. The Julian English role in O'Hara's *Appointment in Samarra* rather appealed to me. We'd live in a large clapboard house with a devoted Dutch couple for staff and I'd wear a Brooks Brothers suit, drive a Cadillac, drink heavily and behave increasingly unpredictably in the country club. This had been my ambition until recently but now, faced with its realisation, the appeal quite drained away. In the last few hours another dream had supplanted it: I wanted to go into the film business and make movies.

'Well, do as you wish,' said Posy, 'But *I'm* going home.'

The film industry, which had boomed in Britain after the war, was now doing less well and the old guard who had held well-padded jobs as directors, art directors, camera technicians and editors found themselves without work. For them, and for many others, the start of commercial TV and production of advertising spots came as the most opportune of lifeboats.

Production, together with the studios and processing laboratories, was rigidly controlled by the ACTT, which demanded a camera crew of five before a frame of film could be exposed. Women were excluded, except in the fields of hairdressing, make-up, wardrobe and continuity. The union would accept no new applicants while a single one of its members remained without work, and the rule had successfully prevented new talent from entering the industry for many years. Film technicians were middle-aged or old, slavishly union minded and, I was disappointed to see, uniformly drab and badly dressed.

The feature-film and documentary business and the new TV companies which had just opened were all located in Soho – a ghetto they shared with restaurants, homosexual and luvvie clubs, a street market and a lively white-slave traffic flourishing under the protection of West End Central police station.

TVA, the company I worked for, occupied a house in Greek Street. I shared a room with the company's three women producers. These days 'advertising' enjoys a stylish high tone; the décor of its offices and appearance of its staff reflect its glossy image. Then it was not the case. Joan, one of the producers whose Brillo-blonde hair was tinged by the fags she smoked without removing from her lips, called her clients 'dear' and knitted baby garments while speaking to them on the telephone.

As assistant to the producers I ran errands, hung out on the studio floor 'making-a-busy', as Milton the Nark had showed me at Lehman's, attended planning meetings with our ad-agency clients (and the excellent lunches they were taken to in the course of production). I found it astonishing I was being paid to do something I enjoyed so much.

I was in at the start of a completely new business; one in

which image and fashion, youth and new ideas, are of the essence – and it was not long before the first signs of this showed at TVA. At a stroke all three women producers were fired and a new man brought in to run production. Jim Garrett was a dynamic Welshman of twenty-eight whose father had been the authoritarian headmaster of a small private school. With him came a couple of younger directors who replaced the old feature-film gaffers TVA had been using.

One of these was Norman Prouting. Witty, good-looking and dressed in trousers even tighter than my own, he was a self-made homosexual from Yorkshire who moved in a world of fashionable faggotry and crossed class barriers easily and most nights of the week. One morning he said to me, 'I won't be here next week, I've had the most mouth-watering invitation to stay in a huge, fearfully grand villa on Cap Ferrat.'

'Sounds fun,' I remarked a little wistfully.

'Oh dear! Too, too tactless of me to mention it. But you can have my flat in Chelsea while I'm away, if you want,' he offered. It was a generous suggestion and I jumped at it. During Mother's continuing absence in the asylum I was living at Gilston Road, but fornication was impossible in the house with Nanny there.

Norman's apartment was the basement of an attractively furnished house belonging to a middle-aged European refugee with a loud voice and theatrical manner. I'd hardly got back on my second evening there when she burst into the flat in a high state of excitement, waving a copy of the evening paper. 'It is *war*!' she announced dramatically.

In the wider world which lay outside my own narrow concerns, history was in the making. A short while before, President Nasser of Egypt had seized control of the Suez Canal, nationalising British and French assets in his country. The headline of the *Evening Standard* gripped in my landlady's fist announced that the Prime Minister, Anthony Eden, had sent British forces into Egypt to regain the Canal.

Only hours earlier I'd been wholly involved in the fun and fantasy of making TV ads. Now, abruptly, another scenario replaced this. Following National Service I was still in the Reserve. The regiment was the obvious reinforcement to send to the Canal Zone, I would be called up. It was disconcerting.

Next morning brought the news that British forces were engaged in street fighting in Port Said. Rodney called me. In the end he'd decided to stay on in the regiment. He was in high spirits. 'Well, we'll be back there next week,' he predicted gleefully. 'Better start getting your kit together, I'd say.'

I telephoned Nanny and after work that day I went over to Gilston Road. She had already unearthed my uniforms from the attic, pressed them and polished the brass and chain mail. 'Your sword's gone rusty, I can't do a thing with it. I'll have to take it to the ironmonger and see what he can manage. Really, Jeremy, you don't look after your things at all,' she told me crossly.

It wasn't so. My Colt .45 and .22 revolver hidden in her trunk together with several hundred rounds of ammunition were in perfect condition. On the frayed carpet in Nanny's room I dismantled them lovingly, cleaning off the heavy grease I'd packed them in before going to America. I'd forgotten what a pleasure it was to handle them. My best toys, they'd shored up my schooldays; it was like meeting old friends. And my uniforms with the buttons and chain mail shined up by Nanny were in immaculate condition. Their narrow trousers which had excited such ridicule in the regiment were now the height of current fashion. Everyone else on the battlefield was going to look pretty silly wearing wide ones, I thought.

My dreams of glory proved short-lived. My sword remained within its scabbard, still slightly stained by rust. The operation foundered; within days the shooting ended and British and French forces slunk out of Egypt, tails between their legs, to ribald catcalls and rude gestures from the triumphant Arabs. The whole bungled venture ended in an ignominious climb-down and withdrawal. It emerged later from political memoirs that Eden was heavily into amphetamines, and, in time, I would discover myself how speed plays with the head. Eden may have invaded Egypt, but one can't be *too* censorious, everybody gets a bit silly when they're stoned.

So I didn't go to war. But, although I'd disliked the army, and my Christian principles told me it was naughty to shoot foreigners, I'd have welcomed returning to the Canal to fight. I enjoyed my job in advertising but I had an addiction to new experience. I longed for travel and adventure, I'd developed a taste for the uncertainties of life, its random encounters and brief intimacies. If I had to choose between the chances, I definitely wished to choose the odd.

13
Jordan

'I gather your mother's been released,' Father remarked while filling his pipe.

We were seated on the terrace of a ramshackle bar by the side of a dusty track. For this was the late 'fifties and Mallorca was a beautiful island as yet untouched by mass tourism. Cala d'Or consisted of a few whitewashed cottages, one modest hotel and the bar/restaurant where we sat, run by an alcoholic Italian not-so-ex-fascist and his long-suffering English wife. A handful of expats had beached here to drink out what remained of their nothing lives at the end of a sandy track that went no further. Such was the spot where Father had chosen to settle.

Yes, Mother had left the asylum several months ago, I told him. Her stay there had been a long one and I'd visited her regularly, though not as often as I should have. It was saddening and awkward to do so, for she sat in bed, silent and withdrawn, making no response to the small talk it became increasingly hard to generate.

'Was it the electric shocks that cured her?' Father asked.

'I think what did it was going there with her lawyer to try to get her power of attorney. Uncle Tony was getting a bit fed up with paying for everything. I needed to write cheques,' I explained.

Father chuckled grimly. 'Yes, she wouldn't want that,' he said.

Most emphatically Mother had not; the suggestion had produced a response not seen in weeks. I was convinced I'd effected her cure where doctors had failed, for she'd got better from that moment on. Within a fortnight she was back at Gilston Road and I realised her recovery was complete when she halved Nanny's wages, which I'd raised to £5 a week in her absence.

Mother was her old self again. And Father, whose whereabouts for so long had been a mystery, had finally come to roost – and invited me to stay. Previously, I'd have done everything in my power to avoid accepting, but curiosity had drawn me to his hideout. In a single year his novel *Sea-wyf* had transformed him into a best-selling author and earned him a fortune. He'd acquired a new partner, Adriana, a slim, voluble Italian in her thirties, inexplicably devoted to him. They had travelled around the world together searching for the perfect place to live, and for a while considered Australia until he found the natives' friendliness insufferable. They were looking for seclusion, no people, beautiful surroundings and the discomfort they both enjoyed.

Standing on a low cliff above a rocky sea inlet, the house he'd bought was constructed on several levels. A flight of steps led down to a private jetty and a boat house where he kept an Indian canoe. Furniture was basic, plank tables and upright chairs; the beds were peasant-style, made from cement and plaster. The house had no electricity or running water but a well instead, and a charcoal-burning stove. It and the waterside setting were enchantingly picturesque but the village was without amenities. The only telephone was in the one hotel.

Father wrote in the morning while Adriana shopped for food and busied herself around the house. During the day I swam, lay in the sun and read, or took out the canoe among the rocky inlets. In the evening the three of us would meet for dinner and conversation, which had grown no easier with the passing years.

After that early and brief discussion of Mother's sanity, mostly we kept to neutral topics affecting neither of us, though I did remark on how well his book had been selling in the USA while I was in New York.

'Yes, it's gone splendidly, I'm told. It's a relief not to have to think about money now,' he said.

'Must be marvellous,' I agreed. 'But do you have to pay tax and things?'

'Oh *tax*,' he repeated disparagingly. 'No, the bank takes care of all that sort of stuff. That's what they're for.' There seemed nothing more to be said.

The tone of our uneasy relationship was not improved by an incident which took place a week after my arrival in Cala d'Or. One afternoon I'd taken the Indian canoe and Father's fishing spear and paddled out to the headland in an attempt to harpoon our dinner. I'd watched the villagers doing so at night with lanterns, but in daylight I was unsuccessful. Getting bored with this, I paddled to the almost deserted beach below the hotel, where Father would meet me later after making a telephone call. Hauling the canoe clear of the water, I lay down in the sun and went to sleep.

I woke to the sound of voices. A photographer with untidy, boyish hair and German accent, together with assistant, make-up, and four models, was at work on the rocks beside me. Three of the girls were wearing swimsuits, one was being fitted into a black rubber wetsuit which the assistant was smearing with a slick sheen of Vaseline. It was an unexpected and welcome sight, I sat up to watch. 'Can we borrow your harpoon?' the photographer called down to me in Spanish.

'Of course,' I told him and he introduced himself: Helmut Newton. The name meant nothing to me, but I was thrilled to meet him and his alluring group. I lent him the fish spear with alacrity. When, a few shots later, he requested the canoe I was glad to give it him. And shortly after, when he asked for my body, I was more than happy to oblige. 'In background only,' he explained, to my disappointment. And so it was at first but, as the models changed into further swimsuits and Helmut's perverse imagination dreamed up yet more highly charged set-ups, I improved my part, becoming ever more entranced within it. At the moment when Father, having made his call, strode on to the beach so that we might paddle the canoe back to the house together, the boat lay overturned at the water's edge and a half-naked model sprawled helpless across its capsized hull. Above her reared a glistening black rubber avenger of flawless Nordic beauty poised to plunge the harpoon into her helpless victim, while I crouched at the fury's feet, clutching her shiny calves in anguish.

Lost in the drama of my role, I did not see Father as he stalked across the sand towards us with a set and rigid face. The first I knew of his presence in the scene was when he snatched his fish spear from the black avenger's hand. With one heave he righted the canoe, sending the hapless model sprawling. Standing among the rest, silent and open-mouthed in surprise, with them I watched his retreating back as, stiff with fury, he dragged the boat into the shallows, clambered in and paddled off.

Dinner that night was more than usually strained. That it took place by candlelight on the house's terrace overlooking the still waters of the *cala* and a view of starlit tranquillity made no difference. Adriana did her best, chattering away brightly in an Italian fashion, but Father remained silent. I said I thought I should go back to London tomorrow.

'Oh yes, your *job*,' Adriana exclaimed, grasping at the opening. 'So interesting, it must be fascinating to make commercials. *Such* a good profession.'

Father grunted. 'Piffling way to spend your life. Frightful second-rate people,' he observed morosely.

I took a sip of wine. 'Actually, I've given up making commercials,' I said in a throwaway voice.

He was wearing his hanging-judge face already; his expression didn't change, but I detected a glint of satisfaction in his eye. 'Fired, were you?' he asked after a long silence.

'No, actually, I left.'

No response but a glance of 'I told you so' to Adriana.

'I've got another job,' I added. 'Writing and producing documentary films. About Britain.'

It took a little while for him to digest this – a pause which was filled with Adriana's Italian enthusiasm. Then he asked, 'Who on earth would want to waste money making films no one wants to look at?'

'The British Government,' I told him. 'I've got a job with something called the Central Office of Information.'

He stared at me disgustedly. 'Good God,' he uttered at last, 'You mean you've become a *civil servant*! Rolled umbrella, bowler hat ... you'll be getting a *mortgage* next!'

The COI was a modern concrete and glass building in Lambeth. The walls of its entrance plaza, open to the street, displayed a vast mosaic mural depicting the labours of Hercules.

Every night at closing time the local residents stumbled from the pubs, fumbling their chalks, to fall upon it with drunken enthusiasm.

Morning would reveal these lurid tableaux. Heroic figures balling with gigantic organs, epically defecating and discharging torrents of highly coloured sperm would greet the stream of civil servants emerging from the tube station to run the rude gauntlet with downcast eyes and reach their desks unsettled. These graffiti formed the subject of lengthy internal memos, but the immutable regulations of government bureaucracy made it impossible for the cleaning staff to start work earlier than other employees in their regular morning task of returning the mosaic to its original design.

Several hundred men and women worked in the building, though only about forty in the Film and TV Department, a half-dozen of these producers. For every person engaged in *making* film, three or more were employed to prevent him or her from doing so – or at least to render it as difficult as possible. Nevertheless, the department's output was prodigious. Each month it despatched a total of four or five hours of cut film to the USA, Canada and the Commonwealth for transmission in a graveyard known as Public Service Time.

My office was large and bare, furnished with a regulation metal desk and filing cabinet. Personal decorative touches were discouraged, though a framed photograph of an unexceptional wife and 2.2 children was permitted. Every Monday an elderly messenger issued each employee with a small tablet of soap and a clean hand-towel. Everyone went home at 5.30 sharp. But the man who ran the department was not what I'd expected. Charles de Vere Beauclerc was a spindly toff with a languid manner and Bertie Wooster voice, who later became the Duke of St Albans and my neighbour in the south of France.

Here there were no perks or client lunches, and the government was a tighter-fisted employer than TVA had been. But I'd become bored by my peripheral role in putting together ads for cornflakes and washing powder. *I wanted to make movies* – a phase in youth as inevitable as acne; moreover, I had the misguided ambition to write and direct them myself, to become an *auteur*. Now I had the chance to do so, though the topics were not those I'd have chosen myself. I'd been at the COI for a couple of months, making two-minute shorts on subjects like morris dancing and Salisbury Cathedral when the department was commissioned to produce a series of four half-hour films on youth in Britain. The reason these were given to *me* to put together was not because I was considerably younger than the other producers, but because the work involved going on location for several weeks. The others were married, the 'living-away' allowance was hopelessly inadequate, and they all hated filming outside London.

'Oh yah, just one more thing,' Charles Beauclerc said, after telling me I had the job, 'The Minister wants a word with you before you start.'

I reported to the Commonwealth Relations Office next day. There was never any question of going anywhere by taxi while working for the COI; they wouldn't pay for it. I caught a bus across the river then walked up Whitehall to the imposing entrance in Downing Street. My name was checked and I took a seat to wait by a bulletin board with a few notices thumbtacked to its green felt. One, which was handwritten, read, *Gentlemen are requested not to play fives on the first floor landing when the Secretary of State is in his office*. Told to go up, I climbed the stately marble staircase. The building was immensely grand. While making my way along a wide corridor from which tall mahogany double doors led into various offices, I overtook an antique cart loaded with brass coal scuttles which was being pushed down it very slowly by a wizened gnome in shapeless gulag uniform.

There was a period in the eighteenth century when it was thought beneficial for people to be reminded constantly of death. The marble effigies of the deceased on their tombstones represent them not in the fullness of life but as corpses well advanced in decomposition. Sir Alec Douglas-Home's shrunken body and sunken features conveyed that same impression. Deliquescence – accompanied by a delightful easy manner and enormous charm. He possessed an instinctive courtesy rare in the British aristocracy; it was impossible not to like him.

His room – large, with tall windows, worn carpet, oil paintings and antique furniture – bore no resemblance to an office. He was dressed for the country in a tweed suit rather too big for him. It was a look I'd considered for myself as this was a Friday, but on the whole I'd thought grey flannel would be more appropriate, with the sixteen-inch rather than the fourteen-inch trouser bottoms.

He gave me a cup of Earl Grey tea. 'Now, about these films …' he began, and I composed myself alertly to listen. Yes, of course they should feature young people, of course they should make their audience want to visit Britain, but this was not their principal objective. In their essence, they should convey the essential and abiding genius of the mother country and the innate virtue of Britishness … and of remaining part of the Commonwealth … the family. I made notes while he talked: *Magna Carta … Houses of Parliament … unbroken tradition of democracy … political stability … constancy … decency* … As he continued, the door opened – there was no knock – and the shrivelled gnome I'd passed earlier shuffled in with a fresh scuttle of coal for the open fire. 'That's what I mean,' Home said. 'This building's been here 150 years and ever since that old chap's been faithfully fulfilling his duty without anyone having to tell him or order him around.'

Essential value of gnomes, I noted on the pad in front of me, enquiring whether these devoted old retainers ever posed a security risk. Not at all, he assured me genially, their ears were cauterised with a red-hot poker and their tongues cut out on starting here as lads.

My briefing completed, he walked me to the door. 'Don't try to be *clever*, will you, Scott,' he added as he showed me out. 'These films have to be understood by our brown brothers, remember.'

For three weeks I travelled the country, staying in third-rate hotels with a two-man 16mm camera crew provided by ITN, filming youth stuff and shooting interviews. I needed a thrusting figure to speak for youthful business enterprise. I asked my school friend Nigel Broackes if he'd come to the studio to be interviewed by Bernard Braden, who was presenting the series.

On the day planned, Nigel arrived at the COI driving a 4.5-litre Bentley, which he parked in the forecourt. It was a while since I'd seen him, he'd put on a little weight and a certain gravitas and he exuded a visible air of prosperity and success. With Braden, we ran through the substance of the interview as Nigel explained his current activities. He'd founded and now controlled a plastics factory with sixty full-time employees and 150 outworkers in Bagshot; he'd started a hire-purchase company, Southern Counties Discount, which he ran from an office above Dr Scholl's shoe shop in the Brompton Road; he'd become a director of a major real-estate agency; he'd entered the West End property market – with two partners he'd bought Green Park House overlooking the Park, which he was converting into ten luxury apartments and two shops.

For someone who, like myself, was only twenty-four, it represented a considerable achievement. Towards the end of the interview Braden asked him what had made it possible.

'A worn-out establishment, antiquated systems, obsolete old men hankering for 'before the war'. We're not crippled in the way they are,' he answered.

On camera, his manner and delivery came over not as boastful but calm and utterly self-confident. It was an impressive performance, but when I ran a rough cut of the interview to Charles Beauclerc he was scathing. 'Pah, bet *he* comes a cropper!' he remarked scornfully. I saw from his face that he was quite worked up about it and realised he was envious.

I'd completed only the first of the youth films when I arrived at Hercules House to work one morning and was called to Beauclerc's office where he sat with a cup of tea and a plate of ginger biscuits on the desk in front of him. He said, 'You probably heard the news on the radio; there's been a revolution in Iraq. They've assassinated Prince Feisal, their ruler.' He nibbled fastidiously on a biscuit. 'In fact, it seems they've eaten him. We think Jordan may go the same way. Last night we sent in a paratroop brigade to secure the country and support the king. Under international law, it's a bit iffy, there's going to be a whole hullabaloo in the UN, the Arab countries, Russia ... We're saying we've been *invited* to go in, but we need favourable news footage showing how popular and welcome the British troops are. Can you go there this afternoon?'

'Of course,' I told him.

I went back to my flat to pack a bag. Before catching a train to Stansted Airport I stopped by Gilston Road to pick up my Colt .45. 'Now you just be careful with that thing, Jeremy. Don't you go shooting anyone,' Nanny told me, unearthing it from her trunk.

I flew to Jordan on a military Dakota loaded with war materiel and supplies. I was the only passenger. I had no camera crew; I'd been told to borrow one from ITN, with whom the COI had a contract. Amman airport had been closed to commercial traffic, but there were several taxis outside. I got into one, telling the driver to take me to a hotel.

'Philadelphia?' he asked.

The name was familiar from a guide book to Jordan I'd consulted before leaving. It was the only decent hotel in Amman, but on my living-away allowance of £3 15s. I couldn't afford the place. 'Not the Philadelphia,' I told him.

We drove into town. Amman was a desolate spread-out slum, stinking of garbage. Knots of ragged restless people hung out in the streets, everyone was waiting for the revolution to begin. We stopped outside a dilapidated building. 'Hotel,' the driver announced. Telling the driver to wait, I went into the hotel and asked a man in a *djellaba* behind the desk if he had a room. Hitching down a key he walked me upstairs. An adolescent squatted on the landing filling Coca-Cola bottles from a jerrycan and wadding their necks with rag. He glowered at me as we went by; there was a strong smell of petrol.

The room I was shown to had a gritty cement floor and walls splattered with crushed flies. It was bare except for a bed. The window overlooked the dusty square, which was filled with a crowd of ragged people milling about aimlessly. A couple of Daimler armoured cars of the type I'd commanded myself were drawn up on the far side, supported by an Arab Legion foot patrol armed with twelve-bore Greener guns. I went downstairs, got back in the taxi and told the driver to take me to the Philadelphia.

This latter turned out to be a pleasant, modern hotel set in a garden of date palms and plants. It was full to overflowing.

The lobby was besieged by press correspondents demanding rooms. More were arriving all the time, entering the country with customary ingenuity. I sought out the ITN crew with their reporter Reggie Bosanquet, and introduced myself. The three of them were sharing a room crowded with equipment; they'd had a bad trip and did not seem especially pleased to see me. Reggie said there was no chance I could move in with them.

At a bit of a loss I went to the hotel bar, still carrying my bag, and ordered a drink. It was amazingly expensive. I had a float of £150 which had been reluctantly advanced by the COI cashier. At these prices my funds weren't going to last long. I realised I had a problem but recalled Christoph's advice on what to do if caught short by a revolution while travelling. Before his father became president of Roche International he'd run their operation from Uruguay, where Christoph had lived as a child. Familiar with the inconvenience caused by a *putsch*, he'd said you must go at once to the best hotel and put yourself in the hands of the hall porter.

I looked for the concierge and slipped him £20 – a small fortune at the time. A little while later I found myself sharing a room with the *Daily Mirror* photographer. A small man with slicked-back, nicotine-coloured hair, he was not happy with the arrangement, but then he wasn't happy about anything because, though he still had his camera bag, his suitcase had been lost in transit.

I spent the next few days hanging around the Philadelphia and sitting on the terrace, drink in hand, with the rest of the international press corps, waiting for the coup to take place. Nothing was happening. The single event to provoke any flicker of interest was caused by the unexplained arrival at the hotel of a stranger who was not a journalist. A taxi drew up, and from it stepped a man wearing an African safari suit, a revolver in a holster and a hat; he was carrying a stick. Without glancing at the crowd of correspondents slumped on the veranda he passed through us into the hotel, followed by his driver with a Gladstone bag. He was an unlikely figure.

'Who's that geezer, then?' The *Mirror* photographer demanded. 'He's a personality, he is.' His eye brightened at the potential.

Apart from this stranger, who avoided conversation and kept to himself, and a party of four Scandinavian call-girls and their pimp who'd been trapped here in their working tour of the Middle East by the closure of the airport, everyone in the Philadelphia was press. Infrequently a bomb would go off and a wispy trail of smoke appear above the roofs of the shanty town in the distance. Downing their drinks, everyone would pile into taxis and go to look, but Amman was such a ruin that a small bomb made little difference to the architecture. Returning to the Philadelphia, everyone would resume drinking and the *Mirror* photographer would complain there wasn't a shot in it. I understood why war correspondents are all alcoholics: they're driven to it by the stultifying boredom of their job.

I sent a cable to the COI requesting money and asking what to do. The reply came back: URGENT DESPATCH FAVOURABLE FOOTAGE SOONEST.

One morning I happened to remark to my room-mate that, years before, I'd once met King Hussein of Jordan when he'd been playing bongo drums in a London nightclub. The *Mirror* photographer was unexpectedly stimulated by the news and suggested we call on him. I thought this a poor idea, unlikely to succeed, but at his insistence I telephoned the palace and spoke to the *chef de protocole*. I was here for COI and would like to do an interview, I told him. Most surprisingly, he called back to say to come at 5 pm.

I couldn't find the ITN crew, who'd gone off somewhere with Reggie Bosanquet, and I was regretting the whole thing by now. If I was to meet the king, it seemed a mistake to pitch up with an uninvited guest in the shape of a pushy tabloid snapper wearing the same soiled suit he'd had on for the last five days. But he wouldn't hear of my going to see the king alone. 'In this game, it's all for one and one for all,' he said.

By 4.30 there was still no sign of the ITN crew. Asking the concierge to send them to join me the instant they reappeared, the photographer and I took a taxi and arrived at the palace gate, which was guarded by concrete machine-gun emplacements. After examination of our documents and a body search we were let through to walk up the exposed drive to the building. It was very, very hot.

A tough-looking major domo showed us into a large ugly room with gilt sofas covered in shiny material standing against the walls and a gaudy carpet. After a while an ADC appeared wearing Desert Legion service dress. 'Where's your camera crew?' he asked.

'On its way,' I told him breezily.

Waiting only for the photographer to come back from the lavatory, the ADC escorted us to a room larger and even more hideous than the one we'd left. Throwing open the door, he said, 'The people from CBS, Your Majesty.'

The king, who was rather a small man covered in medals, was seated behind a desk so enormous it obscured two-thirds of him. I had the impression we didn't resemble the heavy-weight envoys of a US TV network that he'd been expecting.

Clearly, the king had no memory of our meeting, which was hardly surprising. At the mention of Edmundo Ross's Calypso Club, where it had taken place, the royal countenance tightened a little; he didn't respond with the warmth I'd hoped for. The photographer, who'd been squirming in his chair with impatience, chipped in to ask if he could take a shot of what was showing of the monarch above the desk, and was told no.

Conversation flagged; there was still no sign of the camera crew. I attempted to revive things by remarking how handy it must be to have the British army fly in to help out, but he said the Hashemite Kingdom was perfectly capable of taking care of its own internal affairs, adding that this wasn't a very good time to chat as, what with the state of emergency and everything, he was quite busy at the moment ... but he hoped we'd enjoy our stay in Amman.

'A lot of fucking good *that* was!' the *Mirror* photographer remarked as we walked back to the main gate where our cab was waiting surrounded by a gang of urchin beggars who pounced on us, tugging at our clothes and trying to get into our pockets. 'Animals!' said the photographer, and stared moodily at the filthy streets as we drove back to the hotel. He said he couldn't understand how people could live like that, he thought Jordan was a disgusting country, he'd had the runs ever since he'd got here. He said this wasn't his line of work anyway, normally he worked on the sports pages, but no one else had been available to go at such short notice.

Every morning the international press corps got up hoping for revolution, and every night they went to bed drunk and disappointed. The airport stayed closed, water and electricity supplies were erratic. It took four hours to get a call through to the COI. 'I can't pay the hotel bill,' I told Charles Beauclerc.

'Where's the news film? Have you sent it?' he demanded.

'There *is* no favourable footage,' I told him. Scenes of paratroopers playing draughts with Arabs in cafés, fraternising, enjoying a fine time together, dandling kids on their knee, did not exist. 'They don't want to be dandled,' I explained. 'I went out with a para patrol yesterday and they threw rocks at us.'

'We need favourable footage. Organise a football match,' he told me.

It wouldn't have been possible without Noel Barber. He was there working for the *Express*, and God guided me to the bar stool next to him. A generous and engaging man lived behind that creased and well-worn face, who lent me £100 against a receipt I wrote him on COI paper.

I took a taxi to the para brigade tent lines and had a word with the adjutant, who told me his men wanted to shoot the local kids, not play football with them. I said it was a point of view I respected, but I could drop them a few quid. The stately Arab concierge in the Philadelphia put together the opposing team.

The match took place next day on a patch of sandy wasteland outside town. The para side consisted of nine 20-year-olds in peak physical condition, wearing combat boots. The Arab team was aged between twelve and sixteen and barefoot, but there were about thirty of them. At the start, until the Arab supporters poured on to the field to join in, the two were evenly matched.

In normal circumstances competitive sport tends to bring out a particularly vicious streak in people, but in this case the two sides loathed each other already. The match was a grudge fight from the beginning and the uncut footage showed atrocity and slaughter. Nevertheless, until the game degenerated into an all-out brawl, it yielded enough material which the magic art of film editing, capable of turning black to white, could convert to the purpose for which it was intended. And, unusually for the COI, generate worldwide exposure.

Paras £20; *Arabs* £20, I noted in my expenses.

Returning to the Philadelphia relieved that it was over, I discovered a drama had occurred; the *Mirror* photographer had been wounded. What had taken place wasn't clear, for it had happened after lunch when everyone was asleep. But it seemed he'd run into the lobby dripping blood and had been rushed to hospital.

Glad to have the room to myself, I took a shower and a nap. I woke around 6 pm. No sign of the photographer, but the water was cut off again. I dressed and made my way blearily to the hotel veranda. It was empty except for the safari-suited stranger, who sat alone, drink in hand.

'Where are they all?' I asked.

'Those press chaps? They went off to see a bomb.'

Without twilight the sun extinguished itself in the desert. The stranger sniffed the air of evening starting. 'Anywhere decent to go around here?' he enquired.

Everywhere was closed because of the emergency, I told him. 'There's always somewhere,' he insisted. In the taxi on the way into Amman a few minutes later he introduced himself: Richard Crichton. 'Take us to the best restaurant,' he told the driver.

'No restaurant. All finished.' The driver answered.

'Nightclub,' Crichton instructed with authority.

The man's face brightened immediately. He spun the car around. We sped out of town into the desert. 'You have to speak to them loudly,' Crichton explained.

After a few miles we swerved off the road on to an unsurfaced track. I began to feel alarmed. 'Where are we going?' I asked, but the driver, hunched over the wheel, only grunted. Bumping through a featureless landscape of scrub and rock, we came to a small oasis in the desert. We stopped at an unlit collection of tents pitched around some shanty buildings of tea chests and tin. There was no sign of life. A dog howled forlornly.

'What's this?' demanded Crichton.

'Nightclub,' the driver announced.

Crichton regarded the unpromising encampment unperturbed. 'You go fix everything,' he told the driver. 'Tell them who we are.'

The man nodded and disappeared into the gloom. He was gone a long time, undoubtedly making arrangements for our murder, I thought. Inside the building blots of light appeared as lamps were lit to welcome us. The driver materialised out of the darkness at the car window. 'You want belly dancer?'

'Certainly,' said Crichton.

'I fix,' the driver said, and darted back.

A fence surrounded a small sand-floored compound containing a couple of tired palms and a small table. Despite the time they had had to achieve the effect while we waited in the taxi, it bore no resemblance to a restaurant or place of entertainment. A shoeless and toothless man set a candle in front of us. 'Whisky,' Crichton ordered. 'A bottle. And food.' He leaned back in his chair and looked around with satisfaction. 'Not bad,' he commented. 'These out-of-the-way places can often surprise you.'

Over the meal that followed he told me he'd been at Leicester races when he'd learned of the revolution in Iraq – 'bloody wogs ate the king'. In the ensuing week he'd followed the news from Jordan and the troubles facing King Hussein, with whom he'd been at Sandhurst. He'd decided to help. In London's Burlington Arcade he bought a dozen gold $20 coins, minted in the USA, whose obvious worth would be acceptable anywhere. Carrying these in a canvas bag slung inside his trousers he made for the airport, only to discover all flights to Jordan had been suspended. Purchasing a ticket to Beirut, which was more or less adjacent, he left immediately.

To those who assume enough the Gods provide room

service. It was a rule which Crichton exemplified. Lebanon was under curfew and martial law, yet within an hour of arriving on the last flight into Beirut he had been winging out again on his way to Amman aboard the chartered plane of Woodrow Wyatt, member of Parliament and special correspondent.

Whisky had been brought to us some time ago and two plates of something unrecognisable. Crichton had eaten heartily while he'd told his story; together we'd drunk over half the bottle. The waiter cleared the table. Crichton removed a cigar from its metal cylinder and warmed the end in a match flame. 'Pity I can't offer you one,' he remarked, blowing a cloud of smoke in my direction as terrible wails of Arab music started up nearby. The toothless waiter limped up with a wind-up gramophone, already turning, which he set down on the sand beside our table. A motherly belly dancer emerged from behind corrugated tin and wiggled towards us in or out of time with the cracked shriek of the music. Crichton stretched his legs, sucked contentedly on his Havana and settled back to enjoy the floorshow.

People don't always fit the image of their profession. Crichton didn't resemble any character in *The Dirty Dozen*, yet it transpired that he was a mercenary none the less. The previous year he'd passed in Kenya helping with the Mau-Mau insurgency. On his arrival here in Amman he'd presented himself at the palace, offering his services to the king.

'Did he want you?' I asked.

'Of course,' he answered stiffly. 'The Desert Legion's loyal, but the rest of the army's dead wobbly. It's all about to happen, you'll see.'

'No I won't,' I told him. 'I have my football match in the can, my job's done. I'm leaving tomorrow, if I can get a lift out.'

'No! You *have* to stay for the revolution,' he insisted.

It was very hot in the little courtyard. I'd drunk a lot and several times in the course of Crichton's narrative I had caught myself nodding off. The music now was winding to its appalling climax and the middle-aged belly dancer seemed to be coming apart in rolls of fat. 'What actually happened to the *Mirror* photographer?' I roused myself to shout.

'The *Mirror* photographer?' he repeated crossly, tearing his attention from her jellied flesh.

'Someone said he went to your room after lunch.'

'Is that what he was? Burst in, wanting to take a photo. Got him in the bum with my swordstick. Hopeless shot, but I was asleep. Do it correctly across the cheeks and the whole arse falls open like a ripe peach.'

Sometime later I was woken by him prodding me. The moon had moved across the sky. The belly dancer sat at our table. The whisky bottle was empty.

'Time to go,' he said. 'This lady will be coming with us.' He pushed over a grubby scrap of paper. The bill. 'Do you mind doing this?' he asked. 'All I have on me is gold.'

14
Mayfair

The crowded nightclub was dense with cigarette smoke and loud music. On the cabaret stage in front of where my client and I were seated the near-naked, oiled black bodies of the dancers gleamed in the syncopated pulse of coloured spotlights cutting through the pungent haze. He leaned closer to say something.

'What?' I yelled back.

'Ever slept with a black girl before?' Ramage shouted, raising his voice above the thudding rhythm of the mambo.

I shook my head minutely, my eyes fixed on the writhing line of dancers high-kicking to the beat.

'Not the octoroon, she's mine. Yours is Fay – the one in the emerald G-string.' Ramage owned an ad agency in Mayfair which had the Players cigarette account and two identical blonde twins as receptionists. Urbane, articulate, ten years older than myself and driving a Ferrari, he'd left the Colonial Service to enter advertising and was ahead of me on the moneyed road of self-indulgence I had recently embarked on myself with such enthusiasm. He was generous with counsel as he was with his hospitality. I was taking flying lessons; he had already obtained a pilot's licence. 'Are you going to buy your own plane?' I'd asked him.

'No,' he told me. 'There's a rule you must remember. If it flies or floats or fucks, *rent* it.'

For the first time in my life I could truly afford to do so. I was rich. Not long ago Prime Minister Harold Macmillan had addressed the British nation on TV, speaking in his characteristic patrician drawl. 'You've never had it so good,' he told us.

He was talking to *me*. I had a flat in Chelsea and a red E-type Jaguar with state-of-the-art four-way speakers set into the black leather upholstery. I had a high salary and an expense account. Restaurants, bars, theatres, air travel – everything was chargeable to the company, and the company was a goose which had started laying golden eggs. The goose was called James Garrett and Partners, and a quarter of that plump young fowl was mine.

There's a tide in the affairs of men which, taken at the flood ... I hadn't exactly *taken* it, I'd stumbled into the current at the right moment. And it wasn't so much a tide as a time: the 'sixties.

The cabaret Ramage and I were watching was called *Harlem Heatwave*, and, seated beside him in the Pigalle in Piccadilly with the mambo music drowning all conversation, my eyes remained fixed on Fay, the girl he had pointed out to me who was my date. But I was uneasy.

After the cabaret ended, Fay and the lissom octoroon who was Ramage's friend joined us at the table. We drank champagne and shouted at one another above the noise. Fay was twenty-seven and a New Yorker. She was bright, sassy and she'd been around. She was fun, but I was apprehensive about

Father. He taught me garrotting and knife work and how to derail a train. On Easter Sunday he killed and ate a dog.

Mother. She went to Harrods almost every day but got off the bus at the previous stop, a fare-stage, and walked the rest of the way because it saved one penny.

Great-Uncle Bobby. Almost wholly uneducated, he wed an heiress, became First Lord of the Admiralty, and achieved the loss of countless tons of Allied shipping in World War II.

Great-Aunt Sybil. For his bride he chose the large, pathologically shy only daughter of the Birmingham industrialist who had invented the zip fastener. Later he would leave her to marry a younger and smaller woman.

Dumbleton. The drawing room curtains were decorated with a bold motif of Nazi swastikas.

Gino Watkins. What the fashionable skier was wearing in the Alps in 1929. Leading his last fatal expedition to the Arctic the following year Gino also wore a tie.

Tony Watkins. Guns were a part of life. You shot for sport or food, national enemies, game, sick animals, and if necessary yourself.

Brother Hamish. 'This half-term I want you to climb Mont Blanc'.

Father to his sons.

Brother David. 'You want to be a *schoolmaster*? Isn't that frightfully wet?'

The author. Aged seven, I already knew that only God forgives the badly dressed.

Nanny. Her life was given entirely to others in return for a small undependable wage she was not always paid.

Jeremy aged 17. 'This Regiment has a proud and honourable tradition. I want you to know, Scott, that while you are with us nobody wishes to speak to you.'

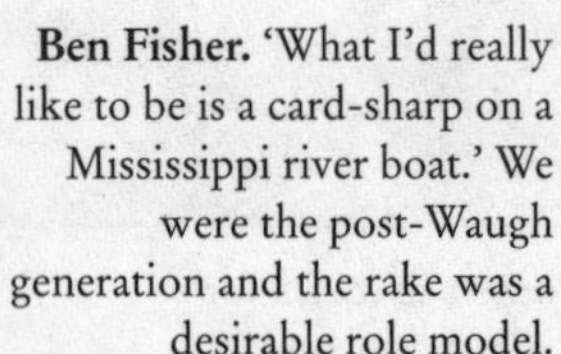

Ben Fisher. 'What I'd really like to be is a card-sharp on a Mississippi river boat.' We were the post-Waugh generation and the rake was a desirable role model.

The COI. Directing James Mason. I wanted to be an *auteur*, a phase of youth inevitable as acne.

Jeremy with Chauffeur. The Sixties. With Rocky my chauffeur, a better dealer than he was driver.

Jeremy with two models. Remarkable what a small cigar will do for a man. An ad for Players Monica cigars photographed by Terence Donovan. The model on the right is Tania, later my wife.

Tania. The word 'relationship' had not been coined. It was a subject we did not discuss.

Daughter Sasha. From Tania and Don she learned character, purpose and impeccable manners; from me she received that inestimable benefit of absence and paternal neglect I had valued so highly myself as a child.

Jeremy working. The Côte d'Azur. A new career meant a new uniform: a pair of khaki shorts – torn and not very clean. Nothing else except a tan.

The pool. Building with water: Walden Pond on completion, with naiad.

Jeremy and Peter Mayle. 'To pay for this, one of us is going to have to write a book.' Life was not *all* toil, for us the Côte was aka Arcadia. On Cap d'Antibes with fellow drop-out Peter Mayle.

Jenny Beerbohm and Edward. With them I lived as a cuckoo in the nest.

Edward Beerbohm.

Fisher. Since childhood his life was passed in a stubborn quest through far-flung and inconvenient places hunting for an elusive prize. Fifty years later he found what he was searching for in Essex.

Gortyna borelii, Fisher's Estuarine Moth, the result of a lifetime's quest.

Nigel Broakes. 'I've bought the QE2. Any ideas what to do with it?'

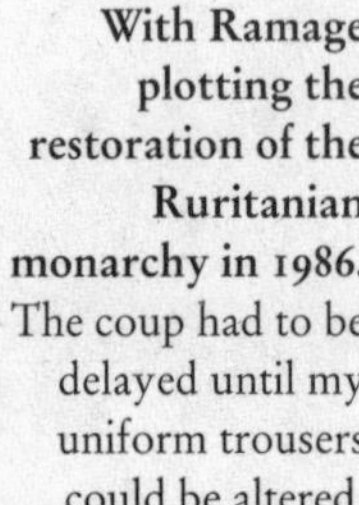

With Ramage plotting the restoration of the Ruritanian monarchy in 1986. The coup had to be delayed until my uniform trousers could be altered.

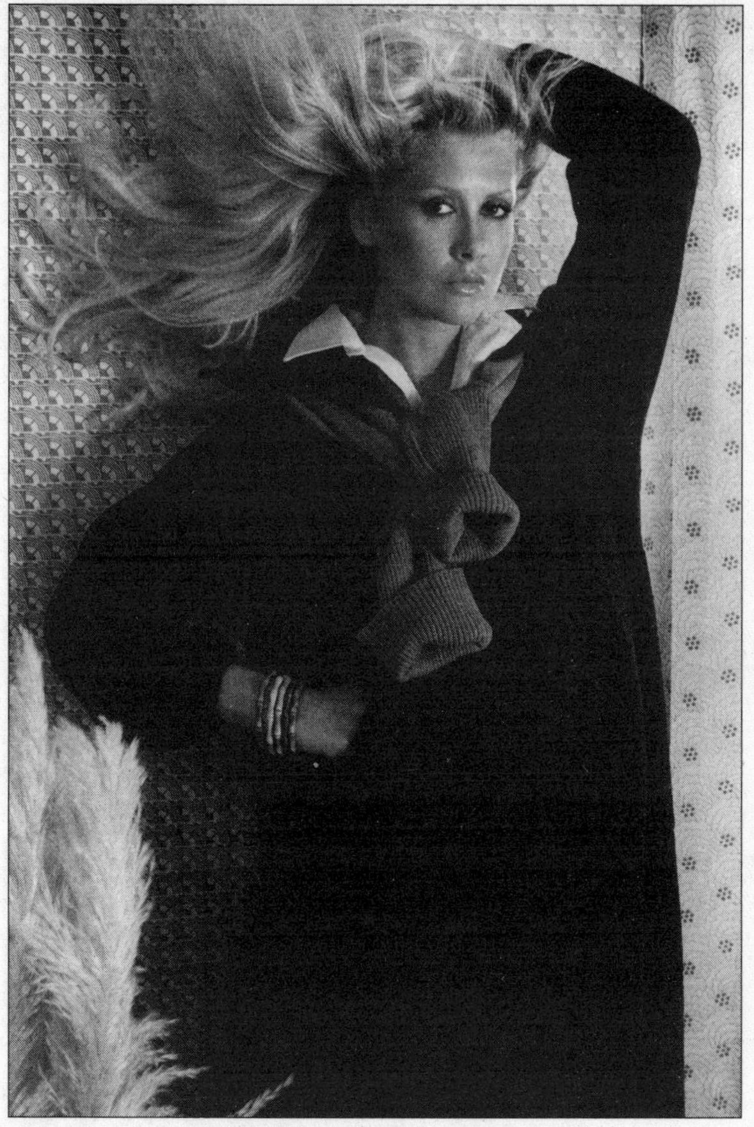

Jamie – my fellow adventurer and soul-mate.
'A fine indifference to money I much admired.'

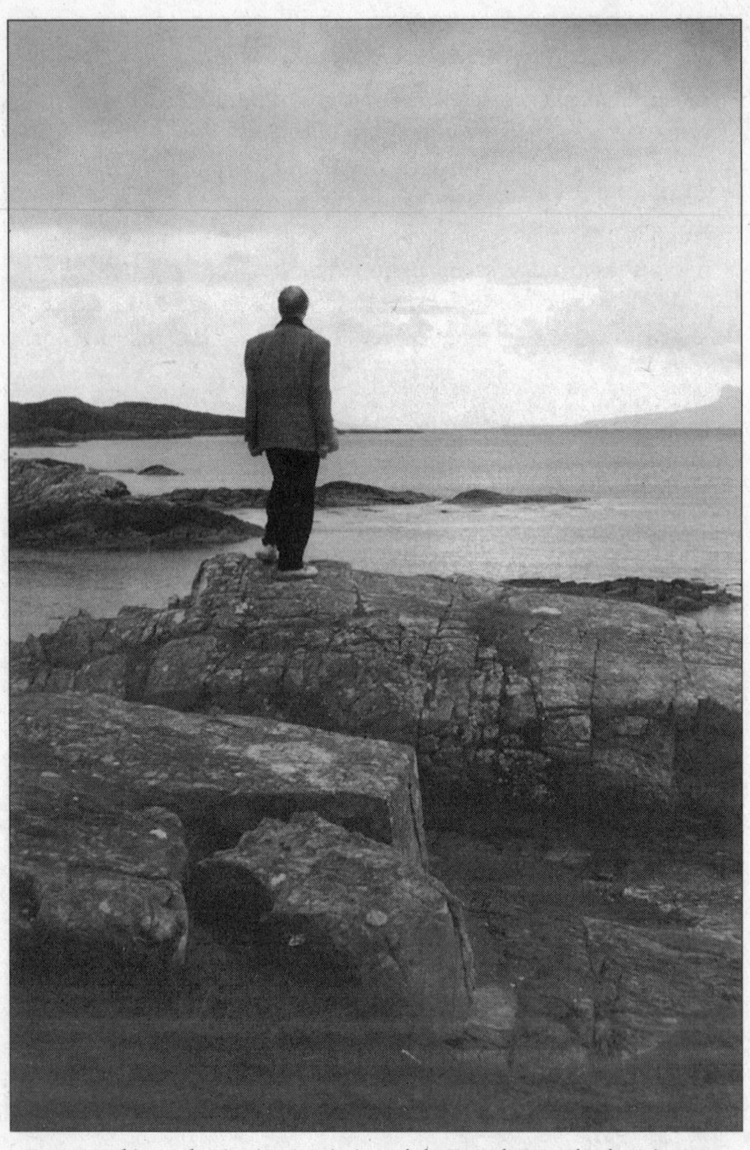

'In my end is my beginning.' Arisaig and the Rough Bounds; the rain swept wilderness of mountains, loch and wilderness that had made my soul.

what lay ahead. A showgirl, she was much more experienced in sex than myself and I knew the reputation blacks had as lovers. Blacks had rhythm; they could dance and love like living dreams. How would I shape up in comparison? At the table with Fay and the others in the Pigalle I talked and laughed and played my most engaging self, but I was as nervous as an adolescent on his first date.

We left the club, saying goodnight to Ramage and his date. '*Mmm* ... nice car,' Fay purred, settling into the deep leather of the Jaguar's passenger seat. At my flat she disappeared into the bathroom, then returned to pick through her bag and set out cigarette papers and a packet of something that wasn't tobacco on the coffee table. I watched her deftly roll a joint. Lighting it, she hissed in a long deep drag. Still holding her breath, she reached out to pass it to me.

I stared at her scarlet-tipped fingers and the slim cigarette she held out to me. This was a seminal moment. I took it with an attempt at easy nonchalance, put it to my lips and inhaled as she had. Acrid choking smoke funnelled into my lungs. A storm of coughing convulsed me, my eyes streamed with tears.

Fay stared at me in astonishment. 'You never *done* grass before?' she demanded, incredulous. 'Man, you white cats here sure is backward and *dee-prived*.'

The alarm woke me at 6 am. Fay's head lay on the pillow next to me, the rest of her firm dancer's body hidden beneath the covers. I got up to make coffee, came back with two cups, 'I have to work. Sleep, you can make breakfast and let yourself out whenever,' I told her.

I went to shower and to dress. Everything had gone OK, miscegenation had taken place. And miscegenation had been terrific, I thought. And so had dope, once I'd learned how not to choke on it. It made music better and sharpened the senses while liquor only blunted them; if this was 'drugs', I was won over. Dope was a real discovery, a watershed event in my life. Making love to Fay while high had been extraordinary. So *I* felt, but how had it been for her? Before I left to drive to work I sat down on the bed and overcame my hesitation to ask her. She knew the reputation of black men, was it true they were, how could I put it ... more outstanding, *better* at sex than white men?

Propped up against the pillows, coffee cup in hand, Fay looked bemused by my query. Her eyes went wide as a startled fawn's. 'Why, ah just don't know, man,' she said. 'Ah just never *bin* with a black boy. Have you?'

Through happy accident, James Garrett and Partners had opened its doors for business the same month that *Time* magazine ran its cover on Swinging London, which is said to have launched the 'sixties.

The purpose of the company was to make TV commercials, and the partners who owned it were Jim Garrett, the director Richard Lester, both of whom I'd known at TVA, and myself – who had by now discovered he was no *auteur* and was happy to join the new venture. The idea was James's who was the driving force of the company. Renting a small house in New Bond Street, we installed cutting rooms, took on the half-dozen people necessary and started work.

Lester was a gifted director. He had an original eye and quick anarchic imagination. Commercials he made had a distinctive quality. He was in demand, and our new company's business was good from the start.

And meanwhile Britain had become transformed. All my life I'd known it as a place of austerity, governed by a mentality born of rationing and the virtue of going without. Now almost everything had changed – money, music, clothes … and drugs. It was another country, and it happened to be mine. I was here with a red sports car, an American Express card and a healthy and not-so-healthy urge to explore *all* of it.

Fay reached for the joint with crimson talons. Taking a deep drag, she stretched luxuriously upon the white sofa. 'There's this cat, Billy, you gotta meet,' she said from behind a cloud of smoke.

'Yes?' I asked.

'Got a pad just down the street apiece from your office. He's crazy, you'd dig him, man.'

'Then ask him for Friday, I've got some people coming round,' I suggested.

'This cat don't go out, the world goes to his place,' Fay said.

After finishing work at Garrett's around 8 pm next day, I picked her up and we went to call on him.

The house was in Mount Street, directly opposite the Connaught Hotel in the heart of respectable Mayfair. A middle-aged housekeeper answered the door. She didn't look pleased to see us, but she didn't ask who we were, either. Leading us downstairs, she showed us into a library furnished with comfortable sofas and chairs to seat a dozen or so people. All were occupied, while further guests sat or sprawled upon cushions on the floor. Their clothes ranged from business suits to hippie beads and flower-wear. Some looked wasted, as if they'd been there for days. The place was dense with marijuana fumes, yet the atmosphere was not torpid and heavy as so often among dope smokers, but charged and vibrant. And in the centre of the group stood Billy, a 35-year-old man with a lean patrician face and the bearing of a Roman emperor – an impression heightened by the fact that he was wearing nothing but a crimson blanket. Wrapped – at times revealingly – in his toga, he was haranguing the room when our arrival interrupted his flow. Abandoning what he was saying, he strolled over to welcome Fay and myself to his circle, but we were no more than a dozen words into the banalities one exchanges at such moments when I felt a thump against my leg. Glancing down, I saw that he'd plunged a hypodermic syringe into my thigh. It had been done with a quick, unaimed flick of the hand and the needle going through my trouser leg into the muscle was so fine I'd felt no prick.

It was startling, though, and, transfixed by the needle, I didn't dare to move my leg. 'That's a diabolical liberty. You do that to all your guests?' I asked him.

'Absolutely,' he assured me cheerfully. 'And you'll feel just great in a few minutes.'

Of course, he was right, my irritation vaporised and I felt *terrific.*

Methedrine, by Burroughs-Wellcome. Speed is a crude name for it; it was the Perrier-Jouët of the amphetamines, compared to which sulphate was the rough Algerian red. Methedrine was magical. It made you realise your entire previous life you'd been suffering from chronic flu and only now were the person you were meant to be. It transformed you into a raconteur and wit and turned quite boring people into your very best friends. It gave you unbounded energy, a pulse rate of 200 and the certainty you could get away with anything. It made the sun sparkle on the greyest day, and the hangover following a binge could last for a whole sickening, gutted week. The cure was to take more Methedrine, of course; it existed in tablet form as well, and was readily available through Billy's pusher.

Apart from the Mayfair flat, Billy also had a country seat in Cornwall, where his father was Lord Lieutenant. His family was rich because they'd owned the London and Great

Western Railway, which had been nationalised to form part of British Rail. The payoff was lush, and along with it Billy had received a London–Cornwall first-class return ticket in the form of a 22-carat gold plaque and valid for his lifetime.

Billy was well educated and well read. Highly intelligent, he could have done well in any field he chose to enter. Instead he had chosen to become a drug addict. He was already quite a way down the path by the time I met him. He went out rarely, but instead he ran a *salon*. Its composition was mixed and broad, sometimes very broad indeed.

His apartment was only yards from my office, but to pick up drugs was not the only reason I went there. He had a free-ranging mind and an original view on the world. Through him certainly I acquired a drug addiction which would last for more than eight years – but also a picture.

His large apartment had several guest bedrooms, one of which had been occupied for months by his personal portrait painter. An accomplished but improvident artist, Costa had started borrowing money from him several years before. Billy lent it generously, insisting only that Costa work it off producing portraits of his patron, views of the Cornwall house and studies of the yacht *Venturer*, which Billy no longer used. But Costa was a gambler and it seemed impossible for his output to catch up with his ever-mounting debt. Billy had long ago run out of original subjects and Costa, working on large canvasses, was kept busy copying family snapshots and old picture postcards.

I had just moved into a new flat. While I was visiting Billy one evening, he asked how it was. 'Depressing,' I told him. 'Modern empty space with nothing in it. I have to get furniture and paintings for the walls.'

'I'll give you a painting,' he offered. 'That one – if you don't mind it being of me?'

On the contrary, I told him. Of the several portraits of him by Costa, it was the one I liked best, a night seascape with Billy on the deck of *Venturer*, wearing a striped blazer and yachting cap. I said I would love to have it, but if he really wished to give it me I wanted to take it with me when I left. Billy's periods of manic exhilaration each lasted seventy-two hours or longer, at the end of which the *salon* was sent packing and he would retire with a carton of milk and a bowl of sleeping pills. The house would be closed tight as a drum, the telephone disconnected, the housekeeper thankfully answering no knock, the master abed. The painting was large and it would be difficult to get into a taxi, but obtaining it later would be impossible.

Billy was studying the portrait critically, as though examining it for the first time. 'No, you can't have it now,' he said.

I knew where I would hang it, I could see it in place. 'Either I take it with me now or I don't want it,' I told him.

'Oh very well,' he said, exasperated but expansive. 'Take it now, if you must, but that get-up looks ridiculous. I want to send Costa round to change my clothes.'

And a few days later he did so. The painting of him hangs on the wall opposite me as I write. Grasping the rigging, he stands on the deck of his black-sailed schooner, hair streaming in the wind and head raised to confront the gale which has flipped back the corner of his fur-collared cloak to expose its crimson lining, the clothes he has chosen to dress in for posterity.

'Here's an idea,' said Kim Waterfield as he navigated his Bentley Continental slowly down the King's Road one sunny October afternoon. 'Let's *do* something together.'

An amusing, good-looking man, he was a leader of the Chelsea set and the greatest fun, for he seemed to take nothing in life entirely seriously, including himself. But he shared with Lord Byron a reputation of being dangerous to know, so I was wary. 'I don't want to go into business or anything,' I said.

He looked hurt. 'I was going to suggest we throw a really spectacular party. As co-hosts,' he added.

'Oh, I think *that's* a fine idea,' I replied.

He brightened immediately and made a call to his PA. It was the first car telephone I'd ever seen. It worked through a radio link and had no number but a call-sign instead. I was very impressed. A few years before, while engaged to Barbara, daughter of Jack Warner the Hollywood mogul, he'd been found guilty *in absentia* for allegedly robbing Warner's Cap d'Antibes villa of some papers. Kim was extradited in 1960 following escape from arrest in Tangier, where he had a night-club and water-ski school, and sent to France to serve a four-year sentence. He obtained release after only a year following the still-unexplained intervention of Warner (who also waived £25,000 damages awarded by the Court). By the date we were cruising the King's Road in his Bentley Kim had more than recovered from this French reversal, and was back in business and enviably rich.

My own approach to throwing a party was haphazard, Kim's was not. In the several meetings necessary to discuss the arrangements for our joint bash he revealed himself to be a perfectionist. 'No, the champagne has to be Roederer Cristal,' he insisted. 'Masses of flowers of course – it will take a day to dress the house. We'll need a very pretty waitress in uniform and a butler – another girl for coats. As to the guest list ... everyone has to be pretty, witty or rich. It does cheer everyone up so.'

I protested, but he was adamant on the rule and by now I knew him to be highly selective – young women must be slim, beautiful and over 5' 8". 'On the celebrities – I'll do Peter

Sellers and Diana Dors and Linda Christian, and I can deliver Bob Hope,' he said.

'Isn't he frightfully old?' I asked.

'Frightfully, and his manager's even older, they've only got half a used heart between them. They're at the Savoy, I'll get Samantha Eggar to bring them.'

Mindful of his diktat, I went through my address book and sent my own invitations: Alex Howard, Ivor and Natassia Mottran, Shirley Were ... Not everyone accepted; Fisher was in East Africa looking for moths, Nigel Broackes said he couldn't possibly attend – the party sounded far too modish, louche and racy for him.

Sixty guests were invited to the event, over 200 came. My date was Tania Edye, a model whose photograph I'd first seen in *Time* Magazine in that seminal article on London. She had invited her 17-year-old brother Anthony, who only the day before had left Harrow. 'Will there be girls there?' he enquired eagerly. He'd passed his last four years in homosexual confinement, women were an unknown race to him.

The party was immensely crowded, hugely successful. Kim's house became so crammed, that near midnight, I grew aware that the 200-year-old building was quivering, its wooden floors vibrating with the weight of so many people; a fine rain of plaster was drifting from the ceilings to dust the guests beneath. Dr Stephen Ward, whom I'd known for years, came with two girls in tow, introducing them to Tania, Anthony and myself: Mandy Rice-Davies and Christine Keeler.

Keeler was dark, beautiful, quiet and composed; Mandy Rice-Davies blonde and bubbly, giving lip good as she got. She was particularly nice to Anthony, who appeared awkward and badly dressed in his schoolboy clothes in such fashionable company.

Not until the next day did I hear how the night ended for him. On leaving the party, he'd gone back with Mandy to Ward's mews house. There she had expertly and imaginatively relieved him of his virginity. He enjoyed the experience enormously, but in the morning over breakfast was mortified to learn that so too had Christine Keeler and Stephen Ward, who'd watched the event with keen pleasure through a two-way mirror. They assured him his performance had been admirable.

Meanwhile, at the house in Chelsea the party degenerated as all good parties should. Peter Sellers grew increasingly jumpy and paranoid, Bob Hope's elderly manager became overcome and had to be escorted back to the Savoy, but the revel was still kicking when Tania and I left. We found ourselves in the street with Linda Christian and Edmund Purdom, the four of us looking for a taxi. They were Kim's guests; I'd met neither of them before, though I'd seen Purdom in Hollywood costume epics, while she was better known for her off-screen romances, widely reported in the press. Before Purdom she'd been married to Tyrone Power, both actors separately described as 'the most beautiful man in the world'. She was quite something herself, I thought.

Now the four of us stood forlorn in the empty street. No taxi passed, there seemed no reason one would ever pass. 'We could try to make it to my apartment,' I suggested.

It lay a quarter of a mile away. Linda grasped my arm and swayed along beside me in high-heeled shoes. I felt I knew her; I'd seen her films through my adolescence and fantasised about her while still at school. She was a few years over her best now, and a little overweight, but there was a ripe magnificence about her. She had a screen-siren sexiness – a swagger and a boldness that said she could drink with the boys and screw with the boys and do anything she damn well wanted.

In the early light our little group made it for 200 yards through the deserted streets before Linda came to a determined halt. 'Fuck this,' she said and sat down abruptly on the steps of a house. We stood around her irresolute. The streets were empty of all traffic and no one knew what to do. The exhilaration of the party drained away, we felt tired and hopeless.

And then – what happened next demonstrated that Fate really does exist. For at that moment there hove into view its instrument and servant. Around the corner appeared a rubbish cart pushed by a burly young dustman. Trundling the cart before him, he plodded towards us in the flat misty light. At the sight, Linda rose from the steps, drew herself to her full height, flicked back her hair. Majestically she swept to the kerb and hailed him. He stopped, he stared. He recognised her, and his mouth fell open. With perfect poise she mounted his vehicle and took her place, proud and straight-backed upon it, head raised high, giving her best profile. The rest of us followed in her train as she rode it to her destination like a queen.

Back at my apartment the curtains were drawn and the lights low. I fixed drinks and put on a Stones record. A little later, as I was freshening Linda's glass and my own, I became aware that we were alone. Linda was seated on a sofa at the far side of the room. 'You queer?' she called over to me.

'Why no, actually,' I told her.

'Then come here,' she said.

The 'sixties was another country. People misbehaved differently there.

15
New Bond Street

All You Need Is Love was playing at full volume over the sound system of the black Aston Martin DB5 which had replaced the E-Type, almost drowning the squeal of its tyres as I gunned my new company car around Belgrave Square on the way to work.

James Garrett and Partners was the hot shop now; we'd become wildly fashionable and successful; six or seven 'name' film directors were under contract to us, all of them busy. Without being able to afford them, I'd always liked good hotels and stylish restaurants; now they were my habitat. I enjoyed the demands of the job I was doing, with twenty or twenty-five commercials in pre-production, shooting, or post-production stage at any one time. I got a kick from skipping lightfoot between different clients and different problems, and the sound of two telephones ringing at the same time.

Leaving the car at the Mayfair garage paid for by the company, I walked the hundred yards to my office. Panelled in pale wood, equipped with drinks cabinet, refrigerator and a slab of illuminated art looking like sucked barley sugar, I shared it with my secretary Jenny McClean.

Today, as most days, began with calls to set up casting, recording and shooting arrangements. We'd been at this for over an hour when James Garrett walked into the room. A big man with red hair, his normally ebullient manner was subdued by the three Americans he had in tow. He seemed particularly overawed by the forceful blonde leading the team he was with – as I soon became myself.

Mary Wells was thirty-something, small, good-looking, fashionably and expensively dressed. She'd risen from the bullpen at Doyle Dane to her present position of total power through a passionate certainty she could achieve *anything*. Tinker, the agency she ran, had none of the usual support services of an ad agency but consisted only of a task force of the most expensive talent in the USA, each paid at least 50 per cent above the going rate. Set up by Marion Harper, owner of the huge Interpublic group of international agencies, if an Interpublic account was in danger anywhere in the world, Mary flew there with a hit team, put up at the best hotel – in this case Claridge's – to throw creativity and money at the problem until it went away.

After introducing me to her and the two men, James said, 'Mary's got this – *Hah,*' he cleared his throat, '– promotion we've been discussing and she thinks – *Hah* – you'd be the right man to set it up for her.'

Mary took a sip from her coffee and put the cup down; clearly it wasn't what she was used to. 'I want you to find me the most beautiful girl in every country in the world,' she said.

Years of practice had gone into not letting my jaw drop and looking wholly gobsmacked, but the vastness of her intention made me blink.

'Below the age of eighteen,' she added.

'*All* the countries in the world?' I asked weakly.

'The *First* World,' she said, impatient at my stupidity; the rest was not a market.

'And the product ...?' I enquired when I'd recovered my equilibrium.

'... Is *Love*,' she told me.

'Er ... what *is* Love?' I asked, bewildered.

'Probably a range of cosmetics ... possibly a perfume,' she answered crisply.

Mary did not believe in long meetings; details did not concern her. Soon after declaring what she wanted she went off with James, who had arranged for a chauffeur-driven car to take her shopping.

Kambannis, a volatile, creative Greek, and John Capsis, an older man in Ivy League sports jacket and flannels, who was Mary's chamberlain and treasurer, remained with me in the office. From a world atlas we worked out a schedule of casting sessions in the various capital cities. The itinerary was enough to make the strongest blanch, but leaving Kambannis and myself to implement it, Capsis strolled off to Savile Row to order a suit. 'OK, so where do we start?' Kambannis demanded. 'You're the fucking guru. So you're a friend of Roger Vadim, huh?'

Vadim was married to Brigitte Bardot. A world-class fornicator, I'd never met him in my life. But, if I wanted to spend the next few weeks jetting around the globe in pursuit of the most desirable girls in the world, this seemed the wrong moment for candour. Over the next few days I briefed casting and model agents across Europe, in Australia, Japan and South Africa, and was booked to fly to Rome the following morning, when I came back from lunch to find Kambannis snorting a bracing hit of oxygen from the cylinder I kept beside the drinks cabinet.

'We got a problem,' he announced, setting aside the black rubber mouthpiece.

I said I was sorry to hear it. Was it serious?

The excitable Kambannis was on his feet now and pacing the room in agitation. 'It's serious,' he said, 'It's Coca-Cola. We got to pull this mother-fucker out the fire. We got a spot to shoot and Love's on hold.'

I concealed my disappointment. What was the spot?

'We got to get this fucking great shiny iceberg from the Arctic and tow it down to the islands and shoot there, right?'

'Right!' I echoed.

'And we got to move *fast*,' he said. 'Get our asses to Norway or Greenland or somewhere and charter a plane and cast the fucker.'

'The iceberg?'

'Right! Mary wants Polaroids. A real fucking ice cathedral, man, and then we lasso the fucking thing and fetch it down.'

'To the Bahamas?'

'Right! We need a ship, and an expert on fucking icebergs. You know anyone who knows about the Arctic?'

I hesitated ... and a monstrous notion blossomed in my mind. The surreal picture of these hard-shopping fantasists aboard an ice-breaker in the frozen North on an expedition led by ... *Father*.

'And you spoke to him?' Fisher asked me over lunch a couple of days later.

'Well, Father's back in England, penniless again, and he needs the cash. But he said it was the most bloody stupid idea he'd ever heard of and hung up on me. When they learned how long it would take, they changed their mind. They want to shoot next week.'

'So you lost the job?'

'No, we're shooting Coca-Cola on the moon. Studio set, I don't have to go there.'

'Not your sort of place anyway, I'd have thought,' Fisher remarked, tucking into his lobster thermidor.

We were eating at Wheelers in Compton Street, at what I had come to think of as 'my' table on the top floor. Fisher's hair had receded somewhat since I'd last seen him, giving him the high forehead and wry face of an ascetic monk. In his sombre City suit he stood out from the trendily dressed advertising and film people filling the restaurant. A slap-up lunch was a treat for him, normally he had a sandwich. Client lunches didn't exist at his level in stockbroking, he explained. And neither did expenses, luxury hotels or foreign travel. His only trip abroad had been a holiday in Nicaragua catching moths, his hobby since childhood; he'd moved around the country by bus to save money.

Unlike today, in 1964 stockbroking and banking were poorly paid professions staffed by former public school boys in bowler hats. God forbid that a woman should enter the profession.

'Whatever made you go into such a dreary job?' I asked him.

'I ran into a friend from Cambridge who's a broker. He said, 'It's all about gambling and practical jokes and fooling around. And you can leave at 5.30 sharp," Fisher explained. But I couldn't see that as an advantage; my own office turned into a bar at 6 pm nightly, and happy hour extended until going on to a restaurant.

During lunch Fisher showed me photos of the run-down country house with grounds he'd bought on the Essex coast. It was a large, eighteenth-century mansion, solid and dignified without being grand, but the photographs brought home to me how different his aspirations were from my own. I enjoyed the exhilarating pace of work, and the ambience and the gloss that went with – but I had no ambitions *beyond* that. My fellow partners in the company were buying houses and holiday homes, they had wives and children. My car belonged to the company and, apart from clothes, I owned nothing and had no plans for the future. I was living in a state of nowness, as Buddhists call it, but mine was no spiritual condition; it was the most material 'now' imaginable. I had no goal, I wasn't navigating my life, but sailing as fast and close to the wind as I could.

The place where Fisher had bought his house was remote and rural. The nearest village, where he'd become a member of the Parish Council, had just one shop and a tiny church seating only twenty people. 'You still go to church?' he asked me.

'Sundays are the only day I get to sleep in, and late lunch is about the only meal I don't have to eat with clients,' I told him.

But, although I'd stopped attending, I still theoretically believed in the faith I'd been entrapped in by Mr Pope. And I still believed in its precepts, though most emphatically I was not following some of them. At moments I experienced fearful hangovers of Methedrine withdrawal and remorse. One of these had coincided with a commercial for the *Sunday Mirror*. The paper's proposed lead story, whose promotion we were filming, was about a homeless, unemployed young Irish couple with a baby dying from an inoperable brain tumour. The point of the story was that the baby had no need to remain in hospital; it was in no pain, it could be at home with its parents – except that they didn't *have* a home. In the studio, surrounded by newspaper execs, admen and film technicians, the pathetic, poorly dressed pair looked cowed and miserable. I watched them sweating and awkward under the hot lights and unwanted attention, while feeling worse and worse myself, for I was coming off speed. At the end of the shoot a godawful hangover coalesced with Christian duty to make me say, 'Well ... I suppose you *could* have my flat to live in.' I'd heard myself speak the words, appalled.

They did, for four months, while I stayed at Gilston Road, but I did not mention this to Fisher. We talked of the times we'd shared in the army and people we both knew, and he brought me up to date on Ivor Mottron who, still awaiting his expected inheritance, had worked for a while as a cinema attendant before taking a job as a travel guide. He'd escorted a coachload of Daughters of the American Revolution he described as 'very very lovely people from St Paul, Minnesota' on an itinerary which included Bologna, Padua and Verona before arriving at Lake Como, where they were to pass a rest afternoon before resuming their demanding schedule. By now thoroughly exasperated by their company, Ivor had installed them at a lakeside restaurant and himself rented a boat so he could escape them for a couple of hours. Unfortunately, while taking his pleasure with the boatboy some way from shore, the group's passports slipped from the hip pocket of his lowered trousers and disappeared into the lake.

'Goodness, whatever did he do?' I asked Fisher.

'He still had his own. He left them in the restaurant, took a taxi to the station and came back to England.'

Ivor's life had always been somewhat mercurial but others we knew were doing well. Christoph had left Connecticut to start a corporation in Munich; Alex Howard had married, and moved to an almost-stately home in the country; Nigel Broackes – also married – was a property tycoon who featured in the financial papers. But somehow Fisher seemed not to be surfing the go-go prosperity of the decade.

'Your life sounds so jazzy and exotic,' he observed rather

wistfully over coffee at the end of our meal. 'It's all going awfully well for you.'

I had to agree it was. As I tried to refill his glass with the last of the wine, he put his hand on it to stop me. 'You've read Henry Miller?' he said.

'Some. Why?'

'That bit when he's sleeping under Paris bridges, cold, hungry and penniless. Then he gets a job washing-up in a restaurant, he has a heated room, food, money. You remember his reaction to good fortune?'

'What?' I asked.

'It makes him fearful. He says it's always at such moments the angels choose to piss in your beer.'

16
Pont Street

Nigel's smile of welcome scarcely flinched as, thirty yards away, the wheels of the alighting helicopter sank deep into his croquet lawn. His greeting was drowned in the racket of the motor.

The party he and Joyce had asked Tania Edye and myself to was at their new house, Wargrave Manor, near Henley. We'd travelled down to it by limo, as did most of the guests, though some came by helicopter, like these whose noisy arrival coincided with our own.

The large, eighteenth-century, white-colonnaded house stood in twenty acres of parkland overlooking the Thames; although this was commuter belt it felt like proper country, for the grounds abutted on their own farm. Nigel was a prominent tycoon now. Trafalgar House, the property business he'd started, had recently become a public company. An article in *The Times* reported that he'd achieved this at the age of only twenty-eight, making himself £1.6 million on the flotation. But going public had been only the first step for Nigel; in the months that followed he took over City and West End Properties, plus a construction company and Hampton's, London's most prestigious chain of estate agencies. In just one year the value of Trafalgar's shares doubled, and had continued to go up steadily ever since.

Tania and I had been living together for more than a year. Raven haired with a dramatic, high-cheekboned face, she was high spirited and liberated – as were most young women and men at that time. Post Pill, the rules governing social etiquette had changed; it was considered bad manners for a gentleman not to sleep with a lady the first time he took her out. And a lady felt mortally offended if he did not sincerely *try*.

Tania and I shared an understanding and enjoyed a rackety good time together. Both of us drank hard and I was using drugs – but by now so too were most people we worked or mixed with. My uncle, Tony Watkins, and his wife raised six-foot-tall cannabis plants beside their swimming pool, generously supplying friends and family, including my now-teenage brother Hamish at Gilston Road. Mother smoked occasionally, and even Nanny enjoyed it puffed in her face during the Queen's Speech after Christmas lunch. And Father, who was writing a book on opium, grew poppies whose crushed seeds he smoked in his pipe.

Tania and I led a busy work and social life. The word 'relationship' had not been coined, it was something we did not discuss. We were seldom alone together, and when we were, neither of us brought the subject up. I'd made no secret about my views on children. As one myself I'd been an inconvenience to my parents, whose children had prevented them leading the lives they wanted. This attitude I understood, for I'd inherited it. I had no objection to other people's, though they bored me rather, but I did not want to father one. I knew

I'd be defective in the role, and my family's genetic heritage was not a desirable gift to bestow on anyone.

On our arrival at Wargrave Manor we'd been led through the house's spacious hall and public rooms into the garden to greet our hosts and join the eighty or so people in evening dress drinking champagne beneath the lamp-lit trees on the lawn, its view over the wide sweep of the Thames valley fading into dusk below. It was, as I remarked to Nigel's pretty blonde wife Joyce, quite some spread.

'You wouldn't *believe* how much work it took to do it up! I'm exhausted!' she exclaimed in her habitual vivid manner, and threw back her head to laugh with teeth and jewellery flashing in the light. And continuing work to run, we learned, for the grounds required four full-time gardeners, and the staff of the house comprised housekeeper, butler, cook and four cleaning women.

Plus a nanny and nursemaids, for the Broackes had three children, who'd made a brief, well-mannered appearance at the start of the evening. 'There'd be no problem about *us* having children if we could afford to bring them up like that,' Tania remarked.

'Mmm,' I murmured unconvinced.

Most of the guests were older than we were and came from the world of property and big business in London, plus a few who owned houses nearby. Not until late in the evening did I get the chance to talk to Nigel alone. 'This house is fearfully grand,' I said. 'The colonnades, the south front ... it reminds me of Stowe.'

He laughed, fanning away the smoke of his cigar. 'Yes, but this house makes sense for us, it's a fine place for the children to grow up. Besides, I want to stand back from Trafalgar's day-to-day operation and be able to reflect.'

On what, I asked, how to live with a Labour government?

Not at all, he preferred them to the Conservatives, the opportunities were greater, he said. 'No, I want to become more reclusive and contemplative here.' But when he *was* in town I could still reach him on his direct number, TRAfalgar 1805, he told me.

It was past midnight when the clatter of departing helicopters hinted that the time had come to say goodbye. As our host was walking us to the front door Tania challenged him. 'You're the richest man either of us know, Nigel. Tell me, what should *we* do to make a fortune?'

Mellow at the close of a successful party, he stopped to answer. Standing in the middle of the imposing hall, he cocked his large head to one side and beamed benignly down. 'The true potential has simply not been fully understood. You must buy the *largest* possible property you can find with the *largest* possible mortgage you can raise,' he told her, and the cigar held between his fingers tapped out the two essential truths, the fruits of his contemplation.

I didn't want to own a flat, I much preferred to rent one; I disliked the idea of commitment and permanence, but when an acquaintance, Tony Carvel, called to say he'd stumbled on this unbelievable bargain in real estate I listened to the tempter.

'There's this old geezer who's been starting old folks' homes, selling the rooms, then burning them down,' he began excitedly. 'He's just gone to jail and there's this house in Pont Street we could pick up the lease of for a couple of grand.'

'That's a frightful story,' I said.

'No, it's a prime location, near where your mate Broackes started,' Tony told me. We'd do up the three apartments and rent them for a handsome profit. So it was agreed; he'd do the work, I'd provide the money.

One warm summer's day a few months later Tania and I were invited to Sunday lunch along with another couple by Robert Pilkington, a new acquaintance. We met for drinks in his fifth-floor Pont Street flat, intending to stroll from there to the Carlton Tower and lunch in the Rib Room.

Wandering over to the window, I looked down at the prosperous sunlit street and the row of small eighteenth-century houses on the other side. The ground floor of number 1 Pont Street, obliquely opposite, was an antique shop (now Drone's restaurant), but the front door to the house itself stood modestly recessed beside it. A good address and a nice little property. And it was mine – or rather mine and Tony's. As I stood, Bloody Mary in hand, regarding the place, it was not without a certain pleasure. Built of mellow brick, unassuming but well-proportioned, it looked a solid, respectable little house. I studied it with satisfaction, I'd come to terms with being a man of property.

Pilkington strolled over to join me. 'See that house,' he said, gesturing with his glass to number 1, 'That's a brothel. Peter Jacobs goes there every Tuesday afternoon to have his ass whipped.'

When I finally succeeded in reaching Tony on the telephone that evening he confessed that he'd inadvertently rented the first-floor apartment to Mrs Wilkinson, who ran two girls there. And we'd just signed a three-month lease. I was appalled – we owned a disorderly house, we could be sent to jail for it. Mrs Wilkinson and her hookers had to go. 'Well, I'm not doing it alone. You've got to help,' Tony said.

We called on her in Pont Street the following afternoon. I knew the flat well; I'd paid for the furniture, tasteful but hard-wearing, and helped Tony put the place in order. But Mrs Wilkinson had rearranged and refurbished it for her specialised trade. Stocks built of heavy planking had been installed in the bedroom. The small living room where she received us was cramped by a leather-topped vaulting horse.

Mrs Sybil Wilkinson – 'Sybs' to her girls – was in her fifties and dressed like the Queen Mother. Her accent was 'naice', a refined south London. She gave us a cup of tea and heard us out graciously. She made no fuss when I told her she had to leave. 'I'll get my movers to take the apparatus out on Friday,' she said. 'But boys, you're being silly. Really, this is unnecessary, my best client is a High Court judge.'

I dismissed her remark, wasn't that what madams always claimed? But it proved to be true, and next week Tony took me to a specialised party given by His Honour and his actress wife in their gloomy Victorian flat in South Kensington. The other guests were already there when we arrived – two couples and a fat, Spanish-looking woman bulging out of a short tarty dress. After welcoming us and fixing drinks, the judge showed us his holiday snaps. We glanced through informal studies of his wife being imaginatively abused on the terrace of their rented villa on the naturist Île de Levant, and fellating the many friends they made while on vacation.

'Interesting composition, what beautiful bougainvillaea,' one murmured, leafing through the lurid deck. The conversation was banal, but held a sinister edge.

Soon there was a general move to the bedroom. This room, though much larger than those in Pont Street, was furnished in a similar fashion with much the same equipment; the décor was striking but oppressive. I was high on Methedrine, otherwise somehow none of this would have been possible. You had to be displaced, the nerves strung tight; the poet Cavafy writes, 'the healthy body is unable to feel what is required'. Assisted by another female guest, the judge's wife secured the fat woman face down across the vaulting horse, obeying his instructions delivered in a cold precise voice to raise her skirt.

The performance was ritualistic, you knew they'd played out this scene many times before. It was disquieting, even menacing, to observe, but also highly erotic. Fastidiously the judge chose a cane from a selection laid out on the bed. With a sense of unease, alarm and appalled excitement I watched him give her a sound thrashing on the bare ass.

Occasionally we entertained at home. A week after Nigel's party I'd asked a few people round to sample some *majoum*. A chewy paste like marzipan, it was made from kif and nuts and honey and tasted luscious. We'd each eaten our portion and were drinking mint tea, the recommended accompaniment. Procul Harum was playing on the record player and delicious warm lethargy was spreading through my limbs when I became aware of the telephone ringing behind the music. I picked it up.

'Jeremy ...'

It was Audrey Watkins, Uncle Tony's wife. She sounded excited, but then she often *was* excited. A fast-moving, petite, pretty woman, excitement was one of the qualities Tony had married her for.

'Jeremy ...' She said something I couldn't hear, something about the swimming pool.

'Hold on,' I told her, and went to turn down the music. 'What was that?' I asked.

Her voice was frantic, 'Jeremy, Tony's shot himself.'

I heard a man's voice speak in the background, the telephone was taken from her by their nearest neighbour, a movie executive. 'He was in the pool, he's gone,' he said.

17
Virgin Islands

The tropical island was a picture-postcard cliché. A tiny atoll, no more than a hundred yards across, it was covered in palm trees and surrounded by calm blue sea. Tania and I were the only figures on the shell-sand beach which formed its leeward shore. The island had only one building, a small hotel, and had been complicated to reach. A six-seater Beachcraft had put us down on the coral airstrip on the neighbouring island of Tortola and we'd come the rest of the way in the hotel's Boston whaler.

We had got married a few months before in St Mary's church in The Boltons, fifty yards from Gilston Road. This we thought was the ideal spot in which to ... no, not exactly *celebrate* the occasion, because celebration and excess were what we wanted to avoid. Deliberately I had brought no drugs. We wanted to eat and sleep and get straight and feel well again. I had been using Methedrine excessively, both for work and to play.

My state of health was fragile, and my mental balance far from stable. I was haunted by the thought of Tony's suicide. He'd had so much to live for: a younger wife who vivified his life, three children aged thirteen, twelve and eight, whom he loved. The house he owned had a two-acre garden with swimming pool and a go-cart track, every winter they went skiing. Tony had capital and was a partner in a successful local business. It was true he had lost money recently on a share purchase, but the amount represented an inconvenience, not a disaster. The reasons for taking his own life were unaccountable.

His mother – my grandmother – had killed herself while he was still at school, jumping from Beachy Head. Her body had never been found, and neither had Gino's when he'd drowned in the Arctic a few years later. Tony too had been drawn to water, though it was a bullet that killed him. His various homes, like my own, had always contained guns. Guns were a standard accessory, shooting a part of life. You shot for sport or food; you shot national enemies, game, sick animals, and, if necessary, yourself. He'd used his revolver for the deed and either he'd got into the pool before he put the gun to his head or sat on the edge so he'd fall forward into the water. Whatever the reason for doing it, he'd wanted to be quite sure.

The Caribbean atoll had seemed the perfect setting for a deferred honeymoon but, as so often, the idea and the reality turned out different. The hotel's main building, a wooden bungalow with veranda, was set on the crest of the atoll; on the slopes below, a dozen empty guest cottages decayed among the palm trees. We were the sole guests; the owner, his wife and daughter the only staff. An accountant in Birmingham who had dreamed of coral seas, on retirement he'd sold up to realise his dream, and it had proved disastrous.

Tiles were gone from our cabana's roof. Inside it, notices were fixed to the mildewed paintwork; regulations which remained unseen, unread, for they had never come here, those sternly awaited guests who would take bath towels to the beach, remove glasses from the bar, play music after 11 pm and put anything other than Harpic down the lavatory. The air conditioning had broken down, the owner said, but the truth was he could no longer afford petrol for the generator. This beautiful horrible little island was a prison and the atmosphere in our falling-apart hotel was grim. A quarrel simmered constantly in the background. The owner and his wife were bitterly discontent, their daughter serving our meals often red-faced and in tears. Only anger kept them from despair, and we were made to feel it was *our* fault.

It was a mistake not to have brought drugs, I realised; combining a holiday with withdrawal from amphetamine was *not* a good idea. We both felt drained; we wanted cool and shade, not heat and blazing rows.

Tania and I lay on the beach, together but alone, each beset by our own monsters though, true to the British tradition of tight-lipped reserve we'd both been raised in, we did not discuss them. Outstretched on the sand with the warm sea lapping at our feet, my state of mind was dismal; I had been in two minds about getting married. Tania had said she was happy with her career and lifestyle ... so why didn't we? And, because I hadn't come up with good cause, I'd gone along with the programme, not wanting to disappoint. It was the very worst of reasons. Naïvely I'd believed it need not alter the relationship. But that's a tendentious way of explaining how the marriage came about; a shorter word is weakness.

Now, in the Virgin Islands, the chill thought of Tony's death was always present; the world was no longer a solid place. My emotions were atrophied, but as I lay on that idyllic white coral beach, sweating and weak and ill in the harsh dazzle of the sun, I stared into an emptiness that seemed to lie at the heart of all things.

18
Chelsea Police Station

'I want a pale, translucent beauty – bring me Richard Lester,' ordered Mary Wells.

She'd winged into town with a crack team to shoot a further series of commercials for Coca-Cola. It was the most elaborate job Garrett's had taken on to date – and Lester wasn't available. With *Petulia* he'd become the highest-paid feature director in the world and was always on a picture.

How about Nic Roeg?' I suggested. He'd made his name as cameraman on *Lawrence of Arabia* and could deliver the visual effects she required.

'Lester,' Mary repeated. 'Lester's why we're here.'

It wasn't entirely true. They and other New York agencies came to us not just for our directors' list but because, filming in Britain, they/we could negotiate buy-out payments to the cast used, rather than pay residual fees. This provided a valid excuse for the *real* reason they came: to visit London, live it up at a swanky hotel and experience the vibrant 'sixties scene everyone was raving about.

Throughout the preparation and shoot of a commercial it was the chosen film director and myself who had to look after them. They enjoyed being close to a big name in the film business, it was glamour-by-association. That director's talent and ability to deliver the goods was vital, but just as important was his line of bullshit and charm, his capacity to suffer clients gladly, enthuse and play back to them. Roeg, Lester, Karel Reisz, Don Leaver were a pleasure to be with and understood the game, knowing when to become carried away by enthusiasm, when to show angst, when to become 'difficult'; but others, such as Ken Russell, resolutely refused to play, showing their scorn for advertising even while they took its cheques.

Seated in my office facing Mary Wells and her retinue, I continued to try to sell her on the merits of Nic Roeg, but without success. She fixed me with a look. 'Lester,' she insisted. I said I'd see what I could do.

The production budget for these spots was bigger than any we'd had before. The job necessitated the large stage at Shepperton, complicated sets, actors and crowd extras. Setting it up had been fraught with problems. For days prior to their arrival the clients had been on the line from New York with changes and anxieties until 11 pm London time. Meanwhile, I'd had other commercials to produce and managed to stay on top of the work only by using speed. Though I functioned capably, just below the surface I was in a state of black depression and experiencing what my soldiers used to describe as 'trouble at home, sir'. Before we were married Tania and I had got on well; in the months since the event we argued all the time.

With difficulty, Lester was induced to take four days out from preparation of his feature to direct. The week before shooting I had numerous production meetings with Mary and her team; in the intervals between she shopped obsessively, always returning with fresh demands. 'I want Orson Welles and Yves Montand for the voiceovers,' she said.

'Welles is available, but I don't think we'll get Montand. Left-wing French actors of that sort take themselves quite seriously,' I told her.

'I *want* him,' she snapped. 'Fix up a lunch and I'll fly to Nice tomorrow and get him.' Her meaning was clear, and she did.

But finally everything had been straightened away, sets built and approved, the spots cast and crew booked. The day before we were to start filming I took my clients to lunch at Tiberio, a lush Italian restaurant in Mayfair. Tomorrow a new and evolving set of problems would arise, but for the moment all was in place for the week's shoot and I was in control. Mario took our order, the wine was poured. As the antipasto arrived a waiter came to say I had a call. I took it in the lobby among the bustle of arrivals. It was Jenny McClean, my secretary at the office. 'There are two men here to see you,' she said.

'Who are they?' I asked.

'I think they're policemen. They have a warrant for your arrest,' she told me.

Several months earlier Tania had called me from the apartment; it was 7 pm and I was still at the office. 'Do you think you could come home? The place is full of policemen,' she said. I did as she asked, picking up our company lawyer on the way. I was driving the Aston Martin, he followed in his Jensen. As we parked our provocatively flashy cars outside, I glanced up at the open windows of my flat; each one framed a large policeman looking down. Inside, the apartment was crawling with them. They'd searched the place thoroughly by then, but what they were looking for was in an antique leather

Buddhist scroll box, prominent on the coffee table. It contained small quantities of Methedrine, grass, LSD and *majoum*, and they took it away with them, saying they would be in touch.

And now they were. Returning to the lunch table, I made my apologies to my clients. I told Mario to charge the bill and I walked back to the office.

On the first floor I peered through the glass wall into the reception area, where sat two men in retro suits and lace-up shoes who were definitely not in advertising. When I was seated in my office Jenny asked them up. Inspector Lynch said they'd come to arrest me, and I said, well, if they must, but there were a few things I absolutely had to do first if that was all right.

They could not have been nicer or more accommodating. They sat down and made themselves comfortable. I offered them a drink, which they politely refused, so Jenny served them tea and Fortnum's cookies. Meanwhile, I made a number of telephone calls. It's not easy to clear your diary for the foreseeable future and ensure the smooth production of a series of very complicated Coca-Cola spots, all in the space of fifteen minutes.

'Actually,' I explained to Inspector Lynch, 'I'm right in the middle of setting up the biggest job we've ever done. I have a huge film crew, several actors and over a hundred extras starting shooting at Shepperton at 8 am tomorrow and, even as we speak, my crucially important clients are halfway through lunch and waiting for me to rejoin them.' I paused to be sure he understood the full complexity of my situation before adding, 'Actually, Inspector, this is a very inconvenient moment to be arrested.'

'It always is, sir,' Inspector Lynch confided in a tone of total understanding ... and led me away to jail.

19
Manhattan

The hotel desk called to say the limo was waiting and I escorted my Collett Dickenson clients down to the lobby and into the car with their luggage, then waved them goodbye on their way to JFK and back to England.

Re-entering the hotel I waited for its single elevator, which was panelled in wood and operated by a uniformed attendant, to take me up to my small suite on the sixth floor.

I was in New York, producing a series of TV spots for Hamlet cigars. The job had come to Garrett's at exactly the right moment. Two months had passed since my conviction for unlawful possession of drugs. It had been alarming to have eight policemen burst into our flat to take it apart. To be arrested and locked up was disagreeable, and waiting for trial knowing I might be sent to jail was especially unpleasant, but in the event my sentence had been absurdly light. On advice, the lawyer I'd taken on to defend me was David Napley. In his stern authoritarian presence I felt nine years old again and that I'd been naughty.

We walked from his chambers to court and were forty-five minutes late turning up. I was nervous this would make a bad impression, but far from it. The half-dozen policemen awaiting me were thrilled to bits by Napley's presence at our humble trial. I hadn't realised he was president of the Law Society, but the magistrate was positively deferential to him. I was fined £200.

Afterwards the police witnesses were gathered in a group by the court exit, they were cheery and matey. The burly fellow who'd played Mr Nice throughout was with them, and as I was wishing him a restrained goodbye I asked, *why*? '*Eight* of you barrelling in! With dogs. Did you think I was Mr Big?'

Overweight policemen are not the most sensitive of plants, so maybe I imagined it, but I thought I detected a hint of apology in his tone as he asked, 'Do you know a William George Bolitho?'

'Why yes, he's a good friend,' I answered.

'Sometimes the people we think are our friends turn out not to be,' he said. I supposed that Billy had been in trouble and obliged to trade off some names: if so it was a disappointment.

My relief at escaping a jail sentence had been short lived. A few days afterwards over breakfast in our London flat, Tania mentioned that she was four months' pregnant and looking forward to giving birth.

My response on receiving the happy news was not that of a normal father-to-be. I was horrified. I hated the idea of having a child, I always had. And I hated the idea of bringing one up. What I'd seen of my own family had not been a recommendation for either role. Also, I believed it was contra-indicated that my brothers or myself should produce children (which neither of them has), because a strain, visible for several generations, existed in the line – an inability to engage, an instability, perhaps a blankness, accompanied in some by an incontinent urge to kill themselves – which it was undesirable to pass on. More shallowly and selfishly, I disliked the notion that, with the arrival of a child, uncertainty was removed from life. The future lay mapped out and I didn't like the look of the country it passed through.

And then had come the job of producing these Hamlet commercials in New York. Gratefully, egoistically, I seized the opportunity and schmeissed. But now, as I rode the elevator to the sixth floor of the Algonquin, I knew my reprieve was over with the completion of the shoot. After settling the last bills on the production I was following my clients back to London next day.

My small hotel suite was very pleasant, done up in vaguely 'thirties style with framed Thurber drawings on the cream-coloured walls. I'd been happy here and was sad at the prospect of leaving it to confront the unwelcome reality awaiting me in London. I'd started to pack my suitcase with a heavy heart when I noticed the message light on the telephone was blinking.

The message was to call back Gary Geyer at Doyle Dane. I did so and a voice said, 'Hi there! You ran your Garrett demo reel for us here a week ago and we have a TV spot we'd like you to make.'

A commercial had delivered me from London to Manhattan ... and now another commercial changed my life and kept me here. For a year and more. While I was setting up that job for Doyle Dane I received calls from other ad agencies in the city and further work came in. Quite by accident the Garrett Company had opened a New York office.

Its premises, my small suite in the Algonquin, seemed to me ideal. The hotel was rich in association for me, the shrine to an era. The same leather chairs furnished the panelled lobby, and the round table where Dorothy Parker, Ross and Bob Benchley had lunched regularly still stood where it had then. Comfortable and expensive, the Algonquin had the sort of shabby chic which only the English understand to be stylish. Located unfashionably mid-town, it stands on the edge of the theatre district, is popular with actors and the cultural heart of Manhattan's English ghetto. At times it felt like an expat club, leavened by the more cosmopolitan of the city's native residents.

I loved living in the hotel, happy to have again no possessions except the clothes I'd brought with me. And I loved New York. When I'd lived here before I could afford to look at life only from outside the window, now I had cash in my pocket and a virtually unlimited expense account. There was vindication in that, as there was in the fact that such profitable work was coming in, the company prospered, and I was so very busy.

My job was to woo clients, and I did it assiduously. Lunch was at Orsini's or the Four Seasons, most evenings took in Elaine's – then at its fashionable peak. Normally I used taxis to get around, but in summer I cruised the sweltering city streets in a black Cadillac with air-conditioning and windows tinted a deep underwater green. There was work, parties, clubs, weekends in the Hamptons, Fire Island, the Bahamas or Mexico, and there was cocaine. The fashion and the music were still coming out of London and there was no disadvantage in being British in Manhattan in the late 'sixties. We were still the flavour of the decade.

Our best client remained Mary Wells, who now ran her own agency, Wells Rich Greene. I was summoned by her to discuss a two-minute spot for Braniff Airlines. She had won the account only two years before and her first move on getting it had been to paint every aircraft pastel pink or pastel blue and transmit a series of commercials each ending with a different but consistently ravishing flight attendant in pastel uniform ogling the viewer with sultry eyes as she breathed 'I'm Tricia/Sharon/Kate, fly *me*!' in invitation. Mary's second move was to marry Harding Lawrence, president of the airline.

Arriving at her agency, I was directed to her private office in what had been Gloria Swanson's duplex. Though the temperature outdoors was in the upper eighties, a log fire blazed in the open hearth, but the air-conditioning kept the place pleasantly chill. The only furniture was a leather chesterfield sofa, a few chairs, and a circular table fifteen feet across, the center of which had been sawn out to create a hole three feet in diameter. 'An interesting piece,' I observed when Mary wafted in, a vision in Pucci, to find me staring at it in mesmerised curiosity.

'Yes, it is,' she agreed. 'I had it made that way so I could put a man inside. For presentations.'

She was looking tanned and well. 'Just got back from Mexico,' she explained. 'Three parties in a week. Emilio Pucci's, the President of Mexico's, and mine – we all have homes in the same locality. Guess which was the best?'

We moved on to the subject of work. The film she wanted us to make was about Braniff's commitment to supersonic air travel. No supersonic commercial aircraft existed at that time; Mary said she wanted Garrett's to build one.

One was used to fairly exacting demands from clients, but this was unusual in that I estimated it would involve head hunting key technicians from Boeing and Lockheed, cost several billion dollars and take between fifteen and twenty years to set up to shoot. As she wanted the spot completed in two months, it was a relief to learn the aircraft did not actually have to fly.

The commercial, which had an enormous production budget, would never be aired on TV. It would be screened only once ... to President Nixon as part of a presentation designed to win Braniff South American air routes in the coming re-allocation among US carriers. Explaining this, Mary leaned forward to look me in the eyes. 'I'm going to take over Lima, Peru,' she confided.

I nodded enthusiastically. 'Great idea,' I told her.

'Turn it into an International Free Trade Area, the number one fashion shopping capital on the planet. One bright island of light in the surrounding darkness of the Third World.'

'*Absolutely*,' I agreed warmly.

The Braniff film she wanted from us was only one of Mary's planned tactical moves towards the realisation of her sovereign intent. To handle the details of the spot's production she appointed her art director, Phil Parker.

I got to know him well, too well, over the next couple of months. He was a small dark man, paid a huge salary. Top creative talent in the newest, flashiest and most fashionable ad agency in Manhattan, he was a star. He had expenses, kids' schooling, medical and psychiatric coverage, perks and benefits; he was thirty-two and *hot* – but he was also under great strain. One major fuck-up and he'd become what's-his-name.

Phil was responsible for the *concept* of the commercial – and its success. Excitable by nature, the pressure of it sent him manic; and it was my job to translate his lavish fantasies into some sort of reality on the studio floor. Over the course of three weeks we flew three separate film art directors into New York from London. Jetlagged, they were whisked through offices and conceptualisations, were abused, rejected and replaced. There'd been scenes of hysteria and high drama ...

but at last designs had been approved, set construction was under way and filming ready to start.

I had the flights to London booked and was ready to accompany the clients there in two days' time when I returned to the Algonquin after lunch to find a message to call Phil Parker.

'I want a meeting. Get your ass round here right away,' he said.

We met in a clinical all-white office. We sat facing each other across a white table, he in one white chair, I in another. He talked, I listened. There was a pad and pencil on the white surface before me, but I did not take notes while he spoke, for all he said had been already discussed and agreed. All he touched on had, in fact, been *done*. And when he paused occasionally for reaction I nodded and smiled reassuringly.

I was agreeing with everything he said. Our meeting should have been smooth, yet it was not. The atmosphere between us in that all-white room was building with electricity; static thickened the air, rage was darkening Phil Parker's face, his hands had begun to shake. Suddenly it became too much for him, the wires that held him together parted with a *twang*. He sprang from his chair, cleared the space between us in a bound. '*Stop it*!' he shrieked.

I stared at him in consternation. His face was purple. What had I *done*?

'Stop it! Stop it,' he screamed. 'Stop being so fucking polite! I've got my ass riding on this job and so have you and all you can do is *be polite*!'

I gaped at him speechless. It was a timeless instant; only after what felt like about an hour did he back off.

The event had a profound effect on me. It was disconcerting to be attacked for *saying nothing*. And I found it astonishing that anyone could get so steamed-up crazy *over a TV spot*.

TV commercials were silly, it was absurd to be making them. Increasingly I was aware that the brisk lunacy of the business I'd found so bewitching no longer held quite the same allure. The expense-account life appealed to me, but I'd come to dislike the work I did.

It felt strange to be back in London for the Braniff shoot after so long away, and to be staying in a hotel as a visitor. Having settled the clients into Claridge's and the Hilton, on my second day there I called Tania and went to visit her at the apartment in Chelsea.

We had tea in the large, starkly modern living room, harshly lit by sun. Both of us were anxious not to touch on anything sensitive; our conversation was casual and surreal. Then Tania asked, 'Would you like to meet your daughter?'

'Why, of course,' I answered, and Sasha was brought in by her nanny. I looked at a tiny, dark-eyed girl; tentatively I reached out to take her minute hand.

An unnavigable sea washes with silent waves between us and things we aim at, converse with, and try to touch. I waited ... waiting for the flash, that current of instinctual rapport said to flow between father and daughter, and did not sense it. Instead I felt only a blankness – an admission I am not proud of, but I tell it like it was.

'I think Daddy's had quite enough now,' said Tania, and the child was taken away. With mutual relief we turned to other subjects.

The nanny was not the usual Norland's type in a lightly starched blue/white uniform but a handsome, craggy-faced man in his twenties, speaking in a West Country accent and answering to the name of Norman. He looked more like a young Mellors than a nanny and, after he'd left with the baby, I asked Tania delicately, 'Is he your ...?'

'Are you kidding! He's a stable hand and brilliant at looking after horses. Sasha adores him.' And Norman was conscientious and devoted to the baby, she told me. 'But he's got the most frightful verbal diarrhoea and he *will* talk. Bangs on endlessly about being buggered by Jeremy Thorpe, and Thorpe stealing his National Insurance card.'

'What an extraordinary story! Could there be anything in it?' I asked.

'Total fantasy, all of it,' Tania assured me. 'But the fact is he's utterly wonderful with your daughter.'

Left to their own devices in London, clients often grew restive and created problems. I had to be with them constantly, pouring oil on the water and liquor down their throats. I was always looking for fresh ways to divert them. A huge anti-Vietnam War protest was scheduled to take place in Grosvenor Square. 'You gotta be there, man,' said my dope-dealer Michael X. 'We're gonna take over the fucking US Embassy, I mean, like, *storm* it. We got weapons, rockets, an armoured car, we're *gonna blow the fucking place apart*, *man*!'

I was in his rancid flat buying dope and I didn't believe him for a moment. Michael de Freitas – I couldn't get used to calling him Michael X – was a compulsive liar, he'd sold me dope and lied to me for years. As a teenager he'd worked as an enforcer for Rachman, the property crook, after whose murder it was said the police had narrowed down the list of suspects to 157. Then Malcolm X had embraced de Freitas on a visit to London, calling him 'my brother', and he'd changed his name and gone progressively more loopy ever since. Raising money from a number of people, including John Lennon, he started Black House. In the months to come another of his backers, the young Nigel Samuel, would go to the police after having been locked in a slave collar and abused; Michael would jump bail and flee to Trinidad, there to found a commune and murder two white women, one of them Gayle Benson, wife of an assistant director who worked for Garrett's.

He was destined to end on the gallows, but just now he was rehearsing to me his battle plans. And the newspapers too were hyping the coming demo; a huge crowd of under-thirties was expected. The combined forces of the counter-culture – including, Michael promised, a whole regiment of stoned black brothers – would be ranged against a battalion of British bobbies, supported by police cavalry, and a crack detachment of US Marines defending the Embassy in the name of American imperialism.

It promised to be an epic battle. My clients wouldn't want to miss it. I decided to book the third-floor corner suite of the Marriott Hotel overlooking Grosvenor Square so they could watch it in comfort while enjoying a buffet lunch. 'It's the most cynical, disgusting thing I've ever heard of,' Richard Lester told me. I agreed with him, but spectators *had* journeyed to take up dress-circle-type seats in the foothills overlooking the Battle of Waterloo, and there was an established precedent. Besides, this was an historic event, and you should always witness history if you get the chance.

In fact, it turned out to be a poor idea. By 11 am on that Saturday the streets surrounding the Marriott were sealed off, and it was only by claiming to be staying there that my clients managed to get through the police lines to join me at the hotel. Once there, they remained marooned, then besieged, and unable to leave for six hours.

By 2 pm Grosvenor Square was packed solid with demonstrators. The bobbies were wearing the endearingly quaint riot gear of the period, and the mixed divisions of the counter-culture colourfully and fashionably dressed for anything but war, but my New York clients were clearly uncomfortable with the threat to their flag and the anti-American slogans the crowd were chanting.

Unsuccessfully I tried to reassure them that we in England adored America and everything American. The mob below were merely expressing a cheerful anarchy, I explained. They were here for the hell of it. Few felt strongly about Vietnam, most would have been unable to find it on a map, I told them as a loud explosion came from the square, followed by a confused noise of shouting and police whistles.

My guests were growing increasingly agitated. The 'sixties weren't about love and flower power any more, the counterculture had become 'political' under the influence of the Red Brigade and angry revolutionaries like Malcolm X. The mood had turned ugly and the flower children grown destructive, tearing apart the fairy-tale fantasy they had created. This was 1968; later that year Robert Kennedy and Martin Luther King were gunned down; at the Democratic convention in Chicago Mayor Daley would order the police to kill arsonists and shoot to maim looters.

I stood with my clients looking down upon the scene. They'd wanted to leave earlier but it was impossible, the crowd were pressed solid around the hotel. They bitched, but there was nothing I could do about it. Now they moved to the buffet set up in the middle of the room and huddled together, muttering and darting glances in my direction. They were behaving as though what was going on was somehow *my* fault.

The sound of explosions drew them back to the windows. A section of the mob were lobbing smoke bombs over the police line, streams of coloured smoke spread across the area. There was a sudden surge of movement. In a perfectly choreographed action the police line opened and a squadron of mounted cavalry cantered out of the smoke towards the crowd.

From the ground it must have been an awesome sight. The mob parted and fell back, running from the horses. The riders did not pursue, they'd achieved their intent. The squadron wheeled and cantered towards another section of the crowd to get it moving.

No force had been used, but the attack on the Embassy had been turned. Thwarted of their objective to take the building, the huge mass of people began to move slowly towards the square's two exits, one of them directly below where we stood. Someone looked up and saw us: 'Pigs!' he called out, and at once the colour of the crowd changed as a sea of faces tilted to look at us. Others took up the cry, 'Pigs! Come down, pigs!'

'Oh my God, they'll tear us to pieces,' I heard an American voice among those beside me mutter.

'You're perfectly safe. Have some more champagne,' I told them. What a craven bunch they were, I thought.

'Pigs ... pigs ... pigs ...' the crowd below was chanting.

A client clutched my arm. 'Jeremy, you've got to get us out of here!'

'Relax! Smoke a joint. Try the chocolate cake,' I said. Below us in the street the baying of the mob was growing louder. What a pitiful occupation we were involved in, I thought. I'd blanked off my mind with drink and drugs and the addictive *pace* of this unwholesome activity, deluding myself I engaged in it with the detachment of a child turning over stones to examine the life forms beneath with fascinated disgust. But I'd deceived myself, seduced by the lure of a gaudy lifestyle and expense-account mimicry of wealth. I was *part* of this world, *I'd become one of these people myself*.

The flow of people leaving the square had halted. Beneath

our window stood a solid, close-packed mass of demonstrators howling, 'Come down, pigs!' They'd forgotten the Embassy, *we* were the enemy.

And then I saw Michael X among them. Got up like a tribal chief, whacked out of his skull and surrounded by a bunch of jiving, wild-eyed soul brothers, he was looking straight at me, shaking his fist and shrieking, 'Eat the rich! Come down, pigs!'

Instinctively I drew back behind my clients cowering in the window. He was my murderous, revolutionary black drug dealer ... and I was ashamed to be seen by him in such company.

A few months later a job came through that was to put the final seal upon the advertising business for me. Garrett's got the contract to produce a series of Volvo commercials for Scali McCabe, their New York agency. A Swedish film of lyrical beauty, *Elvira Madigan*, had recently opened in Manhattan to considerable acclaim and the agency decided that its unknown director, Bo Widerberg, was the man they wanted to direct their spots. I flew to Stockholm to hire him.

A committed communist, he was a cult figure and role model to the young in Sweden. Craggy faced with horn-rimmed glasses, he looked like a schoolmaster and lived in a cabin in the woods twenty minutes from Stockholm with his pregnant student girlfriend. 'She looks good, but she don't talk good,' he explained.

Both were dressed in identical grunge fashion combining urban revolutionary and the older Tolstoy. Seated in their primitive kitchen wearing a Brooks Brothers suit with Turnbull and Asser shirt and tie, I realised my ensemble was ill-considered. Rather frostily Widerberg informed me he never saw TV, he didn't own one. And, on principle, he *never* watched commercials – he believed Western consumerism was responsible for the world's ills. Tucking my Gucci loafers out of sight beneath the crude wooden table, I agreed with him warmly and we talked.

Next day we met again, this time for lunch in the Opera Keller, the superb rococo restaurant in Stockholm's Opera House. As arranged, I had half his fee with me in cash. The dollars formed such a wad in my hip pocket they ruined the cut of my trousers and were uncomfortable to sit upon. I tried to get rid of them early, but he wouldn't have it, stopping me with a nervous glance around him. At the end of the meal we visited the men's room together and furtively the deed was done there. Sweden was a particularly *formal* country in certain ways, he explained.

The commercials were designed to sell the Volvo's hardiness and longevity. One was set on a frozen lake surrounded by forest in northern Sweden, deep in snow. An ancient log cabin stood on the shore – a sauna. The TV spot called for a fit, naked geriatric to step from it, walk twenty yards across the frozen lake to a hole cut in the ice, and jump in.

The temperature was fifteen below; film crew and others at the shoot were dressed in thermal clothing and moon boots. My clients, Ed McCabe plus the agency art director and account director, had been joined by *their* client Le Marr, marketing director for Volvo US. His presence had made them unusually tense, for in keeping Le Marr happy rested an account worth $3 million a year. But he remained chronically restless and discontent. Fear created an uneasy atmosphere in the big Winnebago trailer with observation window which had been positioned overlooking the shoot on the frozen lake. Heated and comfortable, equipped with a rest room, its driver/butler provided a constant supply of coffee and hot grog to the assorted clients and myself sheltering within.

Setting up the first shot had taken an age, but at last the film crew were ready. After a final briefing on network regulations on nudity – 'No tits, no hair, no crack in the ass,' McCabe instructed – Widerberg zipped up his anorak and stepped out into the freezing cold to direct the shot.

The oldster we'd cast in Stockholm, an 82-year-old fitness freak, had meanwhile been roasting in the antique log-built sauna on the water's edge. On Widerberg's call of 'Action!' he stepped from the hut, naked but for a skimpy towel, toddled barefoot across the ice, paused for an instant to shed the towel, and jumped into the hole. His bald head disappeared beneath the surface. A few seconds later I resumed breathing when it reappeared. The old fellow scrambled out on to the ice alive. 'I saw his crack,' Le Marr said.

I went to tell Widerberg we must go for another take, reaching him as the old man stepped to shore. Everyone was staring at him, for he was covered in blood. In the short time required to film the shot, the surface of the hole had frozen over with a skin of ice. Plunging in, the oldster's wrinkled body had been sliced all over by tiny splinters sharp as glass.

The blood was wiped off, he was put back into the sauna to reheat and we went for take two. When the hut's door opened and the old man padded across the ice it was seen that the talcum powder he'd been dusted with all over was effective; to the clients' relief, no blood was visible. But, as he jumped in, all in the viewing trailer glimpsed a flash of grizzled pubic hair. And, irritatingly, the oldster was again streaming with blood when he scrambled back to shore. In less than a minute a membrane of ice formed across the hole, it proved impossible to prevent.

We went for take three. It looked OK to me. 'I saw his cock,' Le Marr said.

'But ...' McCabe began reasonably.

'I saw his *cock*,' Le Marr shrieked. '*I saw his fucking withered cock*!'

We went to nine takes before we had a shot that satisfied him.

At the day's end, when filming was over and the old man had been revived to geriatric half-life, wrapped in cotton wool and blankets and stowed in a station wagon, and as the unit was packing up to return to Stockholm, Le Marr took a closer look at the antique log cabin on the water's edge and said, 'I wanna buy it.'

Next day I negotiated a price with the owner. The log cabin had stood in that idyllic lakeside spot for 300 years, but Le Marr wanted it dismantled, crated, shipped to the USA and reconstructed by the barbecue in the garden of his suburban home in New Jersey.

20

Ten Downing Street

My love affair with advertising had ended. The idea of spending any more time cramming food and drink down the throats of greedy, scared, demanding clients was abhorrent. I ceased going into New Bond Street and sat in my Chelsea flat trying to write a film script.

James Garrett was remarkably tolerant of my defection. I continued to draw a salary, but one day in the spring of 1970 he called to ask if I'd give him a hand making Ted Heath prime minister. Others were pitching for the Conservative party's TV campaign in the forthcoming general election, but James was close to landing it, he believed. He asked me to join him to take a brief from William Whitelaw.

Whitelaw came to that meeting accompanied by two short-haired, pinstriped hounds from Central Office he kept on a short leash, who were not allowed to speak but only bark approval. In his mid-fifties, he was dressed in a blue Savile Row three-piece suit in a retro-toff style no longer truly fashionable. To my eye it looked just a touch too big for him, particularly in the seat – but perhaps it had been built so to allow for growth. His manner was affable, a bland upper-class benignity. He gave off an air of confidence and competence. 'Everyone needs a Willie,' as Maggie Thatcher would later say of him. He was the ideal chief-of-staff, incisive, calm, and seemingly above the battle.

As for myself, I wore pale-grey flannel – the trousers just *slightly* flared in deference to the style then coming into vogue – a wide-brimmed Herbert Johnson hat – which, naturally, I removed on meeting him – and a striped tie matching his own. He could see at once I was the right sort of chap to have on board.

The reason for this meeting was that Harold Wilson had dissolved Parliament, announcing a general election in a month's time. Rejecting suggestions that uncertainty over the economy had led him to choose this early date, Wilson claimed it was prompted by the start to negotiations over Britain's entry to the Common Market, which he believed best handled by a new government.

The timing was opportune for the socialists. Wilson's government had weathered recession and a sterling devaluation, but the economy was now in recovery. A Gallup poll published in the *Daily Telegraph* showed a Labour lead over the Conservatives of 7.5 points, enough to guarantee a very substantial majority in the election. 'The thrust of their strategy will be, "the wind blows fair, the ship is stable, why change the crew?"' Whitelaw informed us, and the pinstripes pricked their ears and growled aggressively on cue.

To counter this the Conservative campaign would sell the policies in their manifesto: to cut back the cost of government and lower tax; restore British forces to the Persian Gulf and Far East; direct social services to those most in need, and improve the economy to the benefit of all ... but also something else ... Whitelaw's voice altered in tone as he spoke of this and, scenting what was coming, the pinstripe hounds sat up and began to shift and wag their bottoms expectantly.

... something less *tangible,* perhaps, Whitelaw continued, but more ... more spiritual, more inspiring ... a new reputable and moral approach ... *a whole new style of government*! Unable to restrain themselves, both pinstripes began to bark excitedly at this point, jumping up in their enthusiasm. Indulgently Whitelaw allowed them to do so before saying, 'One Nation! A Better Tomorrow!' It was the rallying cry of the campaign and the slogan was Heath's own idea, it seemed. In Australia to skipper his yacht in the Sidney–Hobart race, he'd asked his chauffeur, 'Why is everyone in such good form?' 'Because we know tomorrow will be better than today,' the man had apparently told him. Improbable, I thought. *I'd* never met a Strine capable of such shit-licking sanctimony. The man had probably muttered, 'Yer'd be smiling too if yer were sitting with a six-inch nail up yer bum, yer Pom poppie,' and Heath had misheard him.

If Garrett's succeeded in obtaining this account, what we would be providing to the campaign were six ten-minute films to be transmitted at peak time on all channels in the course of the next four weeks. Party Political Broadcasts, the convention had derived from radio, its traditional form an address by the party leader at his desk. The format could not have been more dull. Since the previous election, the nation had rearranged its living room. No longer was the seating grouped around the fireplace and radio but in front of the box. Accustomed as people now were to the cutting rhythms of TV, ten minutes was an enormously long time. Their attention span had shrunk to sixty seconds, and not all could manage that.

James's original and innovative proposal – which he'd masterminded with Barry Day and PR wizard Geoffrey Tucker, plus of course Central Office – was that we should treat each ten-minute length as a mini-programme, incorporating short interviews, clips from ministers' speeches, soundbites ... plus commercials selling particular ideas or policies. It was an excellent notion and one Whitelaw seemed to like. 'I want every major speech throughout the country covered, not just by the networks but by *us*,' he said. 'Reggie Maudling ... Iain Macleod ... Geoffrey Rippon on Europe ... Peter Walker on housing ... and Maggie and, of course, we *must* use Chris Chataway.'

Throughout the meeting I'd been taking notes, for later James and I would have to calculate the number of camera crews, studio space and logistics deriving from our client's requirements. To cover each major speech would necessitate not only a sound-camera team, but a second 'wild' camera and operator to get crowd and reaction shots. Because of the other interviews and commercials required, on some days we'd be providing as many as four, or even five, separate film units. And there would be an intermittent but urgent studio demand; we'd have to book one for the entire period, I realised. We'd need a bench-camera set-up and graphics unit to illustrate the 'negatives' on the economy and the decline in sterling, plus a first-rate animator. At least two cutting rooms and editors would be necessary, and we'd need to provide a 24-hour production capacity. It was some bill our new clients were running up. I caught James's eye: both of us dropped our glance at once.

'The key to winning this election is the TV campaign,' said Whitelaw. 'Ted wants to meet you and take a look at your set-up tomorrow.'

Asians and Germans can meet to do business at any hour, and so can most Americans, but in Britain the idea of discussing any matter unaccompanied by food and drink is unthinkable; no event can take place without. In the worlds of commerce, politics and the arts, alimentation is taken for granted.

'We'll give him a sight of our production capacity as we take him up through the building,' James said to me when we were alone. 'We'll hold the meeting in the library. Will you arrange things, Jeremy?'

I'd been used to doing so in the past. We entertained groups of clients regularly, often screening a new-release movie in the armchair comfort of our viewing theatre before regaling them with food and drink in the large beamed room which had been the library of the Jesuit seminary in Farm Street that was now our corporate headquarters. But I wanted to make this better than those routine events. Not more elaborate, that would be a mistake, but somehow more memorable.

Garrett's had won all kinds of prizes for its commercials, including the Palme d'Or at the Cannes Festival. But this was of a different order, to obtain the Conservative Party account represented a prestigious accolade. James was a highly successful businessman, he'd built up the company to become the leader in its field, but his talents were greater than the cottage industry he dominated and I wanted to help him gain this crown. We'd known each other a long time; he'd been good to me, moreover I owed him. I'd turned down his offer to run the New York office and lately I had not pulled my weight in the company. I would make up for my dereliction now by doing my very best to help win Garrett's the account.

Should I get what was required for this meeting at Fortnum's, I wondered. Unlike the restricted range the store displays today, its delicatessen counter then was unmatched in its spread of treats, some remarkably exotic. But individual Sudanese dried ants encased in chocolate weren't right for this occasion, I considered, and a hundred-year-old Chinese egg had quite the wrong association in the circumstance. No, simplicity was the key: canapés, a selection of tiny sandwiches, sparkling water, fresh orange juice, an unostentatious though stylish white Burgundy ... the catering should be plain but elegant.

At the end of that day I visited Nanny at Gilston Road before going home. I helped her pull out her trunk from beneath the bed and sat chatting to her as she burrowed into its close-packed depths, past the carefully wrapped bundles of postcards my brothers and I had mailed her from school ... and those Gino and Mother had sent when *they* were children, further and deeper than the matchbox containing a cube of her great-niece's wedding cake ... the gala shipboard menu of a Mediterranean cruise I'd sent her on when I'd first started to make money, deeper than my Colt .45 and revolver in their oiled-cloth wrapping ... ammunition ... detonators ... to a bottle of 500 tablets of Methedrine I'd laid down in '66 just before they'd become unobtainable when Burroughs-Wellcome ceased manufacture.

I'd raided the stock over the years but, as with a rare vintage impossible to replace, I'd plundered it solely for important celebrations. Only a dozen and a half of the 10mg tablets remained, but this was no time to be stingy; it was an occasion for the best. Naturally I did not bother James with precise details of the proposed menu. Quite rightly he would have disapproved and vetoed it.

Our new and much grander offices were built in solid ecclesiastical style, their dignified entrance supported by church pilasters. And, though the intervening floors were raucous with the clatter of cutting rooms, telephones and chronic frenzy of production, the library at the top, whose monastic austerity was softened by cut flowers, paintings and comfortable armchairs, was tranquil and serious. A suitable atmosphere for such a gathering as now.

Ted Heath had a portly presence and a florid, well-fed face. He was not a man one warmed to instantly. His bearing and full, rounded tone came over as a rehearsal, but I was puzzled why an intelligent man should have chosen a manner and accent so alienating to so much of the electorate. He arrived surrounded by a small court: Whitelaw, an aide, and the same pair of pinstripe hounds straining at the leash beside them. After the usual social niceties the group took their seats at the table with tacit understanding of their respective pole positions. My role was fulfilled ... but they also serve who only stand and wait. I withdrew to James's office where the sound of the meeting reached me as a muted hum of conversation ...

The minutes passed and I waited nervously, anxious to be sure my carefully prepared delicacies were well received by our distinguished guest. Not that I expected recognition or thanks for the time and trouble I'd put into their preparation – such is not the way of things, I knew. My reward lay in the knowledge of their excellence. The accompanying Chablis, dry and flinty on the palate, was perfectly judged, I thought, and the pinch of Methedrine added to the canapés at the start was an inspired touch; the slight hint of bitterness seemed actually to enhance the rich flavour of the foie gras, introducing a certain *je-ne-sais-quoi,* hard to define in terms of taste yet magical, historic.

But my anxiety was misplaced. The titbits I'd taken such pains to make exceptional were appreciated by all – indeed it seemed our Leader had been quite peckish that morning and they'd gone down extraordinarily well. As I listened to that initial hum of conversation rise in pitch and volume to the lively babble of a party dominated by the confident boom of Heath's voice, I relaxed.

And a very *good* party, I realised with satisfaction. An impression confirmed as the meeting broke up and our guests came to leave, for their mood was quite different to before. People spoke faster, their body language had grown more expressive, their movements more animated. I was, though, a bit worried about our Leader; flecks of spittle showed at the corners of his mouth and he'd turned a rather alarming colour. Doses in the individual treats were low, but I hadn't reckoned on him being quite so partial to the canapés. Yet he seemed to be *feeling* fit, indeed all looked to be feeling wonderfully well. The atmosphere – so restrained and formal at the beginning – had warmed into a joyful shared exuberance. No longer strangers, we were comrades in arms, united in the fray. Champagne amphetamine was the perfect choice for such a moment; all were launched on a month-long high which would last until election night. Such was their exalted state, their blood was up and the race was on. Victory lay just before their eyes and all, all was possible …

A Better Tomorrow … The meeting ended in a jovial flush-faced *au revoir*. Roused and exhilarated, a resolute body of overweight men marched off behind their Leader, their hearts and spirits high, with the pinstripes bounding beside them, muzzles raised and baying for war …

Three weeks into the campaign, with only days to go before the election, bookmakers' odds had lengthened to 3–1 against the Conservatives. The opinion polls, published in all the national papers, played an unprecedented part in the campaign, revealing Wilson to be personally much more popular than the aloof Heath, who, disdaining his opponent's walkabouts and impromptu chats in shopping malls, relied on prepared speeches to a mass assembly and daily press conferences.

Nothing the Conservatives threw into the battle made any difference, nothing they or we came up with served to turn the tide. All the polls showed steady and growing support for Labour. In our tactical planning sessions with Whitelaw the mood had degenerated to manic frenzy underlaid by sweaty-faced desperation.

'Well, what these geezers fucking want, then?' Terry Donovan asked me as he spun the wheel in his big hand to turn the chocolate brown Rolls-Royce into the King's Road.

He was one of the film directors who, along with Bryan Forbes and Gordon Reece, had been hired by Garrett's to direct the footage making up the Party Politicals. A top fashion photographer, he was one of the Cockney snappers who revolutionised photography in the 'sixties (and his later clients would include Margaret Thatcher – whose image he was instrumental in altering – the Duke and Duchess of York and Princess Diana). I had always liked Terry enormously, but this was the first time we'd worked together on a production.

'*Vox populi*,' I said, in answer to Donovan's question. 'They want the C2s, Ds and Es to love them, the proles, the masses. They want to hear *them* repeat the message – the "voice of the common people".'

Terry said nothing for a while, he was thinking. He spent a lot of time driving slowly around Greater London in his Roller, looking out and thinking. A Buddhist with off-centre views, he once got rid of his possessions and *lived* in the car.

He said, 'There's this bird in East Dulwich, she's dead common. Talk your fucking 'ead off, too. Rabbit, rabbit, rabbit all day long, got a slant on everything.'

'Sounds what we need, Terry,' I agreed.

'Speed of light,' he said and, turning the big car out of the King's Road to cross the river, we headed for south London. I asked how he knew the girl we were on our way to visit.

'Her old man's done this an' that for me ... bit of duckin' and diving, know what I mean?' he explained.

Terry's life was characterised by such connections and I knew this was all I was going to get. He didn't *do* explanations, he was entirely instinctive in the way he worked – and he was usually right.

He was in this case. Tracy was the epitome of the down-market consumer whose vote the Conservatives most needed at this critical moment in the last flurry of their, and our, campaign.

She lived in a council estate of post-war modern housing. Yet the development was not dismal and wasted, as often today, but well kept. There were grass and trees, no litter, and no graffiti or signs of vandalism. Modest family saloons stood parked in front of the apartment blocks, far from new but highly polished and clearly lovingly maintained.

Tracy was delighted to see Terry – as everyone always was, for he brought a cheerful ebullience into any room he entered. He had a huge appetite for absurdity and laughter, he was fun. 'The old man out on the job, then?' he asked breezily as he surged into her flat with myself following in his large wake.

'He is an' all, works ever so hard,' she said fondly. It was obvious their marriage was a good one.

If a set designer had to construct a film set typifying the flat of a young working-class couple who had worked hard, done well and earned enough by their own industry to make their modern home really well-equipped and comfortable, even luxurious in its G-Plan way, he would have come up with Tracy and her husband's apartment. The vividly patterned carpet was thick and of good quality, the mirrored cocktail cabinet new and expensive. Their TV set was the largest available, and a later design than we had in the Garrett offices. The couple were model consumers, every available surface was crowded with decorative objects, china and silver. And at least one of them – perhaps both – had taste; some of the pieces were excellent.

Tracy had a vivid, vivacious personality. Aged twenty-six, she was quick-witted and clearly intelligent. With short, dark hair, a pert expressive face and bright eyes, she was very pretty in a wholly ordinary way. No vamp, no threat to other women. Her accent was strong south London, the way she voiced her thoughts uneducated but fluent and forceful; she spoke with conviction. She was exactly what we were looking for. Terry had got it in one.

I used Tracy's telephone to summon up a camera crew and we filmed her two hours later. Keeping the camera running, Terry covered her in mid-shot and close-up responding to my off-screen questions, which would be edited out in cutting. But Tracy had no need of questions to get her going: she was motor-mouth. She talked without pause – housing ... jobs ... health care ... the social services ... the economy ... she had views on everything. And they were the *right* views, the right-wing views our client wanted.

Hardly pausing for breath, she rattled on endlessly. And within that torrent of rabbit pouring from her mouth, precious gems lay embedded. About inflation she said, ' ... go on any longer at this rate and we'll be paying for a bleeding ten-bob loaf by Christmas'. On the Conservatives' policy to restore British military forces to the Middle East she answered, 'Well we're not about to let *that* lot put one over on us, are we? I mean, this country may not be altogether *perfect*, know what I mean, but it's a bleeding sight better than anywhere else.' Her response to my question on race relations – an issue which figured in the campaign as a result of Enoch Powell's notorious 'rivers of blood' speech on immigration – though undoubtedly expressing the views of the majority of the electorate at that time, was judged not suitable for inclusion in the final transmission. 'Send the whole bleeding bunch of them back to Africa, climb back into the bleeding trees,' she asserted roundly.

Aside from that, her opinions accorded with Tory Party dogma, but principally it was her manner that carried weight, the sincerity with which she expressed her Conservative views. That and what she stood for, their home and its evident prosperity, their enterprise and the good life they'd worked so hard to achieve, the fact she was four months' pregnant with their first baby ... the future, the inspiration and the hope.

Edited and put together, the film would network the following night – and would prove to be strikingly effective. But even as we wrapped up and made ready to leave the flat Terry and I were elated. Both of us knew that in those countless feet of exposed film stock we *had* it. Pure gold.

Tracy wanted us to stay, have a cup of tea, and meet her husband when he got back from work. We couldn't unfortunately, though I'd have liked to; he was clearly an enterprising fellow, successful in his job. 'What exactly does he do?' I asked her as we were on the way out.

She shot a glance at Terry. 'Well, he's a ... a real right Jack-the-lad in't he?' she said.

Final opinion polls, published next day on the eve of the election, showed Labour's lead yet further increased. Few, if any, of the Conservative leaders believed they had any prospect of winning, though Heath himself retained a determined positivity.

It had been a crazy month. For those involved in the campaign there'd been little time to sleep. But all of us were sharing a rare level of nervous energy, we were wired. Most of Garrett's people were socialist by conviction, yet they too were caught up in the race. All were still fired up, but when we got together in the seminary library to watch the election results live, no one was unaware that their efforts had been wasted, entirely useless. The other side was going to win. Dressed up for the ball, we were attending a wake.

A few minutes before midnight results started to come in. The first, Guildford, showed a surprising swing to the Conservatives. On TV the pundits discounted it, this was a traditional Conservative seat. But the second, West Salford – traditionally Labour – reflected the same swing. And so did the next ... and as the results streamed in it became evident that the most surprising ballot reversal of the century had taken place. The final results became inevitable, and soon after 2 am Labour accepted defeat.

A fortnight later all who'd worked on the Tories' media campaign were invited by the new Prime Minister to a party at Ten Downing Street. Wearing a dark blue double-breasted suit and the same striped tie, I cut a conservative figure at the assembly. The living room of the house, which was decorated and furnished with the drab neutrality of a reasonably good hotel, was packed with a tightly wedged herd of undistinguished people, pleased as punch to be there.

I was myself. Along with everyone else I hadn't expected Heath to win. I had not been smitten by him or Whitelaw; they seemed to me both bland and brazen, there was something spurious about the attitudes they struck and their complacent breeziness. Yet towards the end, when his disciples were losing faith and he stood embattled by misfortune, he had shown such dignity in adversity I had to admit an unwilling admiration. But I remained a bit underwhelmed by the other politicians I'd encountered. Not a whiff of inspiration came from any of them. And these were the *elite*, the best of them. To be a backbencher, valued only for your obedience, looked a pitiful existence. Badly paid, some of them toiled their entire lives without achieving the rewards of office, the stick-it-on-the-bill delights of a freebie to Barbados or a weekend at the Paris Ritz, the gratification that comes from shovelling the contents of the mini-bar into your briefcase on departure and the satisfied glow of a job well done.

But the campaign had been an extremely interesting experience, I'd enjoyed it immensely. And it was fun to be invited to Number Ten for the valedictory payoff. I wasn't drinking – hadn't in fact since the start of the campaign – but I had brought with me a small packet of coke. I'd dipped into it at times over the past month and only a tiny amount remained. I'd determined to give up cocaine, and this seemed the perfect venue for a final blast. It was only appropriate to mark the occasion, for the whole business had gone so very well for everyone concerned. James Garrett had executed a notable account and been paid, the Conservatives had won, Ted Heath became PM, and Whitelaw Lord President. Terry Donovan had not only been congratulated by the Prime Minister for the best Party Political of the campaign – which, some said, had supplied the final chip that won the pot – but had been presented with a set of five new tyres for his Rolls by Tracy's husband, Jack-the-lad, as a thank-you gift for making his wife famous by putting her on TV.

Everyone had got what they wanted, everyone was happy. Preceding Sir Tim Bell by a full decade into the downstairs lavatory at Number Ten, I set out a long last line, snorted it, and strolled back to join the fun.

21
Côte d'Azur

Fed by melted snow, the torrent roared down the narrow valley to where a natural dam of smooth boulders blocked its course, then surged over them to cascade into a rockpool overhung by trees.

This was my view as I sat at a table by an open window in the south of France, working on a screenplay. It was the spring of 1971. I'd been hired to write a script for Jozsef Sandoz, a Hungarian producer who'd made half a dozen movies, one of them notorious.

I wasn't *totally* unqualified for the job, but near as could be. A ninety-minute script I'd written had been transmitted as a BBC Wednesday Play. Its story – a man going progressively more nuts working for a fashionable ad agency, to end up addressing the world while standing on water in the middle of the Round Pond – was close to my heart, and the writing had been instinctual; I knew nothing of technique or screencraft. But the instant purchase of that script, the speed with which it was produced, its peak-time transmission, reviews, and the fact that payments came in on the nail had convinced me the whole thing was a breeze – a presumption I would come to revise in the weeks ahead.

The old olive mill in which I sat working on this sunny day had walls a yard thick and massive ceiling beams eaten away by woodworm. The flat was in a dreadful state of repair; the water heating yielded nothing above tepid, the Calor-gas cooker in the primitive kitchen was thirty years old and congealed with rust, all the furniture was infirm or broken. The windows looked out on the river and forest beyond and the place was utterly magical.

It was Magda who had found it. A Polish-American fashion model, quick witted, funny and smart, I had met her in New York while I was living at the Algonquin. Always perfectly groomed, she had the unconventional face of the young Bette Davis and Dietrich's Mittel-European voice. Her social talent had been a huge asset entertaining clients in New York, she was immensely stimulating to be with. Intrigued by her, I had asked her to come with me to the south of France.

I'd always enjoyed writing, but I was also attracted by the movie business. I associated it with glamour. Here I believed I would find a larger stage than advertising provided, a more starry cast, a richer and more glittering spectacle.

I had first encountered Sandoz at a meeting set up by my genial American agent, who knew he needed a writer to script a book he'd bought. The producer's apartment spread over two floors of a Mayfair house, the place was overwhelmingly opulent and extravagantly furnished. Every single object within it was glossy and new, including his wife. All four walls of the library where we sat were lined floor to ceiling with fitted wooden bookshelves, filled with leather-bound volumes. Or, rather, their spines glued in place, for none was real.

Not just the library but the entire interior and contents of the apartment had been acquired for nothing, I learned later. A squat man with a face like a smacked arse, Sandoz was an instinctive snapper-up of everything. He'd bought the bare shell of the flat before starting his last picture, which had been shot in Spain. Everyone involved in that production had remarked on the extraordinarily high quality of the studio sets and the luxury of the furniture and room dressings. Film sets usually have two walls, occasionally three, but Sandoz's had *four*. At the end of the shoot the sets were pack-struck, put into crates and trucked to London. The picture's art director and construction crew had worked to very precise plans. Everything slotted exactly into place into the empty apartment ... *clunk* .... *clunk* .... *clunk*. The 1,500-volume library was created in seven minutes and the large flat fully decorated and furnished within an hour.

He was refreshingly candid about these arrangements and his views on life. Admirably free of hypocrisy, he might be said to have possessed an instinctively generous nature. Speaking of women, he once said to me, 'The way I look at it, if something's good enough for me it's good enough for my friends.'

Unlike advertising, where in England most people were respectable and suburban in their lifestyles, the movie business, which was LA led, had exported its West Coast values to London with the several American producers who had moved to this then-lively colony to make pictures. Often to be puzzled by the quaintness of the city's ways. Charlie Feldman, here to produce one of the Bond films, remarked that he couldn't understand all this talk of 'orgies'; to him, any number less than four was an intimate relationship.

And these same liberal values seemed to obtain in the south of France, where Sandoz and his family (wife, new baby, new nanny, newly acquired Mercedes coupé charged to the production as is customary) had rented a villa (ditto) in Mougins behind Cannes, from whose poolside he intended to set up the picture. One day I drove over to his villa to deliver some pages I'd completed. Usually he'd be by the pool wearing only a gold medallion and body hair, but this morning I found him dressed and pacing the house. 'Fuck the script, we got to move ass,' he said. 'Khashoggi's winging in for the Film Festival. We got to find the family a house.'

The financing for the picture was to be provided by Adnan Khashoggi. I'd never met him, but I knew about him – everybody knew about him. You couldn't open a magazine without coming across a photograph of him at some glossy event. His name had surfaced in the Lockheed/Prince Bernhart scandal and would remain notorious in the years to come.

Sandoz, his wife, Magda and I piled into the Mercedes coupé and went to look for a house for Khashoggi and his family. It wasn't easy, most were already rented, but eventually we found a five-bedroom villa with pool, poolhouse and servants' flat, standing on a hilltop near Mougins. The owners drove a hard bargain, the short rental was exorbitant.

Next day the four of us were at Nice airport to meet Khashoggi's plane. He owned his own specially fitted DC8 but arrived in a Boeing 707 lent him by Kirk Kerkorian, president of MGM. The aircraft landed, taxied to the terminal, and off it poured a tide of people. They swept into the arrivals concourse in a human wave. At their head marched the stout, confident figure of Khashoggi attended by his bodyguard, Palestinian business secretary and Lebanese personal assistant. Behind came his English wife Soraya, her social secretary, a nanny, two nursemaids, and three small children. Following them were Khashoggi's two younger brothers, with wives, children and similar retinues ... and in their train shuffled a horde of Arab servants carrying suitcases and large, ill-wrapped bundles.

Khashoggi showed a lordly indifference to the problem of how and where his army was to be housed. He passed only a token two minutes talking to us before getting into a waiting limo with his personal staff and moving to the Carlton in Cannes, where he had a suite reserved. Amid hysteria and confusion his two brothers scattered elsewhere with their retinues. We were left in the airport with Soraya, her secretary, children and nursery staff, and about fifty Bedouin.

Soraya had a dramatic, fine-boned face and long dark hair. The daughter of a London hotel waitress and an unknown father, she'd worked as a telephone operator before she met Khashoggi. 'I want to look at the house first,' she said incisively.

The horde of Bedouin seemed resigned to remain in the concourse until Allah willed otherwise; some had started to brew up and prepare a meal. Leaving them encamped there, we clambered into another of the waiting limos with Soraya and her Scottish secretary and drove off.

Coming out of Cannes into the hills behind, just before the highway joins the autoroute, there was an exhibition of prefabricated homes beside the road. Three examples were displayed: California modern, French eighteenth-century, and Swiss chalet. We passed them on the drive to Mougins.

Soraya inspected the villa we'd rented for her, assessing it in a moment. It was barely large enough for her children and nursery staff; the servants' flat could accommodate another two, at a pinch four, and the pool house a further couple. She did not hesitate. Getting into the limo, we drove back to the display of homes where she bought the three erected by the road. Her secretary would settle in full in cash, she said, but they must be re-sited by the end of that afternoon in the garden of the Mougins house.

They were. And it has to be said, the job was done not only efficiently but rather tastefully. The three contrasting dwellings set down on flower beds looked incongruous but bizarrely interesting. And the fourteen rooms they represented were perfectly adequate if the numerous occupants were wedged in tight. Unfortunately the houses had no running water or drainage, but the fifty desert Bedouin were used to harsher conditions than these; it would be a positive luxury for them to do their business squatting in the shade of the bougainvillaea, and the swimming pool was conveniently at hand for other uses.

Most people wear a mask, an outer manner for the world to see. But spend more time with them and you usually get to glimpse behind it. With Khashoggi, you never did. His voice stayed low, its tone even, his face remained inscrutable. Short and rather plump, he was always starchly dressed in the very latest resort wear, yet he had dignity. His poise was total. He listened well, didn't interrupt and spoke rarely, but when he did, others paid attention. I never got the faintest notion of who and what he really is. His attitude to life seemed wholly pragmatic. The fifteen-strong crew of his yacht were all British. We have the reputation of a seafaring nation, was this the reason he'd hired them, I asked.

'No, the British make the best servants,' he said.

Standing with Magda among a crowd of people on the Carlton terrace one day, I was talking to Sandoz when Soraya hurried over to say, 'Adnan's invited everybody to lunch on the yacht. The crew's off and there's no food. Come – we have to cater.'

It was already past noon but there was no question of telling him lunch would have to be in a restaurant. What is the point of being a multi-millionaire if your whim can't be gratified on the instant? Soraya was skilled in this sort of emergency. We piled into a limo and crawled the *croisette* followed by a back-up car, stopping at every restaurant. 'Whatta you got?' she demanded in each.

The second limo was stowed with assorted dishes and we in the lead car were clutching cold lobsters and salad bowls and accelerating towards the yacht marina when Soraya shrieked, 'Stop! That's Jack Nicholson!'

She'd never met him, but darting from the car she asked him to the lunch party. He came. Lots of people came, all invited in the same random fashion. A hostess in the south of France once said to me, 'I love to entertain, but it's so hard to get the guests.' The Khashoggis experienced no such difficulty, any celeb or wannabe would do.

I stayed on deck throughout that lunch party on the yacht. It had been going on for a while when I saw the director Roman Polanski attempt to come on board. Short and boyish, he was wearing a sweater and crumpled jeans, and had with him a teenage groupie picked up on the beach. They looked like a couple of ragamuffins and a crew member standing security at the gangway tried to shoo them away. 'Not for you, son,' he told Polanski. 'Piss off!'

Polanski blew up and a major row erupted. A frisson of pleasure ran through the crowd safe on deck as they watched the drama develop below. Among us, an ITN camera crew was watching the fun, though not filming it. I realised I knew the soundman. 'So what are *you* doing here, Stan?' I asked him. 'This is *news*?'

He shrugged. 'Khashoggi asked for a film crew. ITN said they couldn't use the item but Khashoggi said to fly down anyway, he'd pay.'

Khashoggi was completely up front about his taste. 'I *like* publicity,' he explained. 'It turns me on.'

Sandoz had made one picture for each of the Hollywood majors; none of them proved keen to repeat the experience. No one was clamouring to cut a deal with him. As for Khashoggi, involvement in film production was a summer flirtation. He enjoyed the fantasy glamour of moviedom and the presence of so many good-looking young women and the attention it won him at the Film Festival; I don't believe he ever intended to finance the picture.

But he got a few months of entertainment from it – and a new employee. Recognising Sandoz's notable talents as a fixer, he offered him a job. And so it came about that a tap-dancing Hungarian chancer relinquished the motion picture business at the age of forty-five to enter a more secure profession. An upwardly mobile Jewish boy, he embraced a new and rewarding career working for Khashoggi – a man whose principal business was providing weaponry to Arab countries dedicated to the destruction of the State of Israel.

And I was out of a job.

22
La Cagne

The sun rose early in a clear blue sky, its first beams flaring on the peaks of the alps twenty miles away, still icy-white with snow, though here in the forested valley it was already summer.

Magda and I were up before seven. This morning as usual I did not bother to shave but had a coffee and a piece of crusty bread, then was at work by eight. I wore a pair of khaki shorts from Prixunic, torn and not very clean, and a battered straw hat. Nothing else except a tan.

I had made a major career move. I'd entered an older and more honourable profession than advertising, politics or movies. I'd become a stone mason – a builder. Kneeling there in my torn shorts I was constructing a curving flight of stone steps – in *style rustique*, as the French say, meaning crudely and rather badly – between the mill and the river coursing in the gorge below the house. I'd been working on the project every day for several weeks now; this was my job.

And the mill was mine, or rather, Magda's and mine. A year after we first clapped eyes on it we'd bought it from the two old English sisters who owned the place, and come to live in the south of France. I'd sold my share in the Garrett Company to do so. It had taken most of that money to buy the property and would require the rest to restore the place into three apartments; but once we'd done so we could rent or sell two of them and live on the proceeds. It was a gamble, but both of us were excited by the idea of a new and wholly different life. We'd committed – and the decision brought a tremendous exhilaration.

I felt the sun hot on my bare shoulders as I worked. There is something elemental and deeply satisfying about building by hand, in choosing the right stone, packing in cement with a trowel, then fitting it into place. The activity occupies the mind at the same level as preparing and cooking a meal, and both provide the same outcome of tangible result. Previously, in advertising, at the end of any day I'd never been able to *see* what I'd accomplished during it. And, if I had actually achieved anything, I could be quite sure it would become unachieved and something else entirely by the following afternoon. Here, the section of stairway I built today had a good chance of standing for a century or more.

There had been a wonderful feeling of liberation in quitting Garrett's, handing back my credit cards and moving to this secluded valley. It was a relief not to have to eat almost every meal in a restaurant with people I didn't want to be with. For so many years practically everything in my life had been chargeable or paid for with Monopoly money. It felt quite odd to be using my own, with it came an adolescent thrill of independence.

Here I worked through the morning, in the afternoons I

lay in the sun and read: Proust, the Goncourt Journals, Madame de Sévigné, Flaubert, Jean Giono, Collette ... To rediscover books was a revelation; they'd been all-important to me when young, essential as solitude. But for so long I hadn't gone to church, or prayed, or read. I'd never listened to music or spent time alone. Now I did all these things. Most of all I read, and it was like regaining a whole section of who I was; I recovered it with a sense of astonishment and joy. I was happy.

I'd gone to visit Mother and Nanny at Gilston Road to tell them of my planned move before leaving for France. The street, shabby and run down when we'd moved there after the war, had become fashionable now. Most of the houses had been restored and repainted, and those that hadn't were encased in scaffolding and being done up. Not ours, however. The grimy paintwork had cracked into a mosaic of flaking scales like eczema and the ceiling plaster in the hall had fallen off to expose the laths.

'Since Mr Baines retired, one can't find *anyone* to repair *anything* these days,' Mother complained. She had asked me to a meal, but when I arrived at 12.30 she was about to set off for the cinema. She thought I'd enjoy the film too.

'Can't we go after lunch?' I asked. No, she explained. Seats for the first performance were only 30p; she always went at this time, taking a picnic to eat in one or other of the local cinemas two or three times a week.

Unwillingly I accompanied her. The large auditorium was almost empty – which was as well, for Mother was a noisy picnicker, scrunching paper and talking loudly through the performance. 'I'm going to live in France,' I told her.

'Really, darling? I've always thought it such a silly shape.

Would you like one of Nanny's lettuce sandwiches? There's only one hard-boiled egg, I'm afraid,' she said.

Her responses were often unsatisfactory, for her mind was elsewhere, but where that elsewhere lay one never knew, though it was evident it was not a happy place. Twice she had become so withdrawn she'd had to return to the hospital overlooking Regent's Park. My brothers visited her and so did I, though not often enough, for it was a miserable experience. She barely responded to anything we said and her muteness numbed the spirit and drained away one's bright intentions.

Father proved easier. Seeing him usually meant meeting on a railway station or some street corner in the rain, but this was my initiative and we met at Wheelers. He arrived in the poacher's jacket he always favoured and the mountaineer's rucksack which he refused to check, instead stowing it beneath the table.

We lunched well. He enjoyed good food and wine, neither of which he tasted often these days. The fortune he'd made from *Sea-wyf* years before had pauperised him. It was a reprise of the rule that had governed his whole existence: success ruined him. Sports hero and head of school ... Cambridge Blue ... an Everest expedition ... Arctic explorer ... author of a best seller ... by the age of twenty-four he'd already peaked. From there his life could only deteriorate – and it had. The success of *Sea-wyf* had revived it only briefly. Following that, he'd travelled the world looking for the ideal place to reinvent himself ... and ended up in Mallorca. The honeymoon was brief, things started to sour almost at once. The sun disagreed with him and the laughter of village children swimming in the creek ruined his concentration and made it impossible to write. He maintained it was the local oil, in which everything was cooked, and garlic – of which he had an extreme, almost religious horror – that caused a prickly rash to spread across his body, but the affliction proved hard to treat. The local doctor had met no other human case, it was a disease caught only by trees. Worst of all – two years into the idyll – he discovered he was liable to supertax at 19s. 6d. (97½p) in the pound on the fortune he'd already spent.

By the date of our lunch he'd been back in England for many years, sharing a cottage with Adriana in a windswept corner of East Anglia. Undermodernised and unheated, their nest was basic; there was only one bedroom and, downstairs, a single, large, low-ceilinged room. Father worked at night and, unable to do so unless alone, a tool shed in the garden had been converted into what few would describe as 'living accommodation', yet served as such for Adriana. After she had washed up their dinner things she'd retire to her hutch and remain there until allowed to reappear to cook breakfast for them both.

People rarely change with age; whatever they are already they become more so. Father and Adriana saw nobody, no one was invited to the house. He remained malcontent as ever, still hounded by the tax man and oppressed by a weight of debt he never could repay. Sitting across the table from me in Wheelers he was broke, his refusal to 'go decimal' with the rest of the country made easier by the fact that he had nothing to go decimal with.

In contrast, my own fortunes were riding high; I'd received the first tranche on the sale of my Garrett shares and was loaded. At the end of an excellent lunch of potted shrimps, sole Colbert, two bottles of Chablis, Stilton and port, I slid him a cheque – not a fortune but enough to sedate the Revenue, or take a trip or do whatever.

Father eyed it lying on the table between us. 'Quite a decent wine,' he remarked, chewing on his port. 'You remember I put down a pipe of Cockburn's '34 for you the year that you were born?'

'Wasn't it bombed in the Blitz?'

'You got the two dozen that were spared,' he replied defensively. A silence followed. He fiddled with the cheque; he seemed quite moved. I realised he was finding it hard to speak. Then, 'Good of you,' he said awkwardly. 'Will change things ... hardly know exactly what I'll do yet.'

And a memory came to me. No slow dissolve but an instant flashback to Nice airport when I'd been eighteen, about to join the army, and he'd handed me a final payoff of £50 ... and his words as he'd done so.

'Father,' I said, 'Personally I don't care *what* you do with it, so long as you don't become a male ballet dancer.'

He flushed ... and then, most surprisingly, he laughed. It was a rare moment. In the rosy glow of after-lunch, briefly he turned into a normal human being and we could talk and joke together.

The property Magda and I had acquired consisted not just of the building we were converting, but the mill further upriver which the old English sisters still occupied. We were buying the place and accompanying land on a French system known as *en viager*. The old sisters received a capital sum plus an annual *rente viagère* until their death, till which they had the right to remain as sitting tenants where they were.

Beside the river at the bottom of a deep valley, the spot the mills occupied was of breathtaking beauty. A tall spire of rock reared up behind, part of the steep mountain range which fed the river. After a storm, and when the snows melted in spring, a torrent of white water thundered past our house. Its power was awesome; standing on the terrace you could feel the ground quiver beneath your feet and had to shout above the roar. In summer the river became a lazy stream plashing over the waterfall into the still pool below, hovered over by dragonflies, where we swam. The sunny air carried the scent of lavender and thyme and for three weeks in early summer the warm dusk of evening was lit by the pulsing glow of a thousand fireflies.

It was an unimaginably lovely place, but I was uncertain how Magda – and also myself – would take to country living. In New York she had been the perfect partner. The few women I've been close to all seem to have come from disturbed backgrounds and dysfunctional families, but hers was particularly turbulent. Her father, a Polish cavalry officer, had been a prisoner of war in Germany. She was only seven when she'd escaped Poland with her mother, crossing Soviet-occupied East Germany on foot. Somehow they had got to England, then to the USA. Her parents barely spoke English; her father was unable to find work except on an assembly line. The apartment they lived in was poor, their friends Polish refugees in the same circumstance as themselves, whose talk was all of the vanished life they'd known before the war. Money was always short but, 'Remember who you are,' her parents told her.

She'd escaped her background by becoming a model. She passed for Scandinavian; it was a look in vogue at the time, there was no lack of well-paid jobs. While working in Paris she'd met a rich young French banker, member of a modish circle drawn from *finance* and *haute juiverie*, and moved in to share his apartment in Avenue Foch. Quick to learn, she spoke French fluently and became an able hostess. She had many skills, but one that struck me because I had not met it before was the ability to take one glance at a woman and *cost* her in seconds, correctly identifying the provenance of dress, shoes, handbag, watch and jewellery.

She was a metropolitan animal and our time together in New York had been highly social; I wasn't sure how she would adapt to a ravine five kilometres from the nearest small town. But she loved the sun and beach as much as I did, and right from the start we were involved in our joint project rebuilding the mill and clearing the overgrown land to lay out a garden. It was absorbing, wholly satisfying work. We felt well, ate well, slept well, and were never without a tan.

We had realised a fantasy common to many with busy city lives; we'd escaped to Provence. At last we had leisure to read, to relax, to eat dinner alone together. Time to get to know the loved one …

Aged thirty-eight, I'd dropped out. The friends of my youth were all still hard at work. Alex Howard was running a major advertising agency he'd started, which specialised in banks and financial institutions. Fisher was still a stockbroker … though no longer with the same firm but already conscious the move was not as satisfactory as he'd hoped. 'One has to keep the old chin up etc., but what with three sets of school fees, it's actually pretty worrying,' he confessed.

In contrast, Kim Waterfield had been riding high when I'd last seen him at a party shortly before we'd moved to France. For a while he'd been obliged to hide his helicopter in a haystack to save it from repossession, but he'd recovered and was again rich. The party where we re-met was lavish and stocked with a select mob of glamorous and modishly dressed people – of which Kim's 21-year-old bride was unquestionably the most striking. What I knew about her came only from reading newspapers, in which her lurid story had unfolded over months. Aged just sixteen she'd married Clive Raphael, a millionaire entrepreneur who – she revealed to me years later – had Mob connections. The marriage was stormy and became physically violent. She left him. He asked her to fly with him in his private plane to Andorra ... she refused. Two days later, with Raphael at the controls, the aircraft crashed in France, killing him, both his parents and another passenger in what may or may not have been an accident.

A will was found in Raphael's safe. Dated two days before his death, it left Penny a one shilling piece and four nude photos of herself. She challenged it in the High Court. The case, which became notorious, was tried at the Old Bailey. Raphael's business partners were convicted of forging the document and sentenced to jail – though one fled the country before the trial. Penny inherited an estate reported by the media to be worth £500,000, which included control of the property company Land and General and, most romantically of all in my eyes, of the Stirling Submachine Gun Company, one of its subsidiaries.

Both she and Kim were remarkably good-looking, they made a stylish couple. Their base was the country estate in Wiltshire he'd owned since the early sixties. By now he'd sold Ann Summers, which he'd founded, and was engaged in setting up a new business. As he was explaining this to me I saw behind him the slender figure of his wife making her way towards us across the crowded room. Moving with a model's unhurried languor, she wore a miniskirt that was no more than a twist of fabric around her hips. She had the longest and most perfect legs I'd ever seen ... and I completely lost the thread of what Kim was saying to me.

On reaching us, her blue eyes flicked over me in what might have been an apology for interrupting before she said quietly ... *what?* Would that one could remember the first words of the woman who, twenty years later, becomes the great love of one's life. The sad truth is that memory is a defective instrument ... and one can't.

Parties, elegance and the social round played little part in Magda's and my own life at the mill. Here the day consisted of manual labour, eating, reading books and sleep, life was reassuringly down to earth and simple. To help us rebuild the mill we had taken on Vincent, a dwarf mason, a carpenter and a *main d'oeuvre,* who were part of a nearby workers' commune inhabiting a stone cottage and shanty outbuildings set in a field of wild flowers and lacking all modern amenities. The commune consisted of six young men and women plus an ancient grandmother, a blond child who looked like an angel, a parrot, hens, dogs, cats and any passing backpacker who chose to share their life. All were communists, pooling what they earned.

We saw them every day and had become close friends.

On Christmas Eve Magda and I spent *réveillon* with them. Their cottage was without telephone or electricity, we dined by candlelight at a rickety trestle table. We ate oysters, traditional at *réveillon*, and drank a great deal of Muscadet. It was a magical evening. I'd grown to know all of them, but Vincent, who was under five feet tall, had become an especial friend. He'd been born Catalan, on the wrong side in the Spanish Civil War. When things got very bad his parents had attempted to escape to France, taking the infant Vincent, his brother and their possessions loaded on a donkey. Crossing the Pyrenees was arduous, twice they were turned back. It took them a month to reach a refugee camp at Perpignan, and by then they'd been so short of food they'd had to eat the donkey.

Magda and I had brought wine and flowers to *réveillon*, and elaborately wrapped gifts for everyone. At the end of the evening as Vincent was walking us back to the mill beneath a night sky clear and brilliant with stars, he told us of the first Christmas presents he'd ever received, at the age of five in the refugee camp. They'd consisted of an orange wrapped in silver paper and a bar of chocolate. His brother had stolen the orange but he'd managed to keep the chocolate hidden. He'd found it so marvellous, so unbelievably delicious, that by nibbling only very tiny pieces he'd made it last until Easter.

It was one in the morning on Christmas Day; I was moved and humbled by his story.

On Sundays throughout that winter I drove to the English church in Nice, then drank *pastis* and played the *tiercé* with a jaunty old tramp who lived and slept in the leafy square outside. The Victorian parish church, its vicarage, garden and graveyard, were as incongruously English as a cricket pitch in the middle of this Mediterranean city. The service was that which I'd known in boyhood, readings from the St James version, and the elderly expat congregation sat as far distant from each other as the pews allowed. The hour and a half I passed there each week brought a sense of stability and order, and a warm enduring gratitude for the life God had granted me in France. Then, early in the new year, on a day that dawned blue and crisp and bright, I rediscovered skiing and my happiness was complete.

Three stations lay within an easy drive from the mill; I could listen to the weather report at first light and if conditions were good I'd strap skis on the car and head into the Alps. Except for weekends and school holidays the slopes were almost empty. Though some of the lifts were closed, the 'egg' to the summit and valley beyond was always running. Once at the top I'd often be alone on the mountain, coming down fast with mind and body one, the sky blue above the icy peaks, the sun warm and glittering on fresh powder snow, and I was exalted and drunk with the sheer joy of it, a *part* of it, and life as perfect as it can get to be this side of paradise.

23
Arcadia

'In summer,' Magda remarked in her distinctive accent, 'people call up all zee time saying can zay come to stay? And often vee are not remembering who zee fuck zey are – let alone friends. But for nine months of zee year vee know only zee commune, vee haf turned into *pecnauds*, country bumpkins.'

Seated in the shade of a parasol, she and I were having lunch on the mill's terrace, from which a handsome flight of *rustique* stone steps led down to the river flowing below. The paved terrace and our own apartment at last had been completed, but even after two years of reconstruction the rest of the mill was still a building site. For the moment we were alone; this was *midi* and the commune workforce had gone back to their cottage to eat. Much as we liked them, it was a relief to be in peace.

'Yes, but the resident expats are so awful,' I said.

On the whole they were; living here had had a bad effect

on them. All were older than us, and retired. Without the job and habit of their previous existence had come an emptiness filled only by drink and food. 'Life's just drinkies and sleepies now,' one had put it. Most lived on fixed sterling incomes, and in two years the pound had fallen from 11 to 7.8 francs. To their disbelief and anger they were poor, and their relentless partying had an edge of desperation. I was going on to Magda about how dreary I found their drunken dinners when she held up a beautifully manicured hand to stop me. 'The telephone,' she said.

I went to pick it up and a voice enquired, 'What's the weather like down there?'

It was Peter Mayle. I'd met him once or twice at the black-tie awards the advertising business stages to celebrate itself, but I knew him only slightly. 'Sunny, how's it in New York?' I asked.

'A foot of melting snow and no taxis. Vile – like advertising. Jennie and I have decided to give it up and live like bums in the south of France. Can you find us a house?'

'To restore?' I asked.

'Absolutely not. I want to write, not get involved in tiresome building nonsense,' he told me.

After several weeks unurgently looking around, I found a small house on the ramparts of St Jeannet, a nearby *village perché*. I mailed him photographs and he asked me to set up a meeting with the local notary. He flew from New York to sign the *compromis de vente.* I met him at Nice airport. He was in his late thirties, slim and extremely good-looking, dressed in a blazer and flared trousers badly creased from the long flight. Coming out into the sunshine he tipped back his head to draw in a deep breath of mimosa-scented air. 'You've no idea how good it feels to be here,' he said.

'Oh yes I do,' I assured him.

He'd taken the job of creative director at Ogilvie and Mather only a couple of years before and moved to New York with Jennie Armstrong, a talented and pretty girl I already knew, for she ran one of Garrett's subsidiary companies. But both of them had now reached the point I had myself some while before; they'd had their fill of neurotic demanding clients and come to loathe the work they did.

Only after signing the *compromis* and paying a deposit did Peter get to see the house I'd chosen for him. To my great relief he loved it. 'Right! So where shall we go for lunch?' he asked.

There was a restaurant on the quay in Nice, I said. Wonderful shellfish.

'Excellent!' he said, rubbing his hands in anticipation. We climbed into the car, collected Magda and drove there. 'The oysters are superlative,' I advised him.

Peter was picking up the check; he was in expansive mood and still on a NY salary. Taking my advice on the oysters, he and we went on to order royally. We had *oursins*, *praires*, *amandes*, *bigorneaux*, sea-snails, and *crustaces*, all eaten with brown bread and a thick slab of white butter.

Normally Magda and I ate quite modestly at the mill. This lunch was a treat, and it was an especial treat to be enjoying it with someone our own age with whom we had so much in common, in both situation and much else as well. It would be eight months before Peter gained possession of his new house. 'I can't stand it that much longer in New York,' he remarked. 'We'll have to rent a place here till it's free.'

'No, no!' Magda and I both cried together. 'Come live with us.'

He and Jennie moved to France soon after, to live for more than a year in one of the mill's primitive and incomplete apartments. The two of them had quit jobs, partners, homes and families to be together. They were often broke – as we were, for restoring the mill was proving far more costly than imagined. Invariably Peter or myself – sometimes both – were waiting for funds to come in. In my case the last payments due on my Garrett shares, in his from books.

'What made you start writing?' I asked him once, settling back for a literary conversation cut short by his answer, 'Sheer desperation.' Boarding a London–New York flight, he'd been seated beside an insistently talkative fellow passenger. To silence her he'd called for paper and hunkered down to authorship. He'd outlined his first book by the time the plane touched down at Kennedy.

Now installed in France he sat in the window of their mill flat and wrote. Meanwhile, I continued working with the commune, and, sometimes alone, on the restoration. At one lunch, following a morning when he'd watched me labouring on a dam I was building in the river, he remarked, 'You should keep a journal.'

'Whatever for?' I asked, reaching for the wine bottle with a callused hand.

'There might be a book in it.'

I considered the idea. 'I don't think so. People fall in love with the fantasy of a home here, but the day-to-day reality is just aggro and dealing with a bunch of feckless Provençal workmen who don't show up.'

'*Mmm*,' he said.

While the Mayles were with us was an enchanted year. For Magda and myself the days were filled by the work and pleasure of rebuilding the mill into something entirely beautiful, and laying out a garden. While Peter wrote, Jennie searched *brocanteurs* for items for their new house. Both were on the run from advertising, like myself; physically occupied, all of us were in retreat from what we'd known before. Deliberately, even a little self-consciously, we embraced a bucolic lifestyle. Hidden away in this forested valley, the river pool became our Walden Pond and Jennie Mayle would launder their sheets by hand, spreading them over the huge boulders on the bank to dry while we swam, lay in the sun and read. For the four of us throughout that summer the Côte d'Azur was aka Arcadia.

Peter's lawyer was coming to visit and talk business. I accompanied Peter to Nice airport to meet his flight from LA. Neither of us had shaved, we were dressed in the disgraceful old clothes we always wore, espadrilles and no socks. Smelling strongly of Calvados and garlic, for we'd eaten a heavy lunch, we drove slowly down the winding country road to the coast. Peter's car matched our peasant image; a beat-up 2CV Citroën plastic jeep, it was the most basic of utility vehicles and definitely unsafe, it had once blown over in the wind. Parking the wreck, we ambled into the airport concourse to welcome Ernie Chapman.

A high-powered showbiz lawyer still operating on LA time, he erupted from the arrivals gate to head in our direction with rampant energy, starting to talk well before he reached us. 'Where's the car?' he demanded and gathered us up in the wind of his pace as he strode towards the exit. A burly figure grasping a leather bag, he radiated the force of a purposeful bear and contracts, sales, deals-in-negotiation poured from him as we trotted to keep up. Bursting out into the sunlight we dashed the few yards to the battered jeep. Still travelling at full speed, Ernie stepped over the buckled side and swung into the passenger seat, in the same uninterrupted motion and, without looking, thrusting his hand down beside it ... to find nothing. He looked up, startled. '*Where's the telephone*?' he demanded in disbelief.

Outside Arcadia life was real, life was urgent, and Ernest its trusty messenger. He was the north wind, gusting into our subtropic Eden, and a further blast from the life we had relinquished arrived in the shape of Frank Lowe, Mammon's ambassador to the Côte d'Azur. A hyperactive *bon vivant*, he'd recently been appointed chief executive of Collett Dickenson, now a public company. Despite strikes in Britain, devaluation of the pound, the three-day week and economic chaos brought upon the country by Ted Heath, the agency – which handled Benson and Hedges and Silk Cut – was doing phenomenally well. Frank had decided its management – himself – required a rustic hideaway in which to replenish its creative juices. Southern exposure and a good view were essential.

He asked me to find him the ideal spot, and after driving around for a while I did so. Four acres of hilltop near Mougins, a thousand feet above sea level, it had a panoramic view of the coast ten miles distant. Rough, rocky land, covered in scrub; a farmhouse built in the style of Jean de la Florette, and just as primitive, stood in a grove of gnarled olive trees. If *I* were a stressed-out CEO it would be exactly the pastoral retreat I'd want, I thought.

Frank bought the property at first glance. On the day following purchase a workforce of twenty men moved on to the site with heavy-duty equipment. By nightfall the farmhouse had been razed to the ground. In the course of the next few months a château of stressed concrete with an imposing *tour* rose in its place, then a team of specialists from Shepperton Studios was trucked down and set to work. The breeze-block and raw concrete structure was sprayed with a mix of stucco and oxide which dried to antiquity over a sunny afternoon. The salon's mirrored walls were faded and stained with acid, its frescoes and eighteenth-century painted ceiling distressed by electric sanders in a choking cloud of iridescent dust. In the space of two weeks the building aged by 250 years to stand venerable and imposing in a ravaged wasteland of torn earth and uprooted trees.

I watched in awe as a swimming pool went in, a stream was added, a boulodrome and tennis court installed, and a carpet of cropped green turf unrolled to make a croquet lawn. When the undertaking finally was complete I stood with Frank and Vincent the dwarf builder – who was in charge of the French crew – on the château's balustraded terrace, looking over the landscaped grounds to a view that embraced the whole coast from Nice to the Estoril, except for a small section of Cap d'Antibes masked by a rise of land at the bottom of the garden.

'Super, absolutely super,' Frank pronounced, then turned to Vincent, 'But lose that hill.'

As Dorothy Parker said, it made you realise what God could have done if only He'd had the money.

But these encounters with the wider universe were rare. The life we followed was active, but hardly social. At the end of a day's work I'd sit on the riverbank, glass in hand, and watch the stream flow by. Confucius had passed his last years doing the same, growing wiser all the while, and Thoreau gained insight from gazing at Walden Pond. I hoped to find a similar enlightenment, but largely it eluded me. In fact quite my most significant *aperçu* came not from contemplation of the river but over lunch with Nigel Broackes.

He and Joyce had a villa on Cap d'Antibes and a yacht plus crew at Cannes. Magda and I were invited occasionally to make up a lunch party. He had earned his knighthood by now, they were Sir Nigel and Lady Broackes. He'd become immensely rich and successful; he owned the Ritz and Berkeley Hotels, the Cunard Shipping Line, half the North Sea's oil, and most things in Britain that weren't actually nailed down. As proprietor of Express Newspapers he was familiar with the corridors of political power, wealthier than his close chum Michael Heseltine and with more successful hair. He stood, as he put it, 'quite close to the centre of things'. The villa's salon contained photographs of him hobnobbing with the Queen.

He'd just bought the *QE II*. The British economy had collapsed, Heath's government fallen, and Denis Healey was threatening to squeeze the rich till the pips squeaked … it looked unlikely anyone in England would take a cruise on a luxury liner in the foreseeable future. 'Any ideas what to do with it?' Nigel asked me.

'Why on earth did you buy it?'

'Because it means the next £15 million we make will be tax free,' he said.

The world he operated in was incomprehensible to me, but our immediate surroundings were comfortably familiar. We sat amid the debris of a large lunch on a shaded terrace overlooking the garden of his villa. Coffee and a glass of brandy stood before each of us as we reminisced.

'What news of Alex Howard?' I asked.

'In fine form. Joyce and I saw him recently in Hong Kong, he lent us a Rolls that broke down.'

'What's he doing there?' I asked.

Nigel shrugged, 'Who can tell? You know how mysterious he is about his life.'

The meal had ended some while before. Magda, Joyce and the Broackes' house guests had gone to take their siestas around the pool, but Nigel and I lingered at the table talking. Still impressively handsome, he'd put on size and weight, he moved with slow dignity. And he'd grown in gravitas. Mentally he was sharp as ever, but over the years he'd become less interested in listening.

Taking a sip of brandy, he leaned back in his cushioned chair to remark, 'Yes ... if pressed, I must admit that on the whole it's all turned out quite well.' The gesture of his cigar embraced the bottle of Napoleon brandy on the table, and the view beyond over the sunlit garden and his life. 'But ...' he added.

But he'd *worked* for it, he went on to say, he'd worked for it very hard from a very early age. In fact, he'd never done anything *except* work. I knew it was true; unlike myself, he'd committed and buckled down from the start. As I listened to him talking about his life the sound of a loud splash and laughter reached us from the pool. For a moment I worried it was Joyce who had gone into the water, the weight of gold she was wearing would have dragged her to the bottom at once. But, unruffled by the danger, Nigel drew on his cigar and continued. He'd never had leisure, or a single life, or a private life; never had the freedom to be irresponsible or act on whim. *He'd never had a youth*. 'I miss it,' he said.

'But why can't you have one *now*?' I asked. 'You can afford it, you can buy yourself a belated randy adolescence.'

He puffed on his cigar. Smoke poured from him, he looked as if he were on fire. 'No I can't,' he explained. 'If I go out at night without taking the Rolls I don't just have to invent a convincing excuse for Joyce, but come up with a story for the chauffeur.'

He'd built himself a golden cage.

The Mayles' house in St Jeannet finally became free and they moved there to set up home. The commune finished work on the apartment they'd been occupying ... and the restoration of the mill was complete. For almost four years Magda and I had devoted our time, energy and money to making it perfect, united in a shared endeavour which had dominated our lives. Now it was done; we had no common interest or work to fill our day. But the weather stayed good even in winter, and I skied.

'You haf more fun zan me,' Magda said. 'You ski, and you stay up late to read, you use more electricity.'

In winter the sun disappeared behind the ridge soon after lunch, and in spring it rained a lot. No TV signal penetrated the gorge we lived in. We had time together ... and time to reflect. Frank Lowe and the Broackes came only in summer; out of season, the Côte d'Azur is a retirement community. It was true we had Vincent and the commune for diversion but, 'What's the *point* of poor people? What are zey *for*?' Magda asked me.

I was stuck for a pithy answer. My attempt at an explanation clearly did not satisfy her, and I found myself brooding about her question afterwards.

One afternoon we were on the terrace idly gazing upstream when she remarked, 'Ven zee old sisters die vee can restore zee mill vere zey are living and sell it for *real* money.'

'That's not going to happen for a while,' I told her.

'It *could*,' she insisted, and I laughed uneasily.

'I could put a curse on them,' she said. 'I haf not told you, but I am a witch.' I looked at her sharply and saw the expression on her face.

She had always been less enamoured by the simple life than the Mayles or myself. She flew to Paris to stay with friends, and on her return mentioned she'd visited Notre Dame. I was surprised, for religious faith played no part in her life.

'I lit a candle zere and prayed zee old sisters would die. I put a curse on zem,' she said.

A sense of dread came over me as I realised she was serious.

On a drizzly winter evening I stood by the river in the dusk and stared at the water flowing by ... and it didn't look like Walden Pond any more. The forested walls of the ravine seemed to close in on me in the thickening gloom. In the dark mass of the mill only a single light was showing, ghostly in the mist. The room where Magda was waiting. The low rumble of the waterfall sounded in my ears like a reproach.

I'd fallen in love with this place. I'd thought there was peace here, and fulfilment and a kind of wisdom, and for a time there *had* been; I'd believed it was Arcadia. But all the while we'd spent making it into that, I'd been building myself a jail. As effectively as Nigel, I'd constructed my own prison. And it wasn't even solitary confinement. I had a cell-mate I'd come to realise I didn't love and did not even especially *like*.

24
46 Lower Belgrave Street

The two tomatoes were each as big as a fist. Cutting them into thick segments, I fried them in olive oil and garlic on the Calor stove. As there was only one pan, I had to remove them to make fried bread and at the precise moment it started to go brown I added a light coating of soft cheese ... Transferring the meal to a plate, I set it on the folding table on the tiny terrace together with a single orange for dessert; dinner was served.

Usually I ate fish, but a money transfer I was expecting hadn't come through. The situation was as familiar as the range of economy menus which went with. Dinner tonight was an especial favourite, well matched by a sturdy red at 400 pesetas a 5-litre jerrycan.

I'd landed here in Ibiza after a winter on the road passed in guest bedrooms and bad hotels. A trail of dirty laundry abandoned in left-luggage lockers through northern Europe lay behind me. I was back to what I could carry in a leather grip.

Provence, the mill, Magda were no more a part of my life and, tonight as every night, I dined alone. I had fled from France.

I believe Magda had an image of her ideal mate which in New York I'd appeared to fit. But I was no longer that man, if ever I had been, nor was she the woman I'd blindly fallen for there. At the mill we'd got to know each other, and that had proved fatal. It was clear to both of us we could not remain together.

The studio apartment I was renting in Ibiza – one of six in a shabby, breeze-block cube – was modern and tacky. Its terrace was cramped, but the view magnificent. The pine forest ended only forty yards away in a cliff that dropped straight into the sea. There was no beach and no one ever came this way to disturb the tranquillity of the scene.

Each day followed the same pattern. I got up, threw back the shutters to reveal the view, made coffee and worked through the morning on the terrace. The only sound was the whirr of insects in the forest as the pines warmed in the sun and the scent of resin grew overpowering. In the afternoon I swam, lay on a rock and read. After a solitary dinner I worked until late. It was an ordered routine and a peaceful life; I was happy.

Tout passe, tout casse, tout lasse ... it was too good to last. On the first of August I woke to the sound of voices, flung open the shutters ... and stumbled back in disbelief. The tranquil view had changed, changed utterly. In place of trees and gleam of sea stood a tented encampment. And the area swarmed with people, young people in shorts busy erecting tents, and all talking at the top of their voices in the way only the Spanish know how. They were Boy Scouts, and there were hundreds of them.

They were close, their tent lines began only paces away, but minutes later I observed them in even greater detail. The scout leader's decision to site their wash house two metres from my bathroom window had been dictated by the block's plumbing. The spine of the rectangular shower tent, whose sides stood open, had been equipped with waterpipes and a double row of showerheads. The wrap-around view revealed to me was of pubescent boys dancing naked on the duckboards, squealing beneath the jets.

Had I been a true, red-blooded pederast, like so many Englishmen I knew, the prospect would have been unimaginable nubile heaven. And even I ... No, no, I told myself firmly, this is no time for such a whim plus a three-stretch in a Spanish jail! Besides, I was here to work. I was writing a book. It was about Lord Lucan.

It's said that a writer does not choose a story, the story chooses him. Four years before in Vence I'd bought a day-old English paper to read on a café terrace. The photograph of 'Lucky' Lucan on the front page was instantly familiar. That haughty tilt to the head, lidded eyes and faint sardonic smile were unmistakable. Often in casinos I'd found myself watching him among his friends, listening to the patrician drawl and manner that said the world was his.

The paper stated that his children's nanny had been murdered, and his wife Veronica savagely assaulted. Lucan's borrowed Ford Corsair had been found abandoned at Newhaven. His whereabouts were unknown; the noble lord had done a runner and disappeared. He was either dead, or somewhere busy reinventing himself ...

It was now 1978 and Lucan's hiding-place was still undiscovered, though a warrant existed for his arrest on a charge of murder. From the start I'd been unusually fascinated by the events of that November night, and I became obsessed, as have so many who have probed the same mystery.

Lucan was a member of a circle of men who were very

close. Some I knew directly or indirectly. Dominic Elwes had married Ben Fisher's cousin; Charles Benson's wife was a friend of Tania's; Tania had dated Jimmy Goldsmith. All I knew by sight. Most of them were old Etonians, most had served in the Guards or a Cavalry regiment, few had been to university. They formed a tight coterie my own age, a small tribe who shared the same upbringing, education, politics, dress, attitude and tastes. Lucan himself was the archetype of the men I'd known and detested in the regiment.

Only once had I seen his wife, Veronica. A small, shy, insecure woman, for her Lucan had been a 'catch'. They had nothing in common except their snobbery; both were prisoners of class. As the marriage deteriorated she'd taken to following him to the Clermont club to watch him gamble. He couldn't stand her near him by then and the evening I saw her she sat alone, outside the circle. Even the women did not trouble to hide their scorn. Her vigil must have been unendurable – yet night after night she put herself in for it. I felt pity for her, at the same time repelled by that bubble of scary alienation that surrounds the mad.

Lucan continued to lose remorselessly over ten years. By the date of his disappearance he was reduced to working as a 'house player' at the casino, he was good furniture. By then his inheritance of £250,000 was long gone; his overdrafts and debts amounted to £20,000, plus legal fees estimated at £40,000.

A year before the murder, Lucan had left the family house to rent a flat. Convinced Veronica was mentally unstable and incapable of looking after their three children, he snatched them from their nanny in Green Park, and kept them with him in his cramped basement apartment until the custody case came to court. Losing it, he was saddled with enormous costs. His bitterness was incalculable. He genuinely loved his children, his feelings for them, and most particularly for his son and heir, were passionate. 'More like an obsession', his mother described them. He'd exhausted all legal recourse – by now the only way to rescue them was for Veronica to die.

I do not believe he planned to kill her himself, I think he hired an accomplice to do so. The evening of 7 November he drove by the Clermont in his Mercedes, speaking to the doorman to give himself an alibi, then quickly back to his own flat where he switched to the Ford Corsair he'd borrowed from his friend Michael Stoop. Then he drove to Lower Belgrave Street to fulfil his intention.

What happened in the unlit basement of that dismal little house is unclear, but something went horribly wrong. 'A terrible catastrophe ... blood ... mess,' Lucan described it to his mother on the telephone an hour later. The wrong woman had been killed, his accomplice fled, and Veronica, hysterical and bleeding, run off down the street. He had only moments to escape before she raised the alarm.

It was 9.45 on a wet winter's night in central London. He was in the most appalling trouble. He had blood on his trousers, very little money and no plan. But he had friends ...

E. M. Forster famously said, 'If I had to choose between betraying my country and betraying my friend, I hope I should have the guts to betray my country.'

To violate the laws of England was entirely alien to the group surrounding Lucan. The idea of 'country' was very important to them. They *were* England, an integral part of its establishment. But in the mid-seventies, the times were gravely out of joint in Britain ... economic recession, strikes, social unrest, kidnapping, bombs. The Left had come to power and the rich were running scared. Colonel David Stirling, who had commanded the SAS, was putting together a private army to combat trade union militancy and 'keep the country going'. Michael Stoop, among others, had volunteered to join, and there was wild talk of mounting a military coup.

They, this group of men and women who'd been accustomed to privilege and deference all their lives, believed the country wasn't *theirs* any more. One of their last strongholds had been breached when the Clermont was bought by the downmarket Playboy Club. The barbarian horde of admen, media people, lesser show-biz, real estate agents, hairdressers and Arabs had swarmed in; *the wrong sort of people* had taken over. Lucan and his set loathed these uppity arrivistes who didn't know their place. They hated what was happening. They felt themselves embattled, an endangered species, and it drew them close.

So, when Lucan went to them that night for help in his desperate need, how had they acted, I wondered. While researching the book I spoke to a number of people, among them David Gerring, one of the two police officers who'd run the investigation. Now retired, he was landlord of a country pub near Gatwick, where he could relax in his twin pleasures of drinking and talking.

'It was a world none of us had met before,' he said, speaking of the enquiry. 'I mean, it was like you had to go cap in hand. There was this snooty old dowager who wouldn't talk to us and I said, 'Madam, this is a criminal investigation, the nanny's been murdered.' 'Such a pity,' she said, 'So hard to find staff these days."

Gerring was convinced Lucan had been hidden, then smuggled to France in a private plane. Equipped with funds and a new passport, from there he'd escaped to East Africa. Gerring had traced and spoken on the telephone to a German doctor who'd been trapped with Lucan by a *coup d'état* in Madagascar. A revolution was going on, the island was in chaos; Gerring was refused the funds to fly there and follow up the contact.

'So what's this book you're doing, exactly?' he asked me late in our first conversation.

'The story *after* the murder,' I told him. 'Where he was hidden, and how his friends rallied round to get him out the country.'

Gerring's face changed expression. 'That wouldn't be clever,' he said.

'It would be *interesting*,' I maintained.

He gave an emphatic shake of the head, 'No, you can't do that,' he insisted. And then he did something extraordinary. The saloon bar where we sat was large and only four other people were in it, at the far end of the room. Yet Gerring glanced left and right to check we were unheard, then leaned towards me, lowering his voice to say, '*You can't upset the Golden Man.*'

He'd been so jovial till then, so bluff and down-to-earth, this shadow of paranoia was absurd yet oddly chilling. Gerring was so in awe of James Goldsmith he would not speak his name for fear of invoking him. He was *afraid* of Goldsmith, I realised.

And perhaps with reason. On the day after the murder a group of Lucan's friends was hurriedly summoned by John Aspinall to lunch at the Clermont. The company included Bill Shand-Kydd (once headboy at Stowe), Daniel Meinertzhagen, Dominic Elwes, Charles Benson and Stephen Raphael. That council-of-war was reported by *Private Eye*, who stated that James Goldsmith had attended the meeting – and in this they were wrong, for he'd been in Paris that day. Goldsmith's response was to issue sixty-three writs against the agents distributing the magazine, including one he owned himself. He then sued Richard Ingrams, its editor, and Patrick Marnham, who'd written the piece, for criminal libel. 'I'll throw them in prison. I'll hound their wives, even in their widows' weeds,' he bragged.

The legal battle went on for seventeen months. In all, Goldsmith brought a total of nine separate actions and issued over one hundred writs, including an injunction to restrain five journalists (Auberon Waugh, Nigel Dempster, Patrick Marnham, Michael Gillard, Richard West) from writing anything about him in any publication anywhere. *Private Eye* was forced to settle out of court for £45,000 damages plus Goldsmith's costs; the magazine barely survived.

Goldsmith was a man implacable in his wars – and dangerous. Gerring's vehemence on this subject was compelling and ultimately persuasive. If I was going to write about Lucan's disappearance and the Clermont set, it would be wise to do so in the guise of fiction, a *roman a clef*, I decided.

My novel, *Hunted,* was published in the UK by W. H. Allen. Before it came out I left the apartment in Ibiza and moved to London to be present at its birth. Because of the years I'd spent in advertising I reckoned I knew something about marketing and promotion, and over lunch with Aubrey Davies, Allen's commissioning editor, asked what plans there were for publicity. His response was evasive, Allen's were in dire financial trouble. There was no money available for publicity or promotion.

'*None?*' I asked, astonished.

Well ... he thought he could get authorisation of a sum up to £25. The news was discouraging.

Just before the book came out *Private Eye* ran a piece saying that 'after representation by person or persons unknown' the publishers had taken the highly unusual step of putting a red wrapper round the book stating that the events described were purely fictitious and not based on anyone, either alive or dead. The next issue of the magazine, only a few days after *Hunted*'s release, stated that all copies of the book had been removed from Allen's stockroom, all remaining warehouse copies ordered in a single order for despatch, and sales reps instructed not to continue to offer the title. 'It would seem that Allen's management has only just discovered what the book is about and has ordered these last-ditch efforts to stop the tome's publication.'

By now I was in a high state of agitation. My baby was being strangled at birth. Aubrey Davies was not taking my calls and I was close to despair when I received a call from a man, who described himself as a freelance publicist. 'I've read your book,' he said. 'I'd like to talk to you about promoting it.'

I'd like that too, I said. We met that same evening in the bar of the Westbury. He was a slightly built Frenchman in his thirties with an air of energy and competence, and I took to him instinctively. We talked for a while about *Hunted*. He'd obviously read it with care, for he spoke perceptively of characters and scenes in it, and I began to warm in that onanistic glow a writer experiences when so indulged. Not only did this fellow have initiative, but also taste and judgement, I thought.

'Now, as to publishing it ... I don't think you should promote it on the Lucan connection,' he said.

I was set aback. The book was *about* Lucan, there was no other way *to* promote it, I protested.

'No, it's really not a good idea,' he said.

'Why ever not?' I asked.

'Because ...' He raised his glass, took a sip, and reached out to replace it on the table, and all the while his eyes stayed fixed on mine, 'Because if you keep trying to do so, one day you will be walking down a street and a stranger will overtake you from behind. Up his sleeve he will have a baseball bat and as he draws level with you he will slide it down till he is grasping the handle. As he steps past he will swing backwards at your leg with all his force. Your leg will be broken, but if he does it correctly and strikes the kneecap it will shatter. The knee is a complicated joint, difficult to repair. You will never be able to bend your leg again and you will feel pain for the rest of your life.' He smiled at me pleasantly.

The situation was unreal. My knowledge of publishing came from Father, who sometimes met his agent A. P. Watt for sausages and mash at the RAC club; no one had ever threatened to break *his* legs. Yet here in the Westbury this man was telling me I would be *kneecapped*! *This* was the literary world? I stared at him in dismay.

Fortunately the above scenario did not come to pass. Six months later *Hunted* was bought by Simon & Schuster and published in the USA; it went into paperback and sold the film rights.

My last conversation with David Gerring took place some years after all this. I'd remained fascinated by the case, as he was himself – he wanted to rename his pub *The Vanishing Earl.*

Like Gerring, I was convinced Lucan had been gotten out of England; he had not committed suicide. Goethe has a poem:

Wealth lost, something lost.
Honour lost, much lost
Courage lost, all lost.

On that wet winter's night, as he stood in blood-spattered trousers in Lower Belgrave Street, wealth and honour were already lost to Lucan, but courage remained to him. And he was a gambler, that was his profession and his deepest nature. He would always go for the outside chance rather than throw in the hand.

But the murder and his escape had taken place five years ago by now. Where was he, and *how was he surviving*? That baffled me. 'All right,' I agreed with Gerring. 'Let's say it's as you claim, Lucan reached Africa, but how is he living now? He's incapable of earning a living or looking after himself, he scarcely knows how to boil an egg. His friends may have helped him escape, but they wouldn't give him a pension for life.'

'Let me put it this way,' Gerring answered. 'In the world of common villains that *I* know they're tight with their muckers too. If one of their mates gets into trouble, they help him. The *once*! But if he then gets to be an embarrassment *they have him taken care of*, know what I mean?'

He paused and added, 'Not that I'd want to say anything to upset anyone, you understand.'

25
Earls Court

Observing the uncertainty of Father's life, I had resolved never to embrace writing as a career.

'Yet as a job it has just about everything,' I said to my old friend Peter over dinner. 'It provides travel on the excuse of "research". You can choose your own hours; you have no boss, the work itself is absorbing. It provides every thing one could possibly want except one – money.'

'That's not *necessarily* the case,' Peter answered with considerable tact as he addressed himself to his order of *pomodori secchi con mozzarella e rucola*.

He'd published several books by now, all non-fiction, slim and profitable. He was in London on a reluctant visit to promote the latest; his day had been a full one in every sense, but he was in boyish form. 'Nothing like a good lunch to give you an appetite for a good dinner,' he'd observed as we studied the menu in La Famiglia.

'All my books were designed in order to make money,' he

explained. 'I had to earn thirty or forty grand a year before Jennie and I had a centime to spend ourselves. However, what I've at last decided to do is write a book which is *not* going to make money ...'

As an ambition it was easier to achieve than most, I thought. For I was broke, the money I'd made from the film sale of *Hunted* was all but gone. On splitting up with Magda we'd decided to sell the mill and divide the spoils, and she had remained to handle its sale. But, though the economy in Britain was booming in the 'eighties, the same was not true of France. And though a number of potential purchasers had visited the mill, no one as yet had wanted to buy a property which had two sitting tenants, in the shape of the old sisters, occupying one of its buildings.

'Why don't you approach Frank Lowe for a job' Peter suggested. 'He picked us up in his executive jet last week and flew us to lunch in Nice. He's running his own agency and is seriously rich and successful now.'

I hated the idea of going back into commercials and reconciled myself to the fact that Peter was of no help with career advice but remained the best of dinner companions. We talked of people we knew in London and New York, most of them still in advertising, and what we'd read and done since we'd last met. He and Jennie had sold their village house and moved to a farmhouse in the Luberon, which they were living in while restoring. 'A total nightmare,' he said. 'Cement mixers and rubble and no electricity and workmen who don't turn up. It's been going on for an entire year now.'

I sympathised; doing up the mill had been the same. Over coffee I asked him about his book which was designed *not* to make money.

'I've pretty much finished it,' he admitted. 'Ernie Chapman showed the draft to Hamish Hamilton, who've come up with an advance of £3,000.'

'That's really stingy,' I said.

'Yes, but they know they won't sell many copies,' he explained.

Peter's previous books had all been better deals than this; it was dispiriting to hear he was going downhill. I must be the one to settle this dinner bill, I decided.

'What's the book called? Have you got a snappy title?' I asked while looking around for our waiter.

'Quite a dull one, in fact. I'm thinking of calling it *A Year in Provence*,' Peter told me.

Finally I succeeded in catching Alvaro's eye, then turned back to Peter. 'Well, you have plenty of time to come up with something better,' I reassured him.

I was invited by the Broackes to their London home.

Set behind a high wall topped with razor wire, only a stone's throw from Harrods, I found an English manor house whose windows opened on to an extensive garden with a swimming pool and even a stream purling through the grounds. The living room was of matching size and opulence, almost overpoweringly big and grand. And so too were the Broackes, both had grown impressively since I'd last seen them in France. Nigel glowed pink with health and well-being, Joyce's deep tan set off her ample jewellery to perfection – they'd just returned from a trip to India.

The couple inhabited a different world from most, but were as hospitable and welcoming as ever. 'Where are you living?' Nigel asked, and I told him with Jenny Beerbohm at her flat in Earls Court.

'The model who married ...?'

' ... Tony Beerbohm, head of school at Stowe, yes that's the one,' I said.

'Doesn't she have a child? I thought you detested children.'

Not *detested*, I corrected him, but I had always found them quite boring. Maybe one grows more tolerant with age, I suggested.

We agreed people do change with the passing years – *some* people. 'Speaking of which, what news of Alex Howard?' Nigel asked.

I could tell him, for as it happened I'd run into his ex-wife, Arabella, outside a newsagent's in the Fulham Road. Tall and gaunt, with long dark hair, she was wearing a sari which covered most of her, but what showed was a most peculiar colour; she looked as though she had spent weeks in a bath of cold tea.

I'd always liked her, I found her artless eccentricity endearing, but I didn't recognise her until she spoke, or rather shouted. Her piercing aristocratic screech, so like Mother's, was unmistakable. Her colour was due to a combination of sun and hepatitis, she explained. She'd passed the last year living under a tree in India with her and Alex's 15-year-old daughter, both of them under instruction from a guru.

'I want to go back to live there, you should try it,' she said, but I didn't think so; the bathroom arrangements sounded less than satisfactory. We stood there chatting on the busy corner, surrounded by people, and I asked if she knew Alex's whereabouts or what he was up to.

'He's in the *East*,' she shrieked. 'Haven't you heard, he's become a *spy*. Doing *frightfully* well.'

Nigel chuckled at the news. Alex's father had been in espionage, but neither of us had thought of it as a family business. I went on to ask Nigel what *he* was up to by way of work and he told me of his current activities as chairman of London Docklands' development, and his plan to build a Channel tunnel. It wasn't until I was about to leave that he revealed his intention to start a charity. I was struck, for, though he served on the board of a major housing trust, actually to found a charity of his own indicated a philanthropic commitment I hadn't met before.

'Well, I've done pretty well from life,' he said. 'But when a man gets to be our sort of age, Jeremy, he starts to think he'd like to *put something back*, to *give* something to society in return ...'

Talking in this vein the three of us strolled from the living room and through the hall to the front door. Outside, a roofed porch gave on to the street. As Nigel opened the door to let me out the three of us saw this was occupied. A bag lady with a shopping trolley loaded with possessions was asleep there. Coming out we woke her and she started up.

Nigel didn't hesitate. '*Out of order!*' he pronounced.

Joyce joined her voice to his. 'You can't sleep *there*,' she said firmly.

'Move along!' Nigel ordered. 'Quickly now! Move!'

I knew that over the years the Broackes had contributed thousands of pounds, and in his case many hours of unpaid work to charity. But how curiously wrong people are in believing it starts at home, I thought.

Jenny and I had been together for the last two years. Her flat was in a Victorian mansion block directly opposite the Coleherne, a notorious leather bar at the heart of London's gay ghetto. Earls Court was the catchment area for Australians, poor Arabs, foreign students and transsexuals who, like opposing species of game, occupied the same territory and used the same watering holes, peaceably ignoring each other except for sudden eruptions of violence at kill-time when the pubs closed.

Aged thirty-six, ten years younger than myself, Jenny was a statuesque, good-looking blonde – 'As a model I got the tits and ass jobs' – of high intelligence, who'd been denied an education; her three brothers had gone to Oxford but she had left school at seventeen. Her mother was Jewish, her father a left-wing writer and intellectual in Berlin. The couple had escaped Germany very late, arriving in Britain as refugees only just before the war. He'd been interned on the Isle of Man, she'd struggled to keep herself and two infants by making toys and doing anything that came to hand. When Jenny was born the war was over but things were just as desperate, and remained so. She escaped her family by becoming a model and she'd married Tony because he spoke in an upper-class accent, had a good job and because his name was spelled SECURITY. Wrong, of course, life's an accidental business however you try to insure against it.

Jenny and I shared a love of books and travel, the same need for time alone, and a strong sexual attraction. My previous relationships had always contained an element of rivalry, yet in this was peace and an unaccustomed stability.

Her son, Edward, was eight. Having been a more than absent father to Sasha, I had never lived in the same house with a child, but he, like his mother, had a taste for privacy; mostly we kept to our own rooms, meeting up for meals. What made the experience fascinating was his talent for music. He spent his evenings listening to and composing classical music. His maternal grandmother, now old, shrunken and living in poverty in Italy, was possessed by the same all-consuming compulsion. Until her death at the age of eighty every moment of her day was passed in sculpting, writing or painting stones and fragments of tile with painstaking skill to transform them into art. The impulse of creativity flowed in her as a palpable force and her energy was phenomenal. And Edward had inherited the same mysterious dynamic.

In Jenny's flat I lived as a cuckoo in the nest, but the three of us cohabited easily. Money came in irregularly; at times there was cash for air tickets and hotels, at others we were flat broke. But in penury was a human warmth and closeness I'd not known before.

Neither Jenny nor Edward came with me, but on Sundays I attended St Luke's church in Redcliffe Square which, a hundred years before, regularly had accommodated 700 local residents at the morning service and an equal number of their domestic servants in the evening. The congregation now numbered sixty, most of them elderly women.

John Barton, the vicar, was my own age, with a vivacious, pretty wife, and a son of five. He had moved to St Luke's from a parish in Dover and a number of his former parishioners were now resident in geriatric homes in an advanced state of disintegration. John continued to visit them, as well as attend to his new parish, and over the course of two or three years I accompanied him on some of these trips to the country, stopping for a pub lunch on the way.

I was aware his marriage had grown thorny, but during one of these drives he let drop that his wife had left him; she'd gone off with another man, taking their son. He mentioned the fact rather than announced it, and we spoke about it for a few minutes in a detached, very English way, as if we were talking about someone else.

In the following fortnight John's father died, closely followed by his mother. An only son, he was very attached to both. He buried them, then returned to an empty vicarage and continued with his pastoral duties. Partly organisational, these consisted mostly in aiding elderly pensioners, the unemployed and the homeless in their struggle with bureaucracy, and in comforting the sick and dying.

'How can you continue to do this, *now*?' I asked him.

'I know I'm in shock. I feel unreal, as if I'm walking on the thinnest, thinnest ice,' he admitted. 'Sometimes I feel like tearing my clothes off in the street and howling at the sky.'

'So what stops you?' I asked.

'*Something*,' he said. 'Grace, perhaps, and prayer.'

I stood in awe of the faith that grounded him and gave him such stability. I wondered if it would do the same for me. As things stood, I doubted it.

Whatever people say, lack of money exerts a pressure on a relationship. 'The perils of the everyday,' Jenny called them. And I too suffered from flashes of nostalgia for that carefree prosperity I'd enjoyed only a few years before.

By now I'd published another novel, *Angels in Your Beer*, which had received fair reviews but sold few copies. The money from a film option had paid for a couple of summers in Spain for Jenny, Edward and myself, but was now gone. And I owed tax on it. It was disconcerting to see how, despite all my efforts to the contrary, my situation had come to mirror Father's, who was still living in penury in his dank thatched cottage attended by the faithful Adriana.

At a party given by a friend of Jenny's I was discussing the shortcomings of authorship with a literary agent, Don Short. He – it transpired – had a lucrative trade selling celebrity revelations into mass-market paperbacks, and lurid exposés to the Sunday tabloids. I was saying to him very much what I'd said to Peter Mayle.

The light was poor in the crowded flat, but I detected a faint gleam come into Don Short's eye. 'If you want some quick cash I know of something that might interest you,' he said.

26
Claridge's

Judy Mazel leaned forward across the table in San Lorenzo to grip my wrist tightly. 'Listen,' she said, 'I'm loved by millions of people all over the world, I've discovered the cure for fat and transformed their lives. I'm a rich, beautiful woman, the number one best-selling author in the universe. I've made ten million dollars, I've bought every item in the Valentino collection and what I want now are orgasms, Jeremy, *orgasms*.'

She was a pale blonde of thirty-eight, thin to the point of emaciation; the skin of her face was drawn tightly across the bones. She never laughed and I'd seen people drop their eyes from hers in embarrassment, disconcerted by the strain of her expression and the fierce intensity of her demanding gaze. She was the inventor of the Beverly Hills Diet; her book had been number one in the USA for thirty-four weeks and topped the best-seller charts throughout Europe, South Africa, Australia and Japan. She'd become internationally famous, a millionaire celebrity.

I was working for her. William Morris, her agent, had proposed she capitalise upon her celebrity and make a second fortune by writing a novel. Her approach was pragmatic. She herself did not write; for her diet book she had hired a journalist, for her novel she would hire a novelist.

On the face of it, the deal appeared good. William Morris believed they could get an advance of $1 million in the USA. Then there was Britain and the rest of the world, probably also a film sale. Judy and I were to split the money 50:50; no fewer than four literary agents were involved, but even after they had taken their percentages my share still looked appealing.

I'd met Judy the week before in Claridge's where she had taken up residence. She swept downstairs and came fast across the lobby towards me, a neat, doll-like woman with a suppressed frenzy in the way she moved. She sat down and ordered a beer for me and an orange juice for herself, but we'd barely started talking when she began to shift and look about her restlessly. Suddenly she sprang to her feet. 'We'll move there,' she announced, and set off rapidly across the room. After a moment I picked up her drink and my own and joined her. 'No, over there,' she said, as the same inner compulsion drove her to change tables yet again.

She was very hard to talk to. A naturally plump child, her doctor had prescribed diet pills in increasing massive doses from the age of eight. She'd remained on them until her conversion to the Beverly Hills Diet. Her concentration span was down to about eight seconds.

She explained to me that the heroine in her novel was herself, this would be *her* story. But it was a biography with a difference, for it would be the life she *wished* she had lived. In it, every humiliation she had suffered – and there were many – would become a triumph, every defeat a victory. 'And I don't want her wishy-washy,' she instructed. 'You heard of Catherine the Great? Like her.'

In San Lorenzo we discussed the plot. The restaurant was crowded with the usual glitterati, many of whom she knew, for she was serviced by three separate PR consultants working concurrently to set up signings, TV appearances, lunches and parties. She was forever springing up to dart across the restaurant to accost someone. It was hard to keep her on track, but what we agreed to do was tape her real story, then alter everything, substituting white for black, adding lurid colour and frothing the mix into a blockbuster.

I asked Judy whether the book would be written in the first or third person. She looked at me blankly.

'Will the heroine be 'I' or 'she'?' I enquired, and explained the advantages and disadvantages of each method, the automatic empathy obtained from the reader if you wrote as 'I', the flexibility and wider range of scenes if related as 'she'.

'I,' she instructed predictably. Then, a few minutes later over coffee, she said, 'I've been thinking and we're going to do my novel in first *and* third person.'

'No, you can't do that,' I said.

She jerked back, it was as if I'd struck her. Her face pinched with fury. She hissed, 'All my life people have been telling me I can't do things and I've proved them *wrong*, *wrong*, *wrong*! I *will* do it!' Her small fist thumped the table so hard the cups rattled.

Fasten your seat belt, I thought, this is going to be a bumpy ride.

'Why aren't you thin and pretty like your sisters?' her mother had asked Judy as a child. Dosed with pills, she had been kept so hungry on her constant diet that at night she picked through her parents' discarded leftovers. Steak fat became her favourite snack. In her thirties, while living on benefit in Venice, California, Judy took charge of her own case. Becoming her own laboratory rat, she reduced her weight from 170 to 98 pounds. 'Being fat,' she stated in her diet book, 'Has little to do with what or how much you eat. Food fully digested can't make you fat, it's only undigested food stuck in your body that accumulates to become fat.' Proteins should be eaten only with other proteins, carbohydrates with carbohydrates, and high-calorie binges can be offset by corrective feasts of fruit. This was the theory she'd developed into the Beverly Hills Diet.

Medical reaction to her book, when it came out, was hostile. 'Ludicrous,' said the Professor of Nutrition at Columbia University, 'Not one element of the diet or one sentence in the book has any scientific basis whatever.' He warned of perforated peptic ulcers together with a risk of cardiac arrhythmia and death. An article in the *Journal of the American Medical Association* identified eighteen major misstatements of simple scientific fact, its authors telling the *Los Angeles Times* they had found ten times that number of errors but the *Journal* didn't have space for any more.

Medical censure seemed only to increase the book's sales; Macmillan followed it with *The Beverly Hills Diet Lifetime Plan*, paying Judy $900,000 as an advance. A week after publication the book was number one in the best-seller list.

In November I went to Claridge's to start taping Judy's life. That morning, as I walked towards her suite along the normally hushed corridors of the hotel, I could hear from thirty yards away the violent row taking place within.

The scene inside was one of remarkable confusion. Every piece of furniture was littered with clothes. An agitated task force of two maids, a housekeeper, assistant manager, and a room-service waiter were searching the piles while, like a demented fury, Judy flew between the rooms shrieking abuse as she tore open drawers and closets to snatch up a further armful of clothes and fling them at the staff. She was so overwrought it was minutes before I could fathom what had happened to cause such drama. The belt to one of her Valentino dresses, the one she wanted to wear *right now*, was missing.

The response of the hotel employees, and their evident terror under the tongue-lashing of this tiny woman, was due to the fact that, only a week before, the hotel had lost a collar to one of her dresses on the way to or from the dry cleaner. On that occasion Judy had insisted a hall porter be sent to Rome to replace it.

Refusing to be drawn into the search, I sat down at the writing desk and started to go through my notes, waiting for the storm to pass. Such behaviour on my part was clearly unacceptable to Judy, for it brought on a fresh paroxysm of fury. My apparent calm before the onslaught – a calm I did not feel – so enraged her that, losing all control, she began to pound her fists upon the wall. At that moment the telephone on the desk started to ring.

No one made a move to answer it. After a few moments I picked it up. 'This is Lady Rothermere's secretary,' said a woman's voice, 'I've just spoken to her in Jamaica. She says she's been eating papayas for three days, she has very bad diarrhoea and her anus is inflamed. What should she do?'

I hesitated ... 'Judy will have to get back to her in that area,' I said.

I delivered the draft of a first chapter to Judy. She started work on it at once with a coloured pen while I sat at the writing desk going through the transcript of what we'd recorded. At lunchtime I said I was going out to get something to eat.

'No,' she told me, 'I don't want you doing that. You can eat here today, but not every day because it's very expensive. From now on you must bring your own food.'

I ordered a sandwich from room service while she asked for three plates of toast. When it came she removed the top from the paprika bottle she carried with her, emptied it in a mound on the tablecloth and used it as a dip. This was merely an appetiser; when it was finished she took from the closet the gnawed carcass of a chicken, scarred by bite marks. Behind it on the shelf I saw vegetables, nuts, biscuits and the bags of boiled sweets which she sucked constantly.

While eating she continued work. When she'd finished she threw the grease-stained pages at me. Some of her changes were good, some were not, but, scrawled in green ink, her words might as well have been carved in granite for she would amend nothing. Amongst other additions, she had put in the sentence, 'In childhood I nailed my foundations.'

'You can't say "nail",' I objected, and she glared at me as I went on, 'You don't "nail" foundations, you pour or lay them.'

'This is *my* book,' she snapped, 'And I'll say whatever I want. A word means exactly what I want it to mean.' She fixed me with a look. 'I'm going to fart,' she said.

Judy's eating habits were eccentric. Sweets, toast, bread rolls ... she ate the entire time. Several times each morning she'd mix a rank-smelling paste of bran and yeast which caused welts to raise across her skin and briefly turned her complexion bright red. She had a metabolism like a furnace and a voracious appetite. I arrived at her suite at 10 am one day to find her clutching a roast pheasant in her hands. She consumed it then wiped her bloody mouth and announced, 'Lord Weidenfeld is gonna publish my novel.'

'Without reading it?' I asked.

'I sucked him off last night and he promised to buy anything I come up with.'

She'd sold the UK rights? I didn't believe it for a moment, but to my astonishment a cheque came through a couple of weeks later. But Judy was discontent. 'He's never asked me out since,' she complained. 'He only screwed me to get my book.'

Only two things calmed her, eating and shopping. She was earning literally millions of dollars from the worldwide sales of her diet book; she spent it with an urgent frenzy. She flew everywhere first class, she would drink only Roederer Cristal champagne, she bought clothes and shoes with reckless abandon. She led me through her closets to view her wardrobe of Valentinos, Ungaros and Halstons, indicating her fourteen suitcases and trunks stuffed with originals still in their wrappings. 'In the next chapter,' she said, 'I want to wear this shirt with these $80 pantyhose and this froufy short skirt which shows off my cute little legs and makes me look thin as a minute.'

The heroine of her novel and her real self became inseparable in Judy's mind, and as her invitations dwindled she grew more and more demanding. After church on Christmas Day she telephoned as I was helping Jenny prepare lunch. 'I want to work, I want you to come round,' she said.

I told her I couldn't and she said, 'You don't understand. I'm alone *and all I got to think about is my novel.*'

One morning we set off for the British Film Institute to research the background of the various Hollywood stars she intended using in her book. On our way there I explained we must be discreet in the library, for we were not BFI members and had no right to use it.

But she wasn't listening. 'I want you to take me to see Randy Newman on Saturday night,' she said.

I explained that I was sorry, but I could not. She said, 'I want you to take me to lunch on Sunday.'

I explained that I had a date, but surely she knew lots of people ... 'No, I want to be with *you*,' she stated. As we drew up outside the BFI she said, 'I want you to marry me, Jeremy.'

I passed it off with a laugh, but I was already wound tight, taut.

She was wearing an ankle-length mink coat and carrying a large paper bag loaded with rolls, bread sticks and pretzels. Marching up to the library counter she issued instructions to a surprised girl who meekly guided her to the shelves, intimidated by such forcefulness. Almost everything the girl produced she rejected as inadequate.

At last we seated ourselves at a table with a pile of film books. While I went through these making notes, Judy took out her food and began voraciously to eat it, scattering crumbs, complaining loudly of the deficiency of the library and upbraiding me for not working fast enough.

In that otherwise silent reading room I felt myself growing more and more tense. She thrust a pile of volumes at me. 'I can't work here,' she announced, 'I want you to take these out.'

I explained we couldn't; it was a reference library, and anyway, we were not members. The reason struck her as irrelevant. She strode to the counter. 'I'm Judy Mazel, the best-selling author,' she announced. 'I want to take these with me.'

Losing this argument drove her to fury. She stamped back to our table and dropped the heavy pile in front of me. 'Go out and buy these,' she instructed. 'Bring them to my suite and we'll work tonight. Or can't you,' she taunted, 'because you're going out with your *boyfriend*? You're a faggot, aren't you, Jeremy?'

I'm a mild man, but something in me snapped. I found

myself on my feet, grasping her by the throat and shaking her like a doll while she shrieked and a wild light of triumph flared in her big blue eyes. Everyone in the crowded library had stopped work and was staring at us. I set her down. This could end very badly, I realised.

By Easter Judy was no longer being interviewed by journalists or invited on to chat shows. Her novel had become all-important; she'd telephone at any hour of the night to discuss it. I'd grown to dread her voice, my nerves would twitch with the effort of restraint. At our meetings she insisted on sitting upon my lap. She had discovered a plot to take her diet book out of the best-seller list; the BMA was trying to suppress her work, she told me.

The conspiracy against Judy spread wider. I arrived one evening while she was changing to go to a first night with Sir Hugh Casson. The BMA had forbidden magazines to publish news of her, she informed me. They had forced the BBC to cancel her TV show. Her skirt was clinging to her thighs, she could not find a slip. She became hysterical, shaking so hard she seemed about to fall apart. 'Hold me!' she ordered.

In horror and pity I found myself obeying, not knowing what else to do.

Finally, I completed taping Judy's life. Now I was faced with the onerous task of changing the real-life Judy Mazel into a bewitching heroine to captivate the reader.

'I've taken a cabana at the Marbella Club for the summer. We'll live there and work on it together,' she informed me.

By now my stomach had contracted to a fist; I felt physically sick when I was with her. Explaining that if there was any hope of turning these crumpled, food-stained pages into a novel I needed seclusion to do so, I told her I intended to install myself in West Malling Abbey, a Benedictine religious order living under a vow of silence which permitted no communication with the outside world. In the whole time I knew Judy this was the sole occasion I saw her lost for words.

She flew to Spain alone, and I did as I'd announced. Over a ten-day retreat I rose at 5 am for matins, spoke to no one, and read nothing published later than the fourteenth century. On my return I holed up in Jenny's flat and went to work. Occasionally in the gossip columns I read of Judy and the scenes she caused in the Marbella Club through the summer. I mailed her my chapters as I finished them. On the telephone to my agent she expressed her displeasure, and set to rewriting them. In September she returned to London. On the 31st, the last date specified in my contract, I delivered the final chapters to Claridge's. When I asked at the desk if she was there, the three hall porters shook their heads and stared at me in a strange, speculative fashion. I left the manuscript with them but remained puzzled by their reaction until next day, when I read that Judy had been arrested.

In Hammersmith Police Station detectives questioned her about a £7,000 cheque which had bounced. There were, it seems, other businesses in London who had provided Judy with goods or services and not been paid. She spent that night locked up in the cells but, next day, her remarkable flair in salesmanship obtained her bail. She fled to California ... and that was the last I ever heard of her or of the book.

27
Gilston Road

Mother died.

Though sudden, it was not wholly unexpected. She was a heavy smoker, attacks of breathlessness had landed her in hospital several times. My brother Hamish, who was living in the basement of Gilston Road, found her – she'd had a heart attack.

My other brother, David, came up from the school where he worked and the three of us sat in the vacated house and felt utterly weird. Unused to being together, we were in shock, possessed by disbelief and that sense that normal rules don't hold and the world is made of glass. In the following days the bureaucracy of death was of help to all of us with its rules and conventions, calls to relatives and family friends, and arrangements that had to be made.

My emotions stayed blocked, but my feelings for Mother anyway were ambivalent. I had never been able to forgive her for how she'd acted at the time of Nanny's death, eleven years before. She had been found in the kitchen, hands still plunged in the sink and her limbs locked rigid with pain. Like a loyal old donkey, she'd gone on working until her body finally gave out and stopped. The hospital found her cancer so advanced it had spread throughout all her organs. The doctor said he'd never seen such an extreme case of malnutrition; for months she had been living on only bread and tea.

'If you're going to be ill you can't be ill *here*,' Mother had told us as children, and the same was said to Nanny, who'd been with her for sixty-four years. She was sent off to die at her sister's house in Clapham. I'd been living in France at the time but flew to visit her there. I was so distressed and grief-stricken I reverted to the uptight, emotionally frozen Englishman I thought I'd long left behind me and was unable to tell her how much she'd meant to me, that I admired and loved her unreservedly, and that any good that might exist within me had come from her alone. But I wrote to her every day until she died.

A week after Mother's death Jenny told me she'd fallen in love with a talented young musician she had been seeing. And this too was not entirely a surprise, but the actual split was horrible, for we'd never fought and still liked each other. But after six years the relationship had leached out through negligence and the perils of the everyday. 'I understand, of course I'll move out,' I told her. We sat at the kitchen table and drank a glass of wine and such a weight of doom fell upon us we could not speak or move but only weep.

I moved into Gilston Road to unpack my single suitcase and leather grip in what had been Mother's room.

Hamish occupied the basement flat, David had the same room he'd had since childhood, which he used only during the holidays, but the family home was otherwise empty. The house was in a disastrous state. Apart from emergency botch-ups, nothing had been done to maintain it for forty years. The 1940s linoleum in the bathroom had cracked into a curled-edge mosaic, the period geyser roared and shook, flaking rust, while discharging a thin dribble of tepid water into the enormous tub. The bomb damage had never been repaired and the top storey, rendered uninhabitable by damp, had been abandoned and shut off.

It was evening when I moved in; having unpacked, I realised there was nothing to eat in the place. I was not at all hungry; shock had sent me manic as it always does, and I had not been able to face food or to sleep for days. But I knew I must eat and went out to buy something from a delicatessen.

I laid a place for one at the Regency table in the dining room, whose leg had given way in 1957 to be refixed crookedly with Seccatine. Swatches of wallpaper bellied from the stained walls, the parchment shades on the light brackets had charred black and two of the forty-watt bulbs were dead. While searching for candles to brighten the room, I found in a kitchen drawer the dried carcass of a mouse imprisoned there when it had shut on him months, perhaps years, before.

Setting the cold turkey, salad and bottle of red wine I'd bought on the table, I sat down to eat. Secluded in its garden, the house was very quiet. I was wired and exhausted, buffeted by recent events, but here was a slightly eerie peace. It felt strange to be eating at this same table where I'd sat as a child, but now alone and at the head of it. The house was full of associations for me; with photographs, letters, school reports, dance cards, invitations, bills, cheque stubs and papers going back 150 years. We'd found an insurance document taken out in New Orleans by Mother's great-grandmother, Héloïse de Mailly, insuring her luggage and two slaves for travel in 1842. And we'd come upon an envelope of love letters to Mother from a married family friend we'd known all our lives. They were devoted to schemes designed to outwit Nanny so they could meet, but there was deep affection there and passion. To read them felt like an intrusion, and to glimpse a stranger who possessed a humanity and capacity for emotion I had not suspected.

The house would not be part of our lives for much longer as my brothers and I had decided to sell it. Despite its dilapidated condition, it was worth a lot of money, for this was the middle of the 'eighties and London property prices were soaring. The value of our eight-bedroomed house in Gilston Road was going up by £2,000 a week.

Over dinner I tried not to brood over the recent past but think positively about the future. In material terms I owned half the mill property, still unsold in France, and a third of a house in Chelsea. My brothers and I lived in squalor but the prospect of wealth was just around the corner. As I mused on my inability to control my own destiny the antique telephone in the hall sprang to life with a particularly loud and strident ring. I went to answer it; it was Susan Newman calling from Los Angeles. She said, 'You've moved house? I called your old number.'

I'd met her on a blind date in New York the year before. The date had been organised by the wife of a director friend, Sally Sapphire, who, after making the suggestion, had called Susan there and then to propose it ... then listened to what was obviously a query about my suitability for a particular event. 'No, no problem,' I heard Sally reassure her, '*You can take him anywhere.*' I thought I'd like the endorsement engraved upon my tombstone.

I didn't really *know* Susan. I'd accompanied her with her father Paul and stepmother Joanne Woodward to the ballet, the theatre and a couple of parties in Manhattan, but no misconduct had taken place, for I was then 'with' Jenny, who would join me in New York. Now Susan was calling me at Gilston Road to say, 'They're giving a party for Dad on Friday. Do you want to come as my date?'

'Why yes, I'd love to,' I told her.

On the flight to LA two days later I still felt displaced, and the sense of unreality was heightened by jetlag. After landing, I looked for Susan, but couldn't spot her among the crowd at the arrivals gate. A figure stepped forward to say 'Hi!' and I stared at her, shaken. In New York she'd been a tall, svelte young woman who had a contract with Estée Lauder. In the months since I'd seen her she'd put on three stones. Dressed in a loose, full-length cotton smock, I'd not recognised her.

I showered and changed at Susan's apartment and we went to pick up her father from the dentist's. A slight figure in Levi's and check shirt, he'd undergone minor heart surgery only a couple of weeks before, and in the car he had the disheveled, slightly traumatised look of someone emerging from a prolonged session of heavy dentistry. His jaw was still numb from anaesthetic and he couldn't speak properly. I thought he could not be looking forward to the party.

The bash was taking place at a hotel in Century City; Susan and I had a drink in Newman's suite while he changed. When he emerged a half-hour later in a tuxedo he was a different man.

Charisma is a quality too elusive to pin down. Though you can recognise it at once, it is impossible to define – yet, seated opposite Newman at the party which followed, I tried to do so. I knew from New York he did not *behave* like a star; he moved unaccompanied by hangers-on, he had no entourage. He was without pretension. Here at the party he bore no resemblance to the somewhat shattered 60-year-old man we'd collected earlier from the dentist; somehow he'd *grown,* his light had come on, he had presence. Surrounded by personable, well-groomed, thirty-something Jewish movie executives and their equally shined-up partners, he gave off a quality utterly different from anyone else. Partly it was his stillness. Others gesticulated while they spoke, fiddled with their wineglasses, or smoked (this was then), he did none of these. Gracefully, without stiffness, he sat calm and still, at ease with himself and the world around him.

The reason for the party was to present him with an award. Accepting it, he gave a speech which was short, deprecatory and funny. After that came a charity auction, its first prize of a mink jacket won by Kenny Rogers, who sang with Dolly Parton as cabaret. Following which the guests circulated and worked the room.

For someone whose adolescence had been passed watching American movies it was an odd experience to meet withered oldsters within whom the icons I'd revered were identifiable only as crumbling ghosts. Old Cary Grant was there, fine and immaculate as ever. Gene Kelly – who wore the red ribbon of the Légion d'honneur given him for *An American in Paris* – had the bull-necked, bull-chested bulk of a retired heavyweight boxer, wrecked and run to fat, and a massive benignity. He was with Robert Wagner, whom I was curious to meet, for reasons I am forbidden to state, but it seemed a bad moment; tired and emotional, he was not in party mood at all. My encounter with Warren Beatty was no more successful. Our only point of contact was David Puttnam. I mentioned that I'd run into Puttnam – whom I liked – the week before in London. Beatty glanced at me without warmth, his mouth tightened. 'And what's that asshole up to now?' he snarled.

Next day Susan and I drove to Big Sur, that mountain wilderness which was home to Big Foot and, at one time, Henry

Miller. The travel lodge was set among giant redwoods, our private deck thirty feet above the ground; it felt like being in a tree house.

'Maybe we should order a bottle of champagne,' Susan suggested. 'Not domestic – imported would be more appropriate under the circumstances, don't you think?'

It was served. We sat on the wooden deck as the warm afternoon faded into evening. Up there among the branches the air smelt sweet and aromatic; surrounded by nature, this was the perfect spot for such an adventure. I moved to sit by Susan on her lounger … and all at once a wave of devastating grief broke over me. A great tidal roller caught me up and pressed me down to the bottom beneath the overpowering weight of it. I was desolate with sadness and regret. Grief for Nanny's death; grief for Mother's, and regret that I'd never been able to like, far less love her. For Jenny, for our break-up and, I knew, *causing* it to happen because we'd grown bored with each other in bed. Sorrow poured over me, I was overwhelmed by sadness. Tears streamed down my cheeks, I wept uncontrollably.

It was not quite what Susan had expected.

Three weeks later, back in England, I received a call from her. 'Joanne and Dad want to visit the women's camp at Greenham Common. We thought we'd come stay with you,' she said.

The notion was startling. How the Newmans, used to Beverly Hills luxury and the comfort of their West Hampton estate, would adapt to mould growing on the bedroom walls, the only bathroom with its shuddering geyser and dribble of tepid water, the lavatories whose sepia-stained pedestals were veined with cracks and inscribed Thomas Crapper and Sons 1848, was hard to imagine. 'It's not that I want to put you off …' I said.

In the end they stayed at the Connaught, and only Susan put up at Gilston Road. Travelling to Greenham Common, Newman and Woodward fraternised with the heavy-sweatered, muddy-booted protesters outside the airbase, raising the tone of the tented encampment considerably. That evening I threw a small party for them at the house, inviting a few guests.

I composed the guest list carefully. Newman had said that if he hadn't gone into movies he'd have liked to teach at Yale; despite his age, he still raced cars. I invited Mark Ramage, who sponsored the Lotus Grand Prix team for Players and could discuss Wittgenstein and Nigel Mansell's cornering with equal authority; I did not ask Nigel Broackes, for two kings at the same court doesn't work, but I did ask Kim Waterfield with his current six-foot girlfriend, for one requires a pinch of notoriety and some beauty. Ben Fisher, for his charm and ease with all; the Stephen Tuckers, because they were pretty and the most determinedly upwardly mobile young couple I knew; my daughter Sasha, aged sixteen; Harry-the-old-lag, a skilled raconteur who'd burgled high society on three continents; Whitepowder Henry, for obvious reasons; and my spiritual counsellor, now become the Venerable John Barton, whom I had need of, for I'd denied Christ over a glass of Chardonnay at a dinner party the night before and was ashamed of how I'd acted.

Gore Vidal had been haranguing the table on the subject of President Reagan, the most powerful man in the world, whose brain was decomposing into cream cheese, whose closest advisers were a dippy, post-menopausal wife and an astrological fortune teller, a President and declared Christian raving about the 'Evil Empire' and professing fundamental belief in the apocalyptic scenario detailed by the Book of Revelation, who knew it was God's will the world should end in a fiery Armageddon ... and who sat day after day in the Oval Office with a red button labelled ARMAGEDDON only inches from his spastically twitching fingers. 'It should be an article of the Constitution that anyone holding the Christian faith should be automatically disqualified from the office of President,' Vidal stated and turned on me. 'Don't you agree?' he demanded.

'Well, Gore, old fruit, actually no ...' I should have said, but didn't. Instead I'd laughed slavishly ... and outside the windows of the Connaught somewhere in the Mayfair dark I'd heard a cock crow twice.

At Gilston Road Susan and I soaked the tarnished silver in hot water then polished it, along with the battered Georgian candelabras. In candlelight the threadbare carpet was unnoticeable unless you caught your heel in it, and the double living room had a shadowy, distressed near-elegance.

Many of our guests I hadn't seen for some while. Fisher was among the first to arrive, explaining he must leave early, he was booked on a 4 am flight to Brazil next day. 'How glamorous,' I remarked, but he assured me it wasn't. It was the cheapest available charter; he was going nowhere near Rio but to camp on a fly-blown swamp in the Amazon delta where he would hunt moths. He could be away only ten days as he worked in the research department of a City stockbroker. 'Not glamorous, and not particularly secure, either; when the Big Bang comes, I think they may axe me,' he confided.

'Never mind, you may discover a new species,' I consoled him, and he laughed wistfully. 'If only!'

I introduced him to Kim Waterfield who – now divorced from Penny Brahms – had brought a striking girl whom he introduced as 'my apprentice mistress' ... causing Susan to tense but others with myself to laugh. His life like my own had plunged somewhat only in his case to soar again in characteristic roller-coaster fashion, for he had founded an international beauty pageant and been travelling South-East Asia to set up the venues. I left him explaining the world scale of the contest to a rather bemused Fisher, almost the only happily married man I knew.

Susan was my date at the party, of course. At one point she, her father, Sasha and myself stood discussing how impossible it was for a child ever to satisfy its parents. Newman then told of how he'd collected his elderly mother and brought her to stay with them in Beverly Hills. He gave a party in her honour. This was in 1970, the year after *Butch Cassidy* had been released; he was the highest-paid film star in the world. The cream of the Hollywood A-list came to the *soirée* casually dressed; he himself was in a caftan. All were at their best and the evening unrolled successfully, but the party failed to make his mother joyful. Towards its end she said to him dolefully, 'Oh, son, you could have been a doctor, a dentist ... You could really have made something of yourself and *become* someone. *And when I look at you now wearing a dress ...!*'

Of course, neither Newman nor anyone else at Gilston Road that evening could fail to notice the ruinous condition of the house. He'd returned from a trip to pee impressed by the many different layers of peeling wallpaper visible in the lavatory, dating back to the early-Victorian original. 'So, what are you aiming to do with this place?' he asked me.

Probably sell it, I told him, though at moments I did think it would be satisfying to restore the house to its original elegance and redesign the garden.

'That would cost a pile,' he remarked.

'Sure,' I agreed. 'But you never know what the future holds.'

He stiffened, his glance went to Susan standing beside us,

then hard to me. His blue eyes hit me with a very sharp look indeed.

Stung by the unspoken suggestion I was a fortune-hunting cad, I reassured him that my intentions towards his daughter were entirely dishonourable.

And therein lay more than a small white lie. For no misconduct had ever taken place between Susan and myself, and since the Big Sur trip it had somehow become impossible. We went out to dinner, to the theatre, to a few parties; we got on together fine, but the fire just failed to spark. We didn't discuss it, but it lay between us limp and scarcely visible.

The problem was solved for me by the photographer Terry Donovan in an unexpected fashion. Susan and her family had flown back to the States, and he had asked me to find a château for him; he'd been contracted to shoot a calendar with three nude models in some rich ornamental setting.

The eighteenth-century chateau I found for him was tiny and utterly magical. The rooms were hung with frayed hunting tapestries; its pre-revolutionary furniture was chipped and infirm, but the place had an ornate, faded splendour. One afternoon I watched him complete the lengthy business of positioning the three naked girls over the distressed silk furnishings; when the tableau was fully lit he reached out to pinch three pairs of nipples between finger and thumb to make them erect, then stepped smartly back behind the camera to press the shutter. He glanced at me and grinned, ''Straordinary to get paid so much for playing with women's tits! Remarkable, really, when you think about it, innit?' he observed.

The setting for one of the months of the year was the royal bedroom, which had been designed for a visit by le Roi Soleil. While the lights were being positioned and the models made up, Donovan and I lounged on the four-poster bed, chatting.

The bed was hung with curtains, covered in rich brocade, and we were sitting side by side with our backs against the headboard and legs extended. He was wearing a suit and tie, I was only slightly less formally dressed myself. One of us an impressive seventeen stone in weight, the other only eleven, we must have looked incongruous and comical. The stills photographer took a Polaroid. Framed in the rich boudoir setting of the canopied four-poster, the photograph gave no indication of the ten or so people, equipment and general busyness surrounding us, but this did not occur to me when I mailed it to Susan Newman with a few words on the back. It must have looked as if we were alone together.

The camera lies, of course. That is what commercials and advertising are *about*, their guiding principle. But sometimes a picture doesn't convey quite the message you intend. I got a letter back from Susan ten days later. Occupying one side of the paper only, it was quite brief:

> *You obviously don't like* softik *women but I'm happy you've found yourself a big fat man.*
> *I wish you both the best*
> *PS You might have told me. – S*

28
Westminster Hospital

It was a bright sunny day in June. Dressed in jeans, cotton blazer and white shoes, I was strolling down the King's Road to buy a couple of bottles of champagne for a picnic with Ben Fisher – who had *not* been fired in the Big Bang as he'd feared. Instead, the stockbrokers where he worked had been taken over by a much larger financial institution and Fisher now held the exalted post of number two at Citibank for an 'obscene salary', he'd told me, though the only difference it had made to his life was that he was now travelling deeper and yet more uncomfortably in Asia and South America in his search for moths.

I was on my way to join him and Bridget for Founder's Day at Eton, where their two sons were pupils. The sun shone brightly and this morning I was feeling particularly cheerful, God was in his heaven, all right with the world. Gilston Road was sold! For over three years my brothers and I had camped there waiting for Mother's estate to be settled while the building decayed around us. A large piece had fallen from the roof, almost killing the postman, and the house threatened to turn into a column of dust before a buyer risked his/her life stepping through the garden gate to fall in love with it. But one *had*, and paid us a million pounds for the place. Nor was that all. Magda had called from France a couple of weeks before to say the last of the two sisters, our sitting tenants, had died. We'd agreed amicably to divide the property; she would keep the mill she was in, I would own the other where the old sisters had lived.

I'd been broke for so long, now all at once I had vacant possession of a house on the Côte d'Azur and one third of a million sterling in the bank. Life seemed a rich feast that sunlit day in Chelsea, the world had become my oyster.

When I came out of the off-licence with two bottles of Moët in a carrier bag a few moments later I sensed the oddest twinge in my chest, a clench, a burning. The pain sharpened as I made my way past the Town Hall. Keep going, I told myself. It was a phrase Nanny had used when I dawdled as a child. *Keep going, it will pass*. But it didn't. Soon it became so fierce I had to sit down on the pavement and prop my back against a wall. I noticed people staring at me curiously as they strolled by. 'Are you all right?' someone asked.

'Fine, just fine,' I answered. Despite the cramp of pain on my ribs, I was aware it must appear odd to be lolling on the pavement in this fashionable spot. I felt very strange by now. The world looked different and darker, as though I were seeing it in a dream. Stumbling to my feet, I teetered to the kerb and waved down a cab. 'Waterloo station,' I told the driver as I got in. The clamp in my chest tightened a further squeeze. 'Better make that the nearest hospital,' I said.

Ten days later I was still in hospital awaiting the result of an angiogram, the only definitive method of assessing the damage following a coronary. To perform the test, a cut is made in the patient's groin and a rubber tube poked through the main artery far as the heart. This is then flooded with radioactive ink whose progress through the startled organ is filmed by an X-ray movie camera.

Back in the ward afterwards I was in a dopey drowse when the young doctor who'd directed the process came to give me the result. Sitting by my bed he said, 'I want you to look at this,' and passed me a cartoon. The drawing was of funny little men at work in a factory; two of the processes they were engaged in had been cancelled out by black crosses. Intended to represent the heart, a child could have understood it; stuperous from sedation, I could not. 'I'm a devoted skier,' I muttered. 'Will it affect that?'

My question only irritated him. 'Oh no, you'll never *ski* again,' he told me with professional certitude. His verdict delivered, the job done, he took up his cartoon and left.

Up to the date I quit Garrett's I'd had a series of sports cars: an XK120, an AC Aceca, a Lotus, an E-Type, the Aston Martin. All belonged to the company, I was spared the responsibility and care of ownership, yet when I crashed or damaged one even moderately my feelings for it changed. I could not stand its imperfection and would replace it at once. I realised I felt the same way about my own body.

After leaving hospital I suffered attacks of chest pain and the fear that comes with as I waited for the pills to work, wondering if this was the big one. I was fifty-four, I felt in shock over what had happened. I could walk no further than a hundred yards without growing short of breath; I didn't know if I could make love, I'd been warned not to try. I hated my decrepitude. The engine was blown, I wanted to trade myself in for a new model.

Under the circumstances that wasn't practicable, but I badgered my doctor to lay on a heart bypass operation. The procedure is surprisingly popular, I learned, no cardiac surgeon had a slot in his schedule for six months. Then one morning I received a call to say one had had a 'cancellation'. Neat euphemism, I thought, as I packed a bag with toothbrush and books and got ready to take the departed patient's place.

The operation involves being sawn in half down the breast bone, split and pinned open flat as a kipper while the job's done. It takes five and a half hours. You are warned that in the days that follow, the resulting pain can be controlled with morphine but the trauma to body and mind is so severe you will experience spells of horror. I was advised to have ready some sure and tranquil mental image to focus on at such moments.

Why – I ask myself now – why did I not choose Arisaig? But it was almost forty years since I'd been there and I seldom thought of that rainswept wilderness of mountain and loch and solitude that had made my soul. Instead I chose the south of France. The mill I'd inherited on the old sisters' recent death was a sprawling, tumbledown ruin. It was vast, it would require a fortune to restore, but it backed on to the river and a waterfall; it was surrounded by the forest and could be transformed into something extraordinary and unique.

In hospital, the night before the operation, I decided that if and when I recovered I would devote myself to laying out a garden by the water, put in a swimming lake, and in that lovely secluded setting restore the ruin into a hideaway for myself and my few sure friends. A retreat: a shared and secret Walden Pond with a library but without a telephone.

Having made the decision I chatted to the anaesthetist when he dropped by, saying I considered his role much more crucial than the surgeon's and would he do his very best not to turn me into a vegetable next morning. He left. I prayed to God along roughly the same lines, read George Herbert for a while, took a pill and went to sleep.

The effect of being sawn open and your heart stopped while someone slices away at it with a knife is, as I'd been warned, profound. I felt as though I'd been gang raped by a herd of bull elephants. I hardly knew who or what I was at times; there were moments of nightmare. I got through them by prayer, and by focusing on the mill and the swimming pool I'd install there, which would be lined in rock, irregular in shape, part overhung by trees ... and if I'd concentrated on Arisaig instead the course of my subsequent life would have been entirely different.

Following the operation, with characteristic generosity Jenny Beerbohm converted her living room into a sick room and looked after me over five weeks of convalescence. With her and Edward I recovered a more-or-less stability and mobility. Then I flew out to recuperate *chez* the Mayles in the Luberon.

They were the perfect hosts, ever tolerant of the chain of small disasters an unwitting guest brings upon a household. At their farmhouse, lying by the pool, eating perfectly cooked meals at the massive stone table in the shaded courtyard, in their undemanding company I regained health and the proper tan.

Since I'd last seen them their lives had turned around completely. Peter's book, *A Year in Provence*, had – contrary to the publisher's meagre expectations – become a runaway success, a huge international best seller topping the charts across the globe. Become bewilderingly rich, the Mayles struggled to maintain a simple life in the place they had chosen for its beauty and seclusion. But it was impossible, for fame had trampled a path to their door.

After lunch one day I was lying with the two of them by the pool. It was a hot, cloudless afternoon, the only sound the hum of insects and occasional call of a bird from the forested slopes of the Luberon at the bottom of the garden. It was in its way perfection, the vision which had led them and myself out of advertising to a hidden corner of Provence. The day was utterly still ... and then, unmistakably, I heard the crunch of gravel and sound of a heavy vehicle pulling up outside the house ... which was followed by a noise as of a flock of birds, a rustling and chirping growing in volume as it approached. And then around the wall of the pool appeared, in orderly column, a horde of small Japanese people. All were dressed in dark clothes, all at first glance looked identical, and each one of them was carrying a hardback book. At the sight of Peter for a second they paused and the twittering rose to a crescendo. Then, all together, chirruping excitedly, they swooped upon him, thrusting out their copies for him to sign. And the same thing happened *all the time*.

There comes a moment when even the best of hosts are glad to see you leave. One morning I packed my trusty leather grip, said goodbye to Peter and Jennie, got into my rented car and drove to the autoroute, taking the direction signed AIX-EN-PROVENCE, CANNES, NICE ...

Moving into the tumbledown mill where the old sisters had lived, I spent the next two years and a fortune doing it up.

By the summer of 1990 the mimosa *quatre saisons* I'd planted was in flower, scenting the air as I stood on the mill terrace with a cup of decaffeinated coffee in my hand, waiting for the man from John Taylor, the leading real estate agents on the coast, who was on his way to value the renovated property. The rebuilding was finished. No, not really *finished*, a mass of detail remained to complete, but 500 square metres of roof had been replaced, the building's exterior walls secured and internal walls constructed, the house rewired and replumbed, five bathrooms and three kitchens installed. Meanwhile, the grounds had been cleared and landscaped, a swimming pool excavated, and a giant boulder hoisted into position as a diving rock. The garden had been laid out, planted, and was in flower.

And most of it had been a pleasure to accomplish. After my brush with the Angel of Death in the King's Road it was good to experience the warmth of the sun and *douceur* of the south, to work physically a little longer each day, to sense vitality returning to my wasted body.

The winter following my return I'd taken up skiing again. I was weak, my muscles feeble, but I persisted and it was exhilarating to defy the doctor's verdict of only nine months before. Strength came back fast and soon I regained a level of skill. I didn't attack black runs with the same reckless abandon as before, but I could come down in the controlled style suitable for a man older than he thinks he is.

It had been naïve of me to think I could return to the south of France and install myself just upriver of Magda without experiencing problems. Before doing so we'd had what politicians describe as 'a full and frank discussion', but it served for nothing. Seemingly straightforward at first, our interaction grew thorny. Also, the cost of rebuilding the place mounted alarmingly higher than planned – as it always does. I'd been obliged to borrow heavily to complete the work and it was this, together with the difficulties posed by Magda, which convinced me that transforming the property into a Walden Pond for myself and friends was not a practical idea. It's not realistic to think you or others can sit contemplating the water in search of the truth that sets you free if someone's concealed behind a nearby bush throwing rocks at you. So I'd sell the place, I determined.

As I stood there I saw a Citroën come up the drive to park below me. A youngish Englishman with wispy blond hair got out. Plying his trade in London, he would have worn a blue striped suit, aping the manner of a merchant banker. Here he'd adopted a blazer and resort shoes, plus that sniffy disdain which croupiers affect that comes from handling large sums of other people's money.

I walked him over my land, showing him the river and the pool before taking him through the house. He looked around, made the usual disparaging comments agents always utter ... and came up with a price of 6.5 million francs. At the exchange rate of the day that was roughly £750,000.

After he'd gone I poured myself a glass of wine. To some £750,000 is not a lot of money; to me it seemed a tidy wad. Enough. That amount of ready cash brought with it something I'd never experienced: financial security. It was an odd, unaccustomed thought. As I stood there, glass in hand, looking at the sunlit view I was feeling pretty ... *smug* is an unattractive word but it's unquestionably accurate.

29
Waitrose

It was the autumn of 1998 and I was standing at the cheese counter of Waitrose supermarket in Chelsea studying the selection. My friend and lawyer Ernest Chapman was about to arrive at my nearby small rented flat. I had a bottle of wine and biscuits there, but nothing to put on them. I chose a piece of Cheddar. The assistant weighed it, wrapped it and slapped a price ticket on the package: 68p. At the check-out I paid with a 50p and 20p piece. I pocketed my change and walked out into the street.

That 2p was all I had left. I had no mill, no assets, no job, no income, no expectations, and I owed over £200,000. I had enjoyed a total reversal of fortune, an experience shared by many in the 'nineties. Property values in the south of France had collapsed. Unable to sell the mill, I'd held on to it as long as I could in the face of mounting debt and mounting anxiety until it was finally repossessed, leaving me with nothing; indeed, less than nothing.

In the course of that eight-year journey from apparent wealth to penury and debt Father had died. He was up an apple tree in the garden angrily sawing off a branch when something broke in him. He was seventy-nine years old. Adriana got him to hospital; I went next day to see him. His bed in a ward on the ground floor was by a picture window which looked out on the snow-covered garden. As I walked in he looked confused, then his face lit up in pleasure. The response was so uncharacteristic I knew something was badly wrong with him. He'd not spoken since his fall, but when I said something he'd react, looking at me with a strangely mild expression I'd never seen before. He was in no pain and I don't believe it occurred to him for a moment that he was dying. Adriana stayed at his bedside throughout the entire week. It was against hospital regulations; nurses and doctors remonstrated with her, insisting she go home, but she utterly refused to leave her post. She said that if they put her out she'd wait in the snow outside the window, like the old dog Greyfriars Bobby in the film. She remained by Father until he died.

Throughout my youth, meetings with him had taken place in inconvenient, usually wet and windy spots, and the remote country graveyard to a disused church in deepest Hampshire where he chose to be buried was no exception. In light, persistent drizzle he was laid to rest in a grave alongside his mother's, his estate insufficient to cover the funeral expenses. A few months later Adriana rallied my brothers and myself to put up a stone, and the question of the inscription arose. His mother's headstone bore two lines he'd chosen for her:

I have warmed both hands before the fire of life,
It sinks and I am ready to depart

I suggested Father's gravestone should be engraved with the same epitaph, but below the couplet we should add a further line: *PS. Please pay coal merchant.*

The Grim Reaper had called on Father, but shortly before that cheese purchase in Waitrose the same hooded figure had also given *me* a sharp nudge in the ribs to remind me he was there and waiting. Since my coronary I'd kept up an active life, walking for a couple of hours or swimming every afternoon, but occasionally I experienced bouts of chest pain. One evening this became so fierce I realised I'd better get to hospital. A week later I was still there, having had the full range of tests measuring the state and function of the heart. 'Your arteries are congested,' a doctor told me, 'You should consider having the operation redone.'

'And if I don't?' I asked. He told me: they would continue to fur up until either a piece of the accumulated gunk broke off to plug and stop the heart, or one of the arterial grafts split – and I would die. *When* this might occur he would not guess.

Promising – falsely as it turned out – to stay in touch, I packed my toothbrush and went home.

I'd have liked to have eaten alone that evening in a first-class restaurant to ponder the implication of his words. I was too broke for that, but I did plunder my living allowance for days to come by buying a half-lobster and a bottle of champagne. I bathed, changed, lit the candles and took my place at table. I drank Perrier-Jouët from one of the two unbroken crystal glasses surviving from Gilston Road, and had dinner with Marcus Aurelius.

The *Meditations* of that second-century Roman emperor and Stoic philosopher had been part of my life for some time; I turned to him quite often. The fundamental lesson of stoicism is that events are merely events, in themselves neither good nor bad. It is how we react to them that defines them so

– and defines us, our character. When we meet with any mishap or reversal, he suggests we call to mind the example of others to whom the same thing once happened: 'Well, what did *they* do, how did they behave? They sulked, they bitched, they blamed. Will you be like unto them and snivel in the self-same fashion? Let your only care be to make a right use of such accidents, for they will prove fit matter for you to work upon ...'

I drank some more champagne and thought about my own life. Or, rather, what remained of it. I did not want to go through another operation. It had been a hideous experience, I couldn't afford it privately now and, because of my age, I'd be low in the NHS waiting list. And *why* clutch at life, trying to extend it? How was I to fund my life, even if I did manage to extend it? The only possible way I had of making money was to write a book, but I'd lost the knack of writing fiction. I had no idea why, but the ability had left me. A life is, in a way, like owning a yacht, I thought. Accompanied by money it can provide enormous fun for yourself and your friends; without funds to maintain the vessel it becomes an inconvenience both to yourself and to others.

So I reasoned over dinner. Not depressed but in a sort of odd limpid calm. I sipped some wine and turned again to Marcus Aurelius. 'What do you desire?' he asks. 'To live long? Why? To experience your own decline, lose your wits and become senile? Ask yourself, is this truly a worthy objective to desire?'

No, it wasn't. But pulling me in a contrary direction back into life was a counter-force. The problem was that, most inappropriately at this untimely moment, I had fallen in love.

One afternoon I'd run into Kim Waterfield in the King's Road. 'I thought you were breeding horses in Ireland,' I said.

He told me he came to London rarely, but later I went for a drink with him and his ex-wife Penny, whom I'd always admired. It was over twenty five years since I'd first met her and thought she had the best legs I'd ever seen; now I realised that was still the case. At the end of the evening she gave me a lift home in her beat-up station wagon.

Following which we'd started seeing each other; she was almost the only person I did see. Dismayed by the notoriety attached to 'Penny Brahms,' she now went by the modelling name of Jamais, or Jamie as I called her, and her life had changed considerably. After the breakdown of her marriage to Kim she'd relocated herself in Paris to resume her modelling career. This went well until she had the misfortune to fall in love with, then marry, David Lyons, an American oil entrepreneur. Based in the USA, the two enjoyed a reckless lifestyle. Lyons fell foul of the SEC, an arrest warrant was issued for fraud. Living on the run, they were hunted, shot at, and finally caught by the police. Lyons was jailed. Wired on amphetamine, Jamie had by now lost the ability to sleep, finally cracking up in the transit lounge between flights at Kennedy and ending up in hospital. Following which she had known bad times but come through them.

Jamie was a loner, addicted to solitude as myself. She was as broke as I was – another bond. In his essay 'On the Want of Money', Hazlitt says that, of all people, actors bear the condition best for it sits light upon them. 'Their life is theatrical ... rags and finery, tears and laughter, a mock-dinner or a real one, a crown of jewels or of straw, are to them nearly the same.' Jamie showed a fine indifference to money I admired. We could never afford to eat out, but occasionally my old friend Mark Ramage – who'd sold his agency to become 'richer than I'd ever believed possible' – would invite us to lunch, always somewhere splendid. There was a childish thrill in dressing up to adventure into the *beau monde*. Neither of us had the least problem in *looking* rich, and there was real pleasure in such good company and superb food costing – I glimpsed Marco Pierre White's bill – over £400 for the three of us; and an ironic savour to enjoying it in the knowledge I had just enough in my pocket for two bus fares back to Chelsea.

Soon Jamie and I were strangely close, coming together with the eerie sense of encountering a twin. Though we were in touch each day we did not meet regularly, but on Sundays often she accompanied me to Westminster Abbey. She was my love and connected me to life ... but how without money to *maintain* that life was the problem occupying my mind that misty autumn evening as I walked out of Waitrose with a remaining capital of 2p and strolled back to my apartment to meet my friend and lawyer Ernest Chapman ...

I already owed Ernest and others a lot of money. Over a bottle of Waitrose red in my run-down flat I borrowed a further £1,500 on the understanding this was the last time I would ask.

The money bought a little time. All my life seemed to have been governed by chance and accidental encounter, something might turn up as it had in the past. I'd never been in quite such desperate straits as these, but thanks to Ernest I had a final stake. Once I would have gambled with it, now I wanted not to challenge chance but give her the maximum opportunity to smile upon me. I determined to live on a budget of £3 per day while I awaited her wilful glance to slant in my direction.

George Orwell, an expert on restricted means, says that 'between an income of £500 a year and £5,000 there is very little difference; between an income of zero pounds and £500 there is all the difference in the world.' He was writing in 1934, one has to scale it up, but I came to realise that, above today's £500 equivalent, poverty and wealth are largely an attitude of mind. What, after all, does one *need*? Shelter, food, warmth, light, fresh air, occupation for the brain ... more than that is wealth. So throw in a couple of suits, half-a-dozen shirts, a pair of re-soled Guccis and consider the lilies of the field, I thought with assumed bravado as I leafed through the pages of Marcus Aurelius.

I'd been short of funds for quite a while and was coming near to broke, but I did not consider myself poor. I did, though, occasionally wonder what my lifestyle would have been if I'd succeeded in selling the mill and had the million or so dollars in the bank I'd been anticipating. I would now be travelling more and eating out when I felt like it, but I did not believe I'd be living much differently from how I was. I'd changed since my coronary; the change was progressive and, in a way I didn't entirely understand, seemed still to be continuing. Before it I'd always sensed an edge of restlessness and boredom behind everything I did; now, though all I did was read, listen to music and take walks, I was never bored.

Most precious in that list of things I possessed was privacy. And I had books. Books had made me. Father and Mother were readers, as were their parents and grandparents. The manse had been crammed with books, some mildewed, some chewed by mice, not all legible. As a child all I had ever wanted was to be left alone to read. Books formed a larger, infinitely more noble universe than the world adults wanted me to inhabit. Then I'd grown up, adventured into the 'real' world of people and events, entered advertising and become so distracted and manic I'd almost lost the ability to read. But now I could: Emerson, Tolstoy's essays, Meister Eckhart, Thomas à Kempis. I craved substance, not diversion, and my small room became my library and cell.

The pages of my address book, photocopied, Tippexed, amended and added to over the years, took up an A4 display binder; the earliest entries dated back to 1956. I'd given my own number only to a handful of those listed in it. Now my telephone remained permanently on answerphone. Not always did I ring back, and over the months my recorded messages grew fewer.

I'd stopped going out. It was not just that I could not repay people's hospitality, but the things they mostly talked about at a dinner party – job, children, politics, exotic vacations – formed no part in my own life. And conversation on any of these subjects soon related to money. It was impossible to discuss anyone's house without learning its current value; people talked about money the whole time. Money is an interesting topic but, as with flogging, religious mania etc., one can hear too much.

My regimen was frugal but entirely adequate. To my surprise I discovered you can eat well and drink wine with dinner on £3 a day. Apart from Jamie I saw perhaps one person a month. She and I exchanged faxes or spoke every day, met sometimes for dinner in my flat and attended the Abbey most Sundays. She was bruised from too much living in the world, so quiet had appeal to her but even then – and more so now – I was astonished and grateful she could accept so meagre a life-menu as I offered.

I'd given up television because I could not afford the licence; now I stopped reading newspapers and listening to the radio. To be free of these distractions – for that is how I had come to think of them – created a wide spread of time but strangely no sense of emptiness or tedium. Without purpose I would have been lost, but I was kept human by the love of a good woman and for purpose I had Marcus Aurelius and the path he and others I was reading lay out.

Stoicism is not anti-possessions, but it recommends you hold them lightly, avoid attachment, and put no faith in them. Thomas à Kempis takes it further: 'Seek to be found naked in all things' ... It wasn't so hard, the work of dispossession had largely been done for me already. The mill was no longer mine, I had no car, my entire wardrobe fitted into two shelves and 15" of hanging space. The only 'things' I owned were a Cartier watch and a few pieces of silver from Gilston Road, and these I now gave away to Sasha, my brothers, friends. All that remained were books, and these too I got rid of sparingly and appropriately, except for a few I could not live without.

There's pleasure in giving things to people, but there was an animated sense of lightness at being back to possessing nothing except a few clothes. I realised it was curiously reminiscent of how I'd felt as an immigrant in Connecticut when I was twenty.

'Forsake all and thou shalt find all,' says Thomas à Kempis, and holds out the promise of 'the truth that sets you free'.

Well that *all* was what I'd look for, I determined. Though there was little merit in my decision – for renouncing the world becomes much easier if the world first renounces *you* – I felt a swell of exhilaration and excitement at having made it. Ahead lay an adventure into the unknown.

'Live lightly in the world, don't put down roots,' Buddha advises. 'Keep thyself as a stranger and pilgrim upon the earth, for here thou hast no abiding city,' says Thomas à

Kempis. Nanny had put it another way: 'A rolling stone gathers no moss,' she'd told me, aged six and afterwards. I'd never known whether moss was supposed to be good or bad.

30
Arisaig

In the Highlands the bracken was rusty red on the heather-covered slopes of the mountains and the leaves had started to turn. The manse was warm and much more comfortable than it had been when I was a boy. It belonged now to my brother Hamish; he and his partner Stephanie had refitted the primitive kitchen and bathroom, installing an efficient hot-water system, and redecorated the house, though much of the furniture remained as I remembered.

In the kitchen at the back, which looked on to the mountains, I sat in the same place at the same scrubbed wooden table I'd sat at more than fifty years before, eating the same meal of baked beans on toast, only that time it had been cooked by Nanny.

Souvenirs of childhood were everywhere in the house, though sadly the arsenal of assorted weaponry, bombs and stocks of ammunition we'd possessed were gone. Brother David had handed them in to the Mallaig police – who were awestruck by the sheer scale of the gift.

Looking through a stack of family albums one evening I came upon photographs of Nanny taken by Terry Donovan thirty years before. As a child, her influence upon me had been greater than anyone's; she'd been the only person I loved. She had worked for the family since she was fifteen. The teenage sweetheart she may have kissed but certainly never slept with had been killed in the trenches in 1914, since when she'd never had any life of her own. It had been given to others – who took her entirely for granted – in return for a small, undependable wage she was not always paid.

'Goodness', I guess, is a short word for it, and Terry had caught it in his photograph. In a wholly different way, I'd loved Terry too for the exuberance of his full-frontal personality. Cheerful, irreverent, he was the greatest fun to be with and always made me laugh.

With Ramage and Jamie I'd gone to his memorial service. The church was packed with the most eclectic mix imaginable, ranging from Princess Diana and Maggie Thatcher to a group of shaven-headed 15-stone karate experts. All were Terry's friends. He'd been such a big, vital and endearing man, the last person in the world I'd have thought to kill himself.

In another album I found photographs dating from my time in the army, including one of Fisher as a cavalry subaltern. Of all those I knew, I thought he was the one who'd completed his life most successfully. He enjoyed an ideally happy marriage to a clever and pretty wife who adored him. His children were grown-up, healthy, happy and loved him. A life fulfilled – but fulfilled *plus*, as he'd disclosed a while earlier over lunch in the Natural History Museum, where he worked unpaid two days a week cataloguing the innumerable private collections bequeathed to the museum. It would take him 140 years, he calculated. He'd just retired from Citibank with a hearty golden handshake. Two of their children were happily married, the youngest had finished university and was in a job. 'Life's going so well, it's worrying,' he said. But there was a further reason for the wry smile on his monkish face; he revealed why after lunch at his workspace in the cavernous upper reaches of the museum.

All his life he'd passed his holidays in far-flung inconvenient places hunting for moths. *And he'd discovered an unknown type*. He showed it me, a pretty little thing with diaphanous outspread wings that looked like a Schiaperelli cocktail dress. It was named *Gortyna corelii*, Fisher's Estuarine Moth. He'd caught it on the marshes below his house near Harwich, where he'd been setting lures for more than thirty years.

As parents he and Bridget had been impeccable. One has noticed this is no guarantee of perfect children, but with theirs it seemed to be the case. And a further example of how a traditional parental upbringing can produce a happy and successful child was my own daughter Sasha, whom I'd grown to know since she became an adult. Articulate, witty and well-balanced, it was always a pleasure to see her, for surprisingly she seemed to harbour no rancour that I had proved so delinquent a father. A tall, dark-haired young woman with spontaneous charm and her mother's legs, her childhood, adolescence and youth had been exemplary; she had caused not a single problem. Tania and Don, her step-father, had proved the best of parents; from them she had learned sound values, discipline, character and faultless manners, while from me she had received that priceless gift of absence and paternal neglect I had valued so highly myself as a child.

By her mid-twenties Sasha had become the youngest director of Union des Banques Suisses and drove a Porsche. She'd asked me to a party she gave, where the other guests were her own age and peer group. Young men and women with short hair, stylishly sober-suited, exhilarated from their day on the trading floor, most of them were drinking mineral water. It was very different from the parties I'd given or gone to when I was their age in the 'sixties, and for Sasha to invite Tania, Don and myself was a gracious gesture, though she must have been aware there was a danger we might lower the tone.

We, the three oldies, had arrived together. Sasha welcomed us and led us to the bedroom to leave our coats. Closing the door, she said, 'I'm so glad you could all come and meet my friends, but just one thing ... while you're here, please, no drugs.' However much you try, parents never turn out the way you hope.

Opposite the photograph of Fisher-the-subaltern was a snap I'd taken of Ivor and Natassia Mottron at the same period. Lounged on the casino terrace at Travemünde, they gave off an air of reckless daring that was pure Scott Fitzgerald; I still thought them the most beautiful couple I'd ever met. Their marriage unsurprisingly had not lasted. She had remarried a financier and lived in Geneva; Ivor I'd last seen in Beverly Hills in 1985. He looked fit and well and was drinking orange juice, but I recognized the same wayward glint at the back of his pale Weimaraner eyes. He too had remarried, as he explained. LA was his wife's hometown, ' ... but we spend most of the year travelling,' he added. I asked him how he liked living here. 'It's the pits,' he said. 'A bunch of demented luvvies surrounded by a vast court of crooked lawyers in designer leisure-wear. With the possible exception of Lagos, Nigeria, this is the most repulsive city in the world.'

On a later page in that same album was a shot of Nigel Broackes in uniform. Along with Alex Howard – last heard of walking over the mountains into Afghanistan with a mule train of weaponry – Nigel was my oldest friend; we'd met as new boys in my first term at Stowe. His subsequent career had been amazingly successful. Trafalgar House, which he'd founded, had grown to become the most profitable of all British conglomerates in the early 'seventies. Later, though, it had gone wrong, and I knew Nigel had resigned as chairman.

Just before coming up to Arisaig I'd decided to call him to suggest we meet. Having lost contact, I thought I'd telephone Trafalgar House to ask where I could reach him. Looking up the number, I found it had an 0181 prefix. Under Nigel's rule their offices had been Cunard House, opposite the Ritz; I was surprised to see they were now in Croydon.

I called the number, requesting to be put through to the Personnel Department. When a woman's voice answered I asked if she could please give me a number for Sir Nigel Broackes. '*Who*?' she queried in a night-school whine. '*Who*?' Never 'eard of 'im.'

And in the library at Arisaig I came across yet another picture that struck a chord. Not a photograph, but the cover of Peter Mayle's book *Anything Considered*. Three years before, when I'd been at the mill, low in money and spirits and fretting at how impossible it seemed to sell the place, he'd called to say, 'I've got this novel coming out about an ageing beach bum on the Côte d'Azur. The sort-of hero is based on you.' The book's cover showed the hero seated alone on the terrace of the Carlton Hotel in Cannes, wearing a white tuxedo. On the table by him stood a bottle of champagne in an ice-bucket and a single glass, three-quarters full. It was evening; beyond him and the palm tree framing his languid pose, the curved sweep of the *croisette* encircled the sable water of the bay of Cannes in a glittering necklace of diamond light. The man's fingers toyed with the stem of his fluted wine-glass; the pleasures of the night were before him and the Côte d'Azur lay at his feet.

Bennett, he was called in the book, and I studied my fictive self with curiosity, for his circumstances were so very different from my own. I'd been living for a year now on £3 a day; nothing had come up and almost nothing of Ernest's loan remained. Jamie had paid for the petrol to get us here in her old car, and again I was facing destitution. I nodded to my alter ego, wishing him well, and put Peter's book back on the shelf.

Bennett was an improvident wastrel who came right in the end, and Fisher had found a new moth. By contrast, in my own life I'd discovered nothing, accomplished nothing. It had been wholly misspent – but my timing to misspend it was immaculate. To have missed the war, caught the 'sixties young with plastic in my pocket, been twenty-six when the Pill transformed young women's overnight habits overnight, and recanted fornication by the date AIDS transformed them back again ... The chronology could not be faulted. And within that chronology lay an event of extraordinary significance. On Christmas Eve 1973, the day after the Arabs raised the price of oil from $5.10 to $11.65 a barrel, I'd stood on Bahnhofstrasse in Zurich, one of Europe's prime shopping streets, *and seen it stationary, with not a single moving car.* I didn't realise it until long afterwards, but that was the moment when people ceased expecting the world to get better and started to believe it would get worse. On that date I saw Western civilisation peak and tip into decline.

During our last day in Arisaig clouds rolled in from the west and it started to rain heavily. The view out to sea from the windows of the manse was closed off and the islands of Eigg and Rum on the horizon were hidden behind the mist.

Shut in by the storm, rain beating on the windows ... it was a familiar condition; throughout childhood the weather had provided long hours in my room with a book. To pass all day there was considered sloth though, and in the afternoon I'd been driven out into the storm. Today after lunch I put on my brother's oilskin coat and set out on a walk. I crossed the stone bridge over a canal. In childhood this was the way I'd come most mornings with my .22 rifle soon after first light to hunt rabbits, and once while crossing it I'd spotted a big sea trout beneath the bridge. It had taken three shots to hit it, for the bullets deflected in the water, but the family had dined well that night.

A half-mile further was a small cove; going by it I saw, only fifty yards out in the bay, a colony of seals on a seaweed-covered reef exposed by the tide. A big bull sprawled on the rocks, keeping watch over his harem. They'd never come so close inshore when I was young. The road I was following ran through a grove of trees, taller and denser than I recalled, then passed by a saddle of land where once had stood a settlement of wretched crofts whose inhabitants were deported in the Clearances. A mile more and I reached the end of the road at a jetty, destroyed by a storm years before and never rebuilt. Here, just short of the headland, I looked on to the ocean. The weather had started to break up; ten miles out to sea the peaks of Rum were taking ghostly shape in the dissolving mist. The wind blew strongly from the west and the sun flared in gaps between the racing clouds.

Standing on the pier's shattered slabs I could see long Atlantic combers breaking on the headland, each wave slamming on to the rocks to fling up a cloud of spray. At the age of twelve, with a similar sea running, I'd tried to take my kayak around the point. Caught in the cross-waves the craft had swamped; clutching my rifle and losing my sneakers, I had to swim to shore.

It was how Gino had died. His kayak was still on display

at the Royal Geographical Society in London. He'd had the Eskimos build it for him; 'Fitted him exactly as a pair of hand-made shoes,' Father said. 'He could flip it over, roll it, make it get up and dance; he could handle it skilfully as they could.'

Father had been staying with me at the mill when – unusually, for always he avoided the subject – he'd talked after dinner about the exploring they'd shared in youth. He said Gino had known it was his last expedition before he'd set sail for Greenland that final time. In Britain there had been the General Strike and hunger marches, America and Europe were in deep recession; no one and no institutions were disposed to fund further expeditions to the Arctic. For Gino, the end of this one meant London, a job, marriage, everyday reality ... and the prospect was unbearable. 'He never intended to return,' said Father.

And now I was facing my own end. Not necessarily from a coronary, but if you have no money to keep a roof over your head and buy food it follows that you do die. I didn't want to, but I saw no way to change my situation.

As I stood on the pier at Rhu, behind me the mountains were still dark with rain, but out to sea the storm had cleared. The islands of Eigg and Rum reared black in silhouette against the blaze of colour behind the clouds. The sun was sinking in the west and a path the exact colour of the molten lead I'd transmuted as a boy tracked across the waves to where they were breaking at my feet.

In my beginning is my end ... home is where one starts from. The end of every journey is to return to the beginning, and this stormy, savage wilderness had been that; this place had shaped my infant soul. Here I'd been entirely happy; sent away to get an education and make my fortune, I'd felt banished. I'd done neither. In the whole course of my life I'd committed to nothing, stayed with nothing. Looking back upon it now, I found it astonishing that, lacking intellect, education or talent, I'd enjoyed such an easy and entertaining ride and dipped into such varied milieus. I'd never felt a *part* of any of them, but only there on a visit. I'd never been a 'player' except in the gambler's sense: one who takes a seat at the table for a spell, to leave it richer or poorer a while later. Here, at the end of my life, I'd achieved nothing, possessed nothing, and had nothing to pass on except the dubious testimony of an accidental witness to our time.

Expelled from this enchanted spot at the end of childhood I'd believed myself exiled from Arcadia ... but it would have been impossible to remain. Then, as now. Tomorrow Jamie and I must get into her car and head south. After that the rest was uncertain.

I remained on the ruined jetty until the sun went down. The night before, in the manse's library, I'd done something I dare to do rarely; the oracle may be consulted only in extremis. With eyes closed I reached to the bookshelves and blindly ran my fingers along the rows of spines. I stopped at one, took the book out, and looked to see: Chaucer. Setting it on the table, I opened it at random, spread the page and read where my eyes lighted on the text:

That thee is sent, receive in buxomness;
The wrestling for this world asketh a fall.
Here is no home, here is but wilderness:
Forth Pilgrim, forth! Forth Beast, out of thy stall!
Know they countree, look up, thank God of all;
Hold the high way, and let thy ghost thee lead,
And truth shall thee deliver, it is no dread.

31
Where the Ghost Leads

Though sparsely furnished, the small flat where I lived was comfortable and quiet. The block was in poor condition; the paintwork was flaking and the decrepit cage-lift often broke down between floors. Built the year I was born, the building was falling apart at the same rate as myself.

It was spring 2000. The money I'd borrowed from Ernest was gone, but since Christmas I'd been receiving a state pension of £124 a month. I used this to pay for electricity and council tax, little went on food. For the last five weeks I'd been living on only boiled cabbage.

I already owed £200,000, there was nowhere to borrow more. I'd ceased making social security and pension payments when I moved to France in the 'seventies, I qualified for no form of benefit. My rent was in long arrears, soon I would be evicted from this flat. Jamie, friends, or my brothers might be willing to put me up for a while, but without prospects, penniless, lacking even the means to move on, truly I would be the houseguest from the abyss. That was not an option. Brahmins believe hell is nothing less than a state of bondage to others; Marcus Aurelius says very much the same, but that truth I knew already.

Jamie did not like what was going on, but she understood where I was and had come to accept my situation. But it can't have been easy for her.

'Conform to Nature' was the founding principle of stoicism. And to them Nature and God were the same. 'Accept. Accept the seasons and whatever comes. Death is but a part of Nature, seasonable and natural. So be ready and willing to leave all things when the day of your departure dawns.'

But the Stoics say you may *choose* that day. Suicide is an honourable option and a number of them died from starvation. If plants and beasts receive no nourishment they conform to nature by departing life. Likewise a man. On hunger strike in Northern Ireland it had taken Bobby Sands sixty-six days. I'd already lost thirty-five pounds from a body-weight of eleven stone. From the day I ceased eating altogether I estimated it would take me two to three weeks.

Surprisingly, the decision freed me of every trace of anxiety. Having taken it, I came to understand what I think Thomas à Kempis meant by 'liberty of mind'. It is similar to the experience of a man who throws himself from a high window; though he is doubtless hurtling down to shatter into fragments on the ground below, to him it feels like flight. And, while it lasted, it was an extraordinarily exhilarating sensation.

I lay on my bed reading. It was Easter, and in the last eight days I had eaten nothing except a single apple, and never once felt hungry. I'd drunk vast quantities of unsweetened tea, walked daily, and peed a lot.

I was physically weak. If I walked for long I became faint and had to sit down and suck a barley sugar to recover. But my mind and all my senses were acute, my awareness of everything felt heightened and intense. Observing the body language of strangers in the street I believed I knew how they were feeling, sometimes even what was in their mind.

Four or five years before, when confronted by loss of the mill, homelessness and poverty, I'd felt I was drowning in chaos and dread. Now to my astonishment I slept well. I dreamt, I dreamt vividly, but my dreams were adventures, never nightmares. I woke calm. I felt physically and mentally light, lucid, detached and *high*. Once you have accepted the worst that can happen, you are in a manner free.

Now, as I lay on my bed reading, the telephone rang, and unusually I picked it up. It was Fisher. I'd seen him a couple of weeks before; he'd asked why I was so thin and I'd told him. At once he pressed money on me and I'd explained that to live by continuing to borrow was no longer tenable. He accepted this after a while and we turned with relief to other subjects. But I'd had few to turn to. Ignorant of current events and having no gossip, I rabbited on far too much about stoicism and Marcus Aurelius. 'No, it's useful,' he said. 'The ground we *all* walk can give way beneath our feet – shit happens in people's lives. This helps, you should give a talk about it.' Not possibly, I'd told him.

Now on the line on Easter Sunday he said, 'I've booked a lecture room in ten days' time. Are you up for it?'

'Of course,' I answered. The response was instinctive, spoken without reflection; but in the circumstances it would have been churlish to refuse.

The rest is brief. I got up, had something to eat and started to make a few notes. I gave the talk to the thirty or forty people the Fishers had press-ganged into attending. It seemed to work, I talked again. And again, in the remorseless way ageing cranks tend to once they get a bee in their outmoded bonnet.

One day Peter Mayle called. 'So what are you up to?' he enquired. I told him. '*Hmm*, might make a how-to book,' he said.

I put one together. Ernest Chapman telephoned. 'There's this publisher Franklin …' he began. 'What's he like?' I asked. 'Harry Potter, doesn't wear a tie, rides a bicycle,' he answered. Ernest is economical with words.

Franklin published Marcus Aurelius as a slim volume in a package with three others I assembled. One day while I was in his office he mused, 'You seem to have led a rather … how shall I put it, *varied* life. Have you ever thought of writing a memoir …?'

Ramage took Jamie and myself to the Dorchester to celebrate. In the high-ceilinged retro opulence of the swanky restaurant he treated us to a lunch of *bélons*, *sole Véronique* and Krug as I related to him the above tale and its denouement. 'So what do you make of that, then?' I asked, when I had finished.

Ramage sipped, set down his wineglass and considered sagely. 'I always think,' he said after a long moment, 'That you cannot ever entirely trust a man who rides a bicycle.'

Index

E

F

G

H